Maybe a
Swan Song

Another Trip Down Memory Lane

Maybe a Swan Song
Another Trip Down Memory Lane

Peter Ellinger

NEW JERSEY · LONDON · SINGAPORE · BEIJING · SHANGHAI · TAIPEI · CHENNAI

Published by

World Scientific Publishing Co. Pte. Ltd.
5 Toh Tuck Link, Singapore 596224
USA office: 27 Warren Street, Suite 401-402, Hackensack, NJ 07601
UK office: 57 Shelton Street, Covent Garden, London WC2H 9HE

British Library Cataloguing-in-Publication Data
A catalogue record for this book is available from the British Library.

MAYBE A SWAN SONG
Another Trip Down Memory Lane

Copyright © 2025 by World Scientific Publishing Co. Pte. Ltd.

All rights reserved. This book, or parts thereof, may not be reproduced in any form or by any means, electronic or mechanical, including photocopying, recording or any information storage and retrieval system now known or to be invented, without written permission from the publisher.

For photocopying of material in this volume, please pay a copying fee through the Copyright Clearance Center, Inc., 222 Rosewood Drive, Danvers, MA 01923, USA. In this case permission to photocopy is not required from the publisher.

ISBN 978-981-98-1465-7 (hardcover)
ISBN 978-981-98-1474-9 (paperback)
ISBN 978-981-98-1466-4 (ebook for institutions)
ISBN 978-981-98-1467-1 (ebook for individuals)

For any available supplementary material, please visit
https://www.worldscientific.com/worldscibooks/10.1142/14353#t=suppl

Desk Editor: Kura Sunaina

Typeset by Stallion Press
Email: enquiries@stallionpress.com

Foreword

I thank my good friend, Professor Peter Ellinger, for inviting me to write the foreword of this book. Two years ago, I had written the foreword of his memoir, *Down Memory Lane*. The memoir was launched on his 90th birthday. It was a very happy occasion, attended by many of Peter's former colleagues, students, friends and relatives.

In 1965, on my way home from Cambridge University, England, I had stopped in Israel, to visit two of my classmates at the Harvard Law School. At Peter's suggestion, I had stayed with his mother in Tel Aviv. Mrs Ellinger was very concerned about Peter's delicate health and well-being. I promised her that I will always be his friend.

One of Peter's hobbies is reading. He can read in German, Hebrew and English. He is a voracious reader and is a fountain of knowledge and wisdom. In addition to collecting porcelain and listening to music, he likes to write, both on law and on non-law related subjects. Although Peter is a secular Jew, he has spent years studying the Bible. Hence, his essay on the book of Job in the Bible.

This book contains six short stories and three essays. I like the short stories better than the essays. If you are an admirer of Franz Kafka, you will like Peter's long essay on him. Taken together, this is an impressive collection of Peter's non-law writings. I am happy to recommend it to readers.

Professor Tommy Koh
Ambassador-at-Large
Ministry of Foreign Affairs

Introduction

Maybe a Swan Song is a sequel to *Down Memory Lane*, published by World Scientific in 2023. This earlier effort related my memoirs, covering my lengthy trip from 1933 to 2023. The new volume encompasses works written during the years I spent in Singapore.

This current tome comprises two sections. The first is a collection of short stories. They are based on aspirations and experiences I have had during my odyssey. Two of them pertain to my collection of European porcelain. The remaining three stories deal with episodes that took place during my trip and with my indulgence as a gourmand.

The second section comprises essays written during my years in the Lion City. All of them relate to disciplines other than Law. These legal contributions were written by me either to guide students or with the objective of dealing with specific issues arising in the law of banking. One of these, a book entitled *Ellinger's Modern Banking Law,* which appeared in five editions, is now in the hands of younger academic lawyers. They are likely to publish the sixth edition in the course of the next year.

Three of the stories included here are based on episodes that took place in Singapore. They taught me an important lesson: real life often gives rise to events stranger than the plots of stories based on a writer's fertile imagination. This ought not to come as a surprise because many fine narrations are triggered by events that did happen, and even famous writers often create heroes resembling persons they have encountered in their travels.

The essays encompassed in the second half of the book deal with issues which arose in the pursuit of my hobbies. Whilst I do not claim expertise in any of the disciplines to which they relate, they may be of use to readers interested in those fields not as professionals but as observers. For instance, my essay about a saying of James Joyce and the article about Franz Kafka deal with problems noted by ordinary readers of these authors. My paper about the Book of Job may interest people with a bible critique orientation who do not specialise in the subject.

Two of the essays, namely those dealing with the Book of Job and with Kafka, are lengthy. Very few readers will read either in a single session. It was therefore advisable to sub-divide these papers into sections with definitive headings. This need did not arise in the case of my less comprehensive paper and my short stories.

Having reached the ripe age of 92, this may turn out to be my swansong. At this stage, though, I hope to complete a further book, to see light on my 95th birthday. The future is not ours to see, but — even at a rife old age — a person is entitled to retain a positive outlook.

Contents

Foreword	v
Introduction	vii
Singapore Stories	1
The Moneylender and the Gambler	3
Darma	27
Shadow of the Gallows	37
A Matter of Compliance	79
An Ageing Gourmet	99
Through the Glasses of My Cabinets	113
Essays by a Non-Specialist	145
Love and Friendship	147
Job: A Reassessment	155
Kafka's Feet of Clay	199
Appendix to Kafka's Feet of Clay	279

Singapore
Stories

The Moneylender and the Gambler

I

That morning in March 1962, I was trying to feel at home in my office located in the Japanese Block of the University of Singapore. Conscience prompted me to concentrate on the examination scripts I had to mark. But as was to be expected, every candidate sought to demonstrate his knowledge of the entire subject and failed to deal with the hidden issues. Worse still, many examinees recapitulated some of the jokes I had cracked in my lectures. Was I as poor a raconteur as my students?

I was about to give up and join two of my colleagues for a cup of coffee in the staff canteen, when the telephone rang. For just a moment I was tempted not to answer. I knew I was late with the results and dreaded the aggressive voice of our examinations clerk. Then, with a shrug, I picked the receiver up.

"Can I please speak with Mr. Peter?" The voice appeared familiar but, for just a moment, I could not identify my caller. A colleague would have left out the "Mr". A student or an administrative clerk would have addressed me as "Dr. Berger" or "Sir". Then the penny dropped. The one and only person who called me "Mr. Peter" was the monumental Sikh porter of the Joyous Bar. But why was he calling?

"Speaking, Pratap," I told him.

"Can I come talk to you today?"

"3 o'clock would be fine. But what is this all about? And do you know our campus?"

"Oh yes, I know campus. And I tell all when I come."

Bewildered, I stared in front of me. Pratap Singh had introduced me to the girl I was dating at the time. He had smiled conspiratorially when I had arrived just before she completed her shift at the Joyous Bar. In all other regards, though, Pratap and I lived worlds apart. As far as I knew, he had no reason to visit the university. What, then, had prompted him to come over?

Right on time, at 3 o'clock sharp, Pratap knocked on my door. Instead of his grand and colourful uniform, which resembled the attire of an officer in the Mogul Empire, he wore a pair of plain trousers, a neat shirt and, of course, his turban. His portly figure dominated my cramped and untidy office. The look in his eyes told me he was ill at ease.

"Well, Pratap, what good spirit has blown you over to our campus?"

"You know Willie Chan, Mr. Peter?" he asked after a short pause.

"Of course. He is one of my best students."

"This why I come. You please see document."

To my amazement, he produced a promissory note — a hand note — in which Willie Chan undertook to pay "Mr Pratap Singh or order" S$18,500 "six months after the date hereof." It looked a tidy and properly worded document. Had it been drafted by a legally trained person or simply copied from a set of standard forms? I was further perplexed by its contents. Was Willie Chan in a position to undertake the payment of a sum that amounted to nearly two years' worth of a lecturer's salary?

I knew Willie well. He was a final-year student, and was enrolled in two of my courses. He was more imaginative than most of his contemporaries, and was further set apart from them by his neat and easy-flowing writing style. He aspired for a First-Class Honours degree and was doing his best to impress me with his insights.

Willie resided in a dormitory called Raffles Hall. At that time, I was a Resident Fellow, which meant that I had a small flat in a choice wing. In this role, I was expected to mix with the students. To this end, I attended parties held at the hall and usually had at least one meal a day in the spacious dining room. Willie and I had breakfast or dinner together frequently. On those occasions, Willie tended to talk about himself. He told me that his parents had died during the Japanese Occupation, but I suspected he might have been an abandoned offspring. Be this as it may, he had been brought up in a Roman Catholic orphanage.

When Willie completed secondary school, one of his teachers, a Miss Winifred Smith, offered to sponsor his university studies. She was a devout Roman catholic who knew Willie well from his childhood at the orphanage. Having remained a spinster, she treated Willie like a son. On many Sundays, he accompanied her to mass and, generally, pronounced his belief in her religion. He had taken his act of faith during his teens.

I had not met Willie's sponsor. Still, on one occasion I spotted him when he accompanied her to church. She was a gaunt, simply dressed woman. Her limp, accentuated by her attempt to walk quickly, indicated that she feared they would be late for mass.

The promissory note produced by Pratap gave me a jolt. How could a youngster, brought up in an orphanage and supported by a secondary school teacher, enter into a transaction which involved a substantial amount of money? Further, where would Willie have met Pratap? The promissory note suggested that they had some joint ventures. Had the two men some alter egos unknown to me?

"You surprised, Mr. Peter," observed Pratap.

"I am. Willie is a believer. Where did you meet him?"

"Sometime he work in Joyous Bar."

"I didn't know this. What sort of job?"

"If barman sick, we call Willie. Also if cook not come."

"So he needs money. But this note is for a very large amount."

"It is. But Mr. Peter, how well you know Willie?"

In the ensuing conversation, Pratap told me that he had lent money to Willie from time to time. Willie lost a great deal of it at the races and in gambling joints. He was not a high-flyer, who wasted money on expensive meals and fast women. As far as Pratap knew, Willie's only weakness was gambling. He looked unhappy as he told me about it.

"I think you like our Willie, Pratap. I can see it."

"I like. He excellent chef. Sometime we invite him and he cook hot curry. Better than my wife curry! He go market buy fresh spices: watches when grind. My wife buy curry powder from grocer."

"He invited me to partake in some lovely curries he made, Pratap. And you know, he loves to throw curry parties. And his chicken liver curry is delicious. Even for my *ang moh* palate, it's not too hot. It's excellent, especially when I take it with yoghurt. But look here Pratap, you like him. So why do you have his note for such an amount? You are a careful chap."

The emerging story appeared unbelievable. As far as I knew, Willie Chan was a sincere man of faith. Then I recalled some notable episodes. One episode took place when I discovered that our hall had a "cafeteria" with mahjong tables. On quite a few occasions I joined the ranks in the hope of enjoying a game of skill with local undergraduates.

Mahjong is not a mere game of chance. Usually four players take part. The tiles, used instead of cards, are shuffled and then arranged as four two-tier rows, one facing each player. Each player takes 13 tiles. In the ensuing game, each player picks up a tile and discards another. The objective is to gather 13 or 14 tiles arranged in one of a number of given sequences, for instance, three sets of identical tiles plus a set of two. A player wins when the last tile he picks up enables him to produce one of these acceptable sequences.

The victorious hand is assessed on its merit. If, for instance, all the winner's tiles are in but one of the available suits, the hand has a "high scoring". A mere termination of a game, with sets from different suits, is a poor win.

I had played mahjong with my classmates in secondary school in Tel Aviv, using a set presented to us by a Jewish tourist from Shanghai. It took us some time to master the complex rules. Once we did, we rose to the challenge. Each of our four players did his best to bring a game to its end by producing a good hand, akin to a royal flush in poker.

We appreciated that a player could terminate a session by arranging all his tiles in one of the acceptable sequences regardless of whether his hand was high scoring or weak. In technical language, he could "pong mahjong" as soon as his "hand" qualified. But a termination with a weak hand was frowned upon.

The players in Singapore had a different philosophy. Their objective was to "pong mahjong" as quickly as possible. In the long run a player made money — or came out as a winner — if he "pong mahjong" often enough. It soon dawned on me that the objective of the players in Singapore was to make a profit. The games in Tel Aviv had involved scoring (or "merit points"), but usually no money.

The players in Singapore were highly skilled. Further, they had a knack for giving misleading signals. Some, for instance, discarded tiles to confuse their opponents. On other occasions, a player held on to a specific tile so as to prevent an opponent from ending with a high score. From his point of view, it was preferable to lose out to a weak rather than to a high-scoring hand.

When the nature of the local game became clear to me, I considered quitting. I knew I was unable to win, especially as my opponents enjoyed ganging up on me. They were teaching their *ang moh* fellow their own mores.

Fortunately, Willie stepped into the gambling room during a disastrous session, just before I resolved to leave. Having taken in the scene, he said something in Mandarin and then joined our table. In no time, the game regained the respectable ambience of Tel Aviv. In the event, each session took longer than the ones prior to Willie's entrance. But the scores of the hands produced by the players were on the high side.

By the end of the evening, I made a marginal profit. All the same, I left with a nagging concern. Had the skilful players of our hall humoured me? A short chat with Willie, when we breakfasted together the next morning, settled any doubts. Politely but firmly, he told me that my way of playing the game was alien to our students. My emphasis was on dexterity; theirs was on profit-taking.

"Should I quit, Willie?"

"I think so, Sir. They will play your way when you join them. But they don't like this. Wilson Wong tells me there is a fine mahjong room in the Tanglin Club. They also have a Bridge room and Chess room. You may find them suitable."

"Do any of our chaps play bridge or chess?"

"I do. But I don't go to European clubs often. You see, expatriates don't play for money."

Willie's idea of directing my feet to games of skill made sense. I was a proficient bridge player. In due course, I became a regular attendant at the Tanglin Club's bridge room. Still, from time to time I dropped into the hall's mahjong room in order to kibitz. On many occasions, Willie was one of the players. More often than not, he came out as the winner.

"Willie plays mahjong," I told Pratap.

"I know," said Pratap.

"He is a champion, I think."

"Maybe," replied Pratap dryly.

Pratap's laconic assent reminded me of another episode. One sunny Sunday morning, I went in the company of some friends to the turf club. We betted on some races. Within two hours I lost the amount I was prepared to risk. So did all my colleagues except one, who invited us to a fine dinner to enjoy the spoils.

Although some secondary events were still in progress, most spectators departed. The aficionados alone remained behind, hoping to make money from betting on the remaining races. As we left, I spotted Willie. He was queuing up in front of the betting counter, with a pre-filled form in his hand. At that time, I considered it a lapse. Still, I was surprised Willie had not chaperoned his sponsor to their church.

However, Singapore was enjoying its school holidays at that time. I assumed that Willie's sponsor had flown to Edinburgh to visit her mother.

"I wonder if Willie likes to bet on horses," I told Pratap.

"Slow horses. He also buy Lottos and TOTOs," muttered Pratap, referring to the few legitimate balloting events. After some hesitation, he added: "And he go some illegal betting places."

"Is he a gambler?" I sought clarification.

"Yes."

"But you like him, Pratap."

"Of course, Mr. Peter. And wife tell me ask over. He always bring something for house. But yes, he gambler."

It dawned on me that, all in all, Willie could be a hardcore gambler. Indeed, some other scenes from my acquaintance with him supported Pratap's indictment. For instance, he placed bets on the outcome of the weekly tugs of war organised by our hall. I had closed my eyes to the self-evident facts.

Further, I recalled that on some occasions Willie had been singularly generous. On others he appeared short of cash and subdued. The cause was now obvious. One point, though, remained unclear. How had Pratap become familiar with our winding and spread-out campus? In my early days in Singapore I had, occasionally, lost my way in it.

"I look after Willie when fell ill last year. One day I take to clinic. On way, he showed me Japanese Block and say your office there."

"You looked after him when he was ill?"

"Of course. Willie is friend."

"But then, Pratap, why this hand note? Why do you need such a document from a friend?"

"But, Mr. Peter, friendship is friendship; business is business."

"I don't understand," I prevaricated.

"If Willie no food, I invite or take out. But loan is business. So, he must pay back."

"How much did you lend him?"

"Is not so simple. You see, first time I lend \$2,000 and he promise pay \$4,000 at end of month. When he not pay, he ask me "roll it over". So I tell him: pay \$8,000 after another two months. Then borrow more. So I think better get hand note."

I looked at him with amazement. In terms of real annual interest, the rate was phenomenal. Was Pratap a usurious moneylender? Did he hold a licence? Moreover, why had he turned to me? He knew I was unaware of Willie's nefarious activities.

"It's not a nice story, Pratap. But what can I do about it?"

"Willie respect you."

"So?"

"Please ask him pay. He win; so I can get money back. And, Mr. Peter, I cannot let go. You see, other borrowers can then also say "no". I cannot be hard on some and soft on others."

"You are not going to use the piranha tank, surely?" My reference to the carnivorous fish, which would gnaw off a hand forced into their tank, did not baffle Pratap.

"No need," he observed solemnly. "My men beat him up. And I not want this. I like him."

"Why on earth did you demand such a high rate?"

"You think Willie get money from bank?"

"Of course not. A gambler is a bad risk."

"So, you see, Mr. Peter, I take risk."

"So, if you lose out, why not forget about it?"

"You know what happens if other debtors find out. I told you."

For a few minutes I reflected. Then I gave way. "Alright, I'll talk to him."

A few days later, I spotted Willie in the mahjong room. His smirk and radiant expression convinced me that he was going through a winning streak. When the game was over, he invited me to join him for dinner. As often before, we proceeded to the Chinatown Market, where the food was reasonably priced and excellent.

"This was a sumptuous meal, Willie. Thanks."

"You love our local dishes, Sir."

"I do, if they are not too spicy. But now, Willie, I've got to talk to you about a different matter."

"So, you came to our den to see me?"

"I did, rather. You see, Willie, I had a visit from a mutual friend of ours."

"Wilson Wong, by any chance? He stopped coming over to the hall when the new term started. He moved in with his auntie."

"No, Willie. It wasn't Wilson Wong. I, too, haven't seen him for weeks."

"So, who was it?" asked Willie awkwardly.

"Pratap Singh, Willie. I know him from the Joyous Bar. He showed me that hand note of yours. You owe him a lot of money. Is it really your note?"

"It is, Sir."

"How could you? It's S$16,500, what I earn in roughly two years."

"I understand, Sir. But you see, I cannot help myself."

"Why?"

"I always try to give the table a miss. Sometimes I escape to the church. But many times I can't control my urge. Have you never placed a bet, Sir?"

"Only from my own money, Willie. I never borrow."

"Then you don't have a gambling streak. You are lucky."

I was aware of the nature of uncontrollable drives. One of my friends in Israel had been a compulsive gambler. He solved his problem by taking his life. A girl I knew well was a compulsive drinker. She had serious liver problems before she reached 40. Drugs and sex too could be compulsive.

The few who managed to kick their habit usually relied on their own internal resources. Others did so by making an act of faith and turning to providence. Most addicts, though, were beyond help. I suspected that Willie fell into this group. Still, I tried my best to solve his immediate problem. His next words indicated that there was a remote chance.

"If Pratap came over to see you, he is still a friend, Sir."

"He is. But he draws a distinction between friendship and business. We need to mollify him. How much did he lend you?"

"There were a few rollovers, Sir."

"He told me. Still, how much cash did he give you?"

"About $5,500, I think. The balance is interest. It's his usual rate."

"How much can you pay him?"

"I have $8,000. But I can't give him all my capital. I must try to win some money back."

"Do you owe money to others?"

"Not much," he told me frankly.

I saw no point in getting further information. In any event, I found the episode distasteful. Both Willie and Pratap were good acquaintances. I liked them. At the same time, I had no wish to get embroiled in their affairs. Once I sorted out the current problem, I would be entitled to avoid any further entanglements.

In more than one way, I was treading on thin ice. Under the law of Singapore, Pratap's lending transactions could not be enforced by a legal action. Once it was established that he had lent money to a number of people so as to make a gain, he would be deemed an unregistered moneylender. He could be prosecuted and fined. In addition, his job as a *jaga* (porter) in the Joyous Bar was in jeopardy. No hotel in Singapore would employ a "criminal".

Willie, too, was in a cul-de-sac. If his gambling activities became public knowledge — for instance, by a reference in the press — he might not be allowed to practise law. Regardless of any success in his studies, the law society might decline an application for his admission. He could also incur the displeasure of his sponsor. She was making a financial sacrifice to see him through. Would she forgive the squander of funds in gambling?

My own standing, too, was on the line. The university's authorities were bound to take exception to staff members involved directly or indirectly in gambling or illicit moneylending. The renewal of my contract of employment would be in jeopardy. I could, of course, protect my back by telling both Willie and Pratap that their affairs were none of my business. But I was loath to take such a stand.

"There is only one way out," I told Willie. "You must have a chat with Pratap. He may agree to settle on friendly terms."

"Can I meet him at your office, Sir? He will listen to you."

To my relief, the protagonists faced each other cordially. I was certain they wanted to clear the air. Both feared the limelight and the ensuing notoriety involved in publicity. In addition, they liked one another. Initially, Pratap was adamant. His transactions with Willie were made in good faith, and he had done Willie a favour.

"But Pratap, why did you ask Willie to execute the hand note?"

"I want things be clear," he replied after a pause.

"I thought it was?" I let my surprise show.

"Amounts and dates can confuse," explained the huge *jaga*. Then, after another pause, he added: "Sometime man confuse friendship and business. When have document all clear."

"I can see Pratap's point," volunteered Willie with a tinge of bitterness. "But Pratap knew where I was going to spend the money."

"But if you win, you share profit with me?" asked Pratap.

"Of course not. I repay your money with interest."

"You see," summed up Pratap.

His last words cleared the air. The deal involved moneylending. Pratap did not enter into a joint venture. He was not a partner to Willie's gambling activities. He was too cautious, too worldly, to throw his money onto the roulette table.

All the same, his words provided an opening for negotiations. As was to be expected, Pratap conceded that his rates were high. Still, ordinary financial institutions, or even licensed moneylenders, would not advance funds for gambling purposes. After some probing on my part, he accepted that he had lent Willie less than half the amount of the note. Initially, he insisted that all this — including the high rate — had been clear from the start and resisted any attempt to accept less than the amount of the note. Willie, in turn, pointed out that he simply did not have that much money. If he paid back all he had, he would have no chance to win money back. In the end, I persuaded both that we ought to re-open the set of loans.

"You see Pratap, you took the risk of losing, didn't you?" I reasoned with him.

"Of course. This my risk. But you see, Mr. Peter, I know Willie has money. He win a lot last week."

"How do you know?" asked Willie.

"My men watch you."

"You never trust anybody. Did you think I would run away?"

"I want be sure. I trust friend but not gambler."

Both were getting acrimonious. I sensed that before long they would reach the point of no return. It seemed best to step in.

"I can see the points of both of you. Let's leave the morals out. You, Pratap, lent money at a very high rate. And you, Willie, went ahead and borrowed. Now you have money. Let's see how much you can pay back."

To my relief, Willie produced his roll. He offered to pay Pratap $7,000 out of his $8,000 "stake". He needed the remaining $1,000 for the next race. Pratap took the money, but changed his mind.

"This is enough — $6,500. Good luck next race," he told his bewildered friend. He then produced the hand note and tore it into shreds. The matter was over.

II

A few months later, I got married. Later still, a university in New Zealand offered me a professorship. Both Pratap and Willie were far away from our new abode. Still, I remembered both with affection. I intended to look them up when I became eligible for a few months of sabbatical leave. As my wife's family resided in Singapore, we were bound to spend a few days there.

Shortly after our arrival in Singapore, I went over to the Joyous Bar. The new porter told me that Pratap had retired. At my request, he went to their office and brought me a slip with Pratap's address. I got the news about Willie when I called on one of his classmates, who had been elevated to the local bench. His Honour looked displeased when I asked about Willie, and produced a cutting from a newspaper. It showed a blurred photograph of Willie and included a report about his sad case. He had misappropriated clients' money and been convicted of criminal breach of trust. Having pleaded guilty to the charges, he was sentenced to six years in prison.

"I didn't expect this!" I let my disappointment show.

"Didn't you know he was a gambler, Prof?"

"I knew, but thought he would get over it."

"They never do, don't you know?"

"But why did he have to steal the money? Why didn't he borrow?"

"Who would have lent him? Everyone had a glimpse long ago."

"But didn't he know he was bound to get caught?"

"He hoped to win it back — they always do."

"Hopefully prison is not too rough on him. I'll visit him," I muttered.

"I don't think he'll see you. Quite a few of his mates called on him. He said that he wasn't well enough to cope. I suppose he's too embarrassed. But you know, he sees some church people. They say he is repenting."

Initially, Willie agreed to see me. But when I arrived at Changi, using my brother-in-law's car, the officer in charge told me that the prisoner was ill. As I left the complex, my eye caught sight of a woman, well past her prime, wearing a shabby old-fashioned skirt and holding a worn-out handbag. She was limping in the direction of the bus stop. As I recognised her, it also dawned on me that she might have just visited the very man I had been hoping to see.

"Miss Winifred Smith?" I asked with hesitation.

"Well?" she looked startled.

"Have you, per chance, visited Willie Chan?"

"Why do you want to know?"

"I was his teacher. I'm just passing through Singapore on my way to Frankfurt. He told me a lot about you when I was a warden in Raffles Hall. Can I give you a lift?"

As I steered the car through the traffic, I told her all about Willie's days at the hall. I had hoped he would get over his gambling drive, especially as he topped his form and got his first-class degree. He was bound to get a good job.

"What drove him back to the gambling tables?" I wanted to know.

"I have no idea. He was, I think, alright in school. It started when he enrolled in university. We talked about it often. He always promised to mend his ways. For a while I insisted on taking him to church every Sunday. But it was no good."

"Do you know anything about his parents? Who were they?"

"The orphanage doesn't ask, and if they know, they don't tell. But why does this matter? Surely gambling is not hereditary. I'm sure Willie does not know his parents."

"I suspect they abandoned him. How could they do that?"

"You assume they were married. Suppose his mother made a mistake?"

"Even so. How could she? And, come to think of it, where was the father?"

"He might have escaped as soon as he realised the girl was in trouble. Some men are like that." She did not display any annoyance. She was doing her best to remain objective.

"Did you sponsor him because you felt sympathy?"

"Not really. You see, he was such a bright spark: articulate, charming when he chose to be, and I thought he had a good core."

"Would you have done it if you had suspected he had a gambling streak?" I asked tactlessly.

"I think so. I would have tried to influence him. And, you know, he was — still is — a decent fellow. He married a really nice girl, and she told me that he was a model husband and a good father."

"I thought she divorced him?" I told her, startled.

"Her parents' decision. She wanted to stick it out with him, but they refused to support her unless she dropped him. Perhaps they were right. And she reverted to her maiden name."

"I am pretty sure he wanted to see me. How come he changed his mind? The warder told me that he has taken ill. But surely, he saw you."

"He is ashamed of his past. He sees only Father William, who preaches solace in faith, and me. Some of his classmates had the same experience as you. He was keen to see them but then couldn't."

I had no further questions to ask. Willie's willingness to talk to a priest did not surprise me. Many a rake sees the light when the right opportunity comes up. In most cases this inner light extinguishes itself when he has the chance to revert to his misdeeds.

"You don't think much of his future?" asked Winifred, who had been watching me keenly.

"I suspect I don't. But you see, I still like Willie. He is a nice chap. I remember how he treated me to some fine meals; his curries were excellent. I never wondered how he got his cash. I was too fond of him and, frankly, of the treats. I still can't understand why he was unable to stop himself. And I hate to see him down. Candidly, I do wish he had a fresh start. But I am pessimistic."

"Let's hope Father William succeeds where others have failed," she said resignedly.

I dropped her outside a run-down apartment block in the vicinity of the orphanage. She proceeded to the staircase without turning back.

III

When I arrived back at my room in my brother-in-law's house, I found the slip of paper with Pratap's address. I must have dropped it when I changed my trousers, but the conscientious maid placed it back on my bedside table.

Pratap was not surprised when I called on him. He knew I had gone down to Changi to see Willie. One of the warders, an old buddy, had told Pratap about it.

In more than one way, Pratap's appearance gave me a jolt. He was wearing neither the uniform I had come to know so well, nor the simple Western clothes he had put on when he had come to see me in the university. Instead, he was wearing a sarong and a batik shirt. He was not wearing his turban. I also noticed that he had aged and had put on weight. But his glance told me that he had retained his vigour and zest for life.

After the common pleasantries, I went straight to the point.

"Have you seen Willie after his scandal?"

"Only one time, Mr. Peter, before they give him six years. He told me bad luck. He wanted one break. If he win one race, he say he pay all of it back. After that, he told me, he quit. They always say this."

"Did you lend him any money after he finished law school?"

"He never ask."

"But would you have given him some if he had asked?"

"No, Mr. Peter. I know he never stop."

"And you never saw him in Changi?"

"No. I sure he not want see old friends. And what for? He serve out sentence. But I ask friends be kind to him. They treat well and is model prisoner."

"So you have friends in the prison?"

"Two warders."

"It is good of you to help him. But what will happen when Willie comes out?"

"He leave Singapore. But have friends in Kuala Lumpur. They find job where cannot take money."

"What is he doing in the prison?"

"He work in kitchen. He good chef."

I sensed that Pratap did not want to tell me any more about Willie. He had not abandoned him. Further, the idea of getting Willie employment as a chef made sense. He would thrive on any job that would keep him out of trouble.

"And what are you yourself doing these days, Pratap?"

"Same old business, Mr. Peter. I make good money and, you know, I very careful."

"But how do you know if a fellow will pay you back?"

"I try judge him. Like I knew Willie pay me back if has money. I take risk when borrower cannot pay."

"Do you ask your men to take care of him?"

"Depends," he prevaricated.

"And why did you leave the Joyous Bar?"

"Tough job; stand hours in hot sun. And pay poor. Now my boy and girl good jobs. I take things easy."

"Your boy and girl?"

"Daughter take your course in Wellington. She tell you tough teacher."

"And your boy?"

"He doctor; work in General Hospital."

"They live with you?"

"Both married. Wife and I have big house empty."

Pratap invited me to have supper with them. I gratefully accepted. Pratap's wife was a pleasant woman. The conversation flowed but steered clear of Willie. Pratap had told me what he thought I should know.

IV

A few days later, my wife Pat and I flew onward to Europe. We used to travelw to Singapore frequently during our years in New Zealand and Australia, but normally proceeded to Europe or Canada after. The visits were short, and so I had little time to enquire about Willie's whereabouts. And I did not call on Pratap. Eventually, though, we spent a year in Singapore when I got tired of the administrative functions associated with my post in Australia.

Some two months after we resettled in a university flat, I visited Pratap. This time he was surprised to see me. I, too, was perplexed. Pratap had shaved off his beard. He was bald and looked smaller. Had he shrunk with age?

The Moneylender and the Gambler

"I saw you in street, Mr. Peter. You not recognise me."

"You look different Pratap. Why did you shave off your beard?"

"Is nuisance. Very itchy."

As before, Pratap invited me to have dinner in his spacious bungalow. To my surprise, the food was served by an amah.

"Wife died two years ago. Heart attack."

"I am sorry, Pratap," was all I could say.

"She good wife. And so sudden."

"Better than suffering before you go, Pratap."

"I know. But house empty. I want sell and buy small flat in condo."

The amah brought in the dishes. The curries had a lovely smell. But they were bound to be hot. Pratap grinned when he saw my expression.

"These two, near you, not so hot," he assured me. "But you try this one. Is hot but take with yoghurt."

"It's excellent," I conceded. "Where did you get these spices?"

"From Willie. You see, Mr. Peter, son and daughter not come see me. Perhaps they ashamed. But Willie come over every time he fly down."

"What became of him?"

"He chef of curry restaurant in K L, very posh."

"Who lent him the money? He is a bad risk, isn't he?"

"So I refuse lend him. But you know, I little to do now. So we become partners. I fly up every two week. And he cannot take money from account without my signature."

"And if the business fails, Pratap? You used to say that lending is a better business than a partnership!"

"But Mr. Peter, I really not mind. So boy and girl get less when I go. But business not fail. Willie excellent chef and customers love restaurant. So don't you worry."

"And how about your old business?"

"Boy and girl say moneylending not respectable. So, Mr. Peter, I retire."

"You were always a smart fellow," I told him. "But can you afford to lose your investment?"

"Sure can. Have some houses. But, you know, I like help Willie. He good fellow and friend."

"Has he stopped gambling?"

"I not know for sure, Mr. Peter. I not ask. But he cannot take money from restaurant. And you see, my lawyer tell me register it as private company."

"So you are not liable for debts," I grinned.

"True. Make profit, but no loss!"

Just as I was getting ready to leave, the telephone rang. I wondered whether the caller was either Pratap's son or his daughter. Then I heard Pratap's reply.

"Good hear from you, Willie. And you know who here? ... No, Willie, no! Ranjan and Mali busy. They always is. Your old teacher, Mr. Peter. He like your curry."

For a few minutes they conversed. Then Pratap told me that Willie would like to speak to me.

"Long time no see, Sir. I hope you are fit and well."

"Oh, I'm okay, Willie. But last time I came to see you, you were ill."

"I have put all this behind me, Sir. Please get my address from Pratap and come and have a meal here. I'll make the chicken liver curry you liked so much, with yoghurt."

"You have a good memory, Willie."

"Always had, Sir. I remember how you pushed me to my first-class."

"You could have been a courtroom virtuoso, Willie."

"Perhaps. But I enjoy life here. It's just the right job for me. I love it when patrons savour my dishes and come back. It feels great."

"So fortuna smiled on you again, Willie."

"Fortuna?"

"You call her karma. But she is the same lady."

Darma

The bed, with the guards on both sides and the gadgets mounted on top, revealed that I was not in an upmarket hotel. I was in a room in Ward XX of a local hospital.

I was initially taken to Emergency. However, it was bound to take the physicians a few days to determine the cause of my fainting spell. The functioning of my heart, brain and vascular system required assessment. Accordingly, I had to be transferred to a ward.

Shortly after my wife, Pat, and relatives left, a nurse came to monitor my blood pressure and sugar levels. When she was done, she mentioned that a patient in an adjacent room recognised me. His door had been ajar when I was taken to the ward.

"I think he would love to see you. Let me wheel you over. He is bedridden."

The patient I went to visit was a dark Indian fellow in his mid 60s. His pie bald head, sagging shoulders, wrinkled face and skinny arms projected an aura of defeat. He was clean-shaven, but the occasional stubbles showed that his beard had gone white.

I was initially unable to recognise him. Then I observed the twinkle in his dark eyes and the ghost of a smile spreading over his face.

"Have I changed that much?" he asked in a husky, alien voice.
"D… d… ar… ma," I stammered.
"At your service, Sir," he chuckled.

It took me a while to recover from my shock. When I knew him in the old days, Darma was a broad-shouldered, heavy-set giant. The bedridden man in the ward was an emaciated shadow of my erstwhile student. He had aged less gracefully than me or any of his contemporaries.

"I thought you had settled in Sydney, Darma," I tried to salvage the situation. "When did you return to our shores?"

"Ages ago, Sir," he grinned; then added awkwardly, "You see, my Australian wife, Jill, ran away. I planned to stay put but then I met Lynn, a nice dental nurse who came over from Singapore to visit her sister. She took me back to Singapore."

"But wasn't that rather sudden?"
"It was," he nodded.
"How did you settle your affairs?"
"There wasn't much to settle," he said flatly. "A young colleague took over my files. So all I had to do was to give up my office and sell my house. No big deal!"

"And how did you re-settle in Singapore?" I ventured.
"Not too well. Most of my old friends had long forgotten me."

As he spoke, I recalled that Darma had acquired a dubious reputation in Sydney. He was regarded as tricky and untrustworthy. This type of information travels fast. Back at home nobody wanted to take him in as a partner or even as a legal associate.

"How about your family?" I asked Darma.

"They washed their hands of me when I married Jill."

Having failed to secure a post in an established Singapore law firm, Darma started to practise on his own. Although none of his old friends had offered him a post, some kept referring to him undemanding and usually not too remunerative matters. There were also some walk-in clients who engaged him for simple matters such as traffic offences. Work was not abundant but, at the very least, he eked out a living.

Darma's main comfort was his home life. Lynn was not a beauty, but she was a self-assured, vivacious, supportive and understanding wife. She kept Darma happy. Further, her contribution to the household expenditure enabled them to enjoy a comfortable existence. Then, unexpectedly, Lynn developed cancer of the stomach. For a few months she struggled on but, in the end, passed away.

Darma was devastated. Friendless and lonely, he started to hit the bottle. Often, he was too inebriated to go to his office. Before long, he lost most of his clients. One morning he collapsed in a supermarket and was rushed to Emergency. Like me, he was admitted into a ward.

Darma's sad story contrasted sharply with his joyous life during his university days. I had come to know him well when I was appointed a Residential Fellow of Raffles Hall. Darma, who was in his third year of studies, shared a room with Dan, a Chinese student from a middle-class background. Their corridor was adjacent to my flat.

Shortly after I joined the hall, Darma organised a welcome lunch at a well-known eatery owned by a fellow called Gomez. The grapevine had it that Gomez stirred his pots with his "leprous finger". Still, his South Indian curries were so hot that the bacteria succumbed.

Gomez' curries were, indeed, pure fire. To consume them, I had to drink one glass of iced water after the other. Darma cherished my profuse thanks but, on future occasions, led us to a North Indian eatery. I enjoyed the mild chicken livers and sea food curries while Darma and his gang ordered such hot dishes as were available.

Once a week our two corridors engaged in a contest of strength, known as a tug of war. Two teams pulled a rope in opposite directions. Unfortunately, some problems arose from the terrain. Usually the team stationed on the upper part of the slope lost out to the team on the lower part. As the teams changed their position after each tug, the general outcome per afternoon was a draw.

Darma and I were the "heavy weights" on each side. As he was some 10 kilos heavier than me, we ensured that our team included some husky fellows. Initially both teams used the same tactic. Each had a timer who, upon the blow of whistle, yelled "one ... two ... three: pull". Seeking to gain an advantage, I induced our timer to forego the count to three and, instead, shout "pull, ho" as soon as the whistle was blown. Taken by surprise, Darma's team lost that tug although they were stationed on the favourable lower terrain.

They took their revenge the following week. When our timer yelled "pull, ho", his counterpart commanded: "let go". As our team members stumbled over each other, Darma's group pulled us up the slope. I recall Dan, who teamed up with us that afternoon, dangling at the end of the rope and yelling "this was a mean trick, Darma".

Darma's reputation as a student was, alas, mixed. He could work hard but often failed to see the wood for the trees. Occasionally, he lost the thread of the lectures he attended. On one such occasion, the lecturer — a well-known bully — was irked by Darma's patent failure to concentrate. In the end, he asked Darma to explain the last point covered in class.

"Sorry, Sir," confessed Darma, "I can't."

"Darma," roared the enraged staff member, "why don't you jump out of the window?"

"After you, Sir," retorted Darma.

Darma maintained a low profile at the faculty. In the hall, he was one of our bright sparks, always happy to mastermind the organisation of our numerous functions and parties. In my first year in residence, Darma took charge of the preparations for our annual festive dinner. The Master of the hall contributed by raising extra funds for drinks.

As was to be expected, everybody partook. By 9 p.m., most of us had more to drink than was recommended. Some slept it off under the huge dining table; others danced merrily on its top and the few semi-sober fellows withdrew discreetly to their quarters where, in the very least, they had beds.

As the proceedings turned chaotic, I saw Darma dancing happily on the stage. Being well stoned, it occurred to me that it would be nice to get Darma's smart green turban.

Acting on my whim, I offered Dan S$10 for the trophy. Dan hesitated but, when I doubled my offer, his eyes gained lustre and he cold-bloodedly demanded S$25 — a substantial amount in those remote Golden Days. Reluctantly, I closed the bargain.

A few minutes later, all of us were startled by a haul of anger. Dan, who was a small chap, made a triple somersault, coming to rest against a sliding door. Anxiously, Darma rushed over to his side.

"Oh my God," he wailed, "what have I done?"

"You, Darma, better learn to reckon with your own strength," muttered Dan as he rose back to his feet, dusted himself and proceeded in the direction of the conveniences.

Later in the evening, I discovered the entire truth. Dan had told Darma about my offer and suggested that they share the spoils on a 50-50 basis. Darma insisted that, as the object of the transaction was his turban, he deserved S$15. When Dan called him "a turbaned skinflint", Darma lost his temper. He did not punch his friend but simply pushed him out of the way.

Two days later, when I returned to the hall after work, I was surprised to find a neatly folded green turban on my table. The card accompanying it read: "Sorry for the fuss, Sir."

In the following academic session, Darma became my problem. Contrary to my advice, he enrolled in my Advanced Banking Law course. The subject was hard and the problems and issues were complex. Occasionally, it was difficult to reconcile the mass of judicial pronouncements found in English and local authorities. Even the brightest students were frequently struggling.

By the end of the first semester most students came to grips with the convoluted subject. Darma was the exception. His mid-year exam revealed that he had remained out of depth. I feared that if his final-year paper was to be of a similar calibre, he would have to be failed. The problem was serious: Dan had told me in confidence that if Darma failed, his father would withdraw his financial support.

The only way out was to give Darma some extra tuition. When I went over to his room to make the offer, I was flabbergasted to see Darma leaning against the wall whilst standing on his head. His eyes were closed and he was chanting words in an alien language. Had he gone off his rocker?

It seemed best to withdraw quietly and think the matter over. To soothe my nerves, I went over to a nearby cafeteria and ordered a cup of the strongly brewed local coffee.

"I must have given you a start, Sir," said Darma, who sneaked in while I was sipping.

"You did, rather," I affirmed. "What on earth are you up to?"

"Look here, Sir: I know I'm not a bright student. But my Guru assures me that I'd have a chance if I stood on my head for half an hour every morning and said some prayers!"

Notwithstanding the Guru's counsel, Darma's final- year paper was even worse than his attempt at mid-year. If my own assessments were final, I would have had no option but to fail him. Fortunately, we had at that time a regime of external examiners. It seemed best to pass Darma and settle the matter when our "external", a well-known scholar of London University, put in his appearance.

"I have approved all your marks, except this one," the "external" told me when we met. "Do you really think this candidate deserves a pass? Was his class performance outstanding?"

"Well …" I stammered, "… actually it wasn't. He was a marginal candidate throughout."

"On what basis do you then recommend a pass?"

A twinkle crept into the external examiner's eye when I told him how I found Darma standing on his head. His stern expression mellowed as I expounded the Guru's advice. When I finished the story, our seriously minded "external" was grinning from ear to ear.

"We can't possibly slight the Guru," he concluded and added his signature to mine.

A few days later, when the results approved by the Board of Examiners were posted on the notice board, I saw Darma hailing a taxi.

"Where are you off to, Darma?"
"Downtown, Sir," he confided. "I've got to pay my Guru."
"I understand," I muttered when I found my voice.

"Those were great days," said the bedridden invalid.
"Weren't they ever?" I affirmed.
"They were the best years of my life, my heyday. Now life is full of uncertainties," he told me sadly.

Back in my room, I reflected on Darma's unfortunate life. Where did he go wrong? Was it his move to Sydney? It then dawned on me that the rot had set in earlier than that: Darma opted for the wrong profession. He had the makings of an excellent entertainer or hotel executive. He was a shrewd individual but lacked the "machinery" to make it in the world of the law. Passing him was misguided. In reality, the external and I myself delivered the coup de grace! We aimed to be kind but enabled Darma to proceed with a career for which he had no aptitude.

The next morning in hospital, I was wheeled over to the main building for the last and final test. On my way, I noticed that the door to Darma's room was wide ajar and that his bed was empty. Was he, too, going to be subjected to further tests?

My own test, conducted with the objective of determining the flaw of blood in my brain, was singularly unpleasant. When at long last the procedure was over, I was glad to be wheeled back to my room.

"I'd love a cup of coffee," I told the nurse. "And then it would be time to look Darma up."

"I am afraid that's not on," she told me. "You see, Sir, your friend passed away late last night."

"What happened? How did he die?"

It turned out that after I had returned to my own room following my chat with Darma, a staff member of the cashier's department called on him in order to obtain a deposit. It was actually her third visit. When Darma could not pay the amount demanded, they moved him to a Class C Ward. Late at night, Darma suffered an attack of breathlessness. The nurse-in-charge called the duty physician. By the time he arrived, Darma had given up the ghost.

I feared that Darma's funeral would be modest, perhaps even nondescript. To my delight, I discovered that I had been wrong. My wife, who at my request had attended the function, kept me informed. She told me that Darma's remains had been placed in an elegant coffin. An ageing, sparse but still energetic looking man, acted as the master of ceremonies.

"Dan?" I asked her.

"I think so," she affirmed. "Darma's old classmates and friends congregated for the occasion."

Initially I was surprised. I then realised that Darma was remembered by all of them. Due to his tarnished reputation, nobody offered him a job. But quite a few of them donated generously when Dan passed the hat around to commemorate Darma.

A few days later the ward doctor signed my discharge. Pat came to take me back. Whilst we waited in the queue for a taxi to take us home,

I kept reflecting about Darma. His sad end was the culmination of an unsuccessful career. His friends, though, remembered his heydays. In their eyes he remained — to the very end — the cheerleader of his contemporaries at Raffles Hall. And they recalled him affectionately, as, indeed, did I.

Shadow of the Gallows

I

The banking law conference I attended in Hong Kong in 1999 was over. The flight back to Singapore was crowded. Fortunately, I managed to secure an aisle seat near the bathrooms. A group of young Australian tourists who, I suspected, planned to make a stopover in our town on their way back from holidays in the People's Republic of China (PRC) "enlivened" the flight by mooing like cows and singing *Waltzing Matilda*. The other passengers, including me, suffered in silence.

I was aware that this noisy group could not be described as typical Australians. In my nine years in Melbourne, I found the middle-class locals, like my Australian neighbours and colleagues, a considerate and friendly lot. But I soon discovered that certain neighbourhoods and streets were unsafe. The holidaymakers on our flight reminded me of the type of person you had to avoid.

Unexpectedly, the young woman who occupied the window seat in my row asked me to swap seats with her. She was informally dressed and, obviously, was one of the Australian holidaymakers. You could sense from her bearing and self-assured manner that she was used to having her way. She explained that she was keen to take part in the festivities and hence wanted to step from time to time onto the aisle.

When I refused, she asked the flight attendant to find her a seat near her fellow holidaymakers. Eventually, she exchanged places with a Swiss tourist, who was relieved to get away from the unbearable noise. After a while, my new neighbour and I started to chat in German, talking mainly about banking and finance.

As we approached Changi Airport, the loudspeakers announced that the use of drugs carried heavy penalties in Singapore. A person proved to be in possession of more than the prescribed quantity of drugs may be presumed a drug dealer and may face the death penalty.

Shortly thereafter, the Australian girl, who had originally occupied the window seat in my row, came over and asked whether we could take her hand luggage through the customs. The Swiss tourist explained that he was transiting on his way back to Zurich and I told her that my own carrier was heavy and as much as I could take.

Having bestowed an unkind glance on me, she took her bag, which she had left in the overhead compartment. Walking back to her current seat, she took out a parcel and asked a young member of her group, who struck me as less vulgar than the rest, to carry it for her. He placed it in his own hand luggage. Shortly thereafter, he accepted parcels handed to him by other members of the group.

Before long, we arrived at our destination. The efficient arrangements at Changi Airport enabled me to complete all the formalities within 20 minutes. However, I noticed that the young Australian, who had taken the parcels entrusted to him by his fellows, was prevented from going through the gates after being sniffed out by trained dogs.

His fellow holidaymakers were waiting for him in the arrival hall. I suspected that he was being subjected to a body search.

My own priority was to get home as soon as possible. My wife was waiting for me and I wanted to have a good rest. The taxi queue not being long, I was on my way within five minutes. On arrival, my wife mentioned that a recent news broadcast announced the arrest of an Australian drug trafficker by the airport police.

"I hate these gangsters," she observed.

"I couldn't agree more." I was, at the same time, wondering whether the offender was the young fellow who had carried the parcels. In the event, I concluded that this was not my business.

Supper was ready and I retired shortly thereafter. But I was unable to fall asleep. I was concerned about the cul-de-sac in which my wife existed. True, her family was in Singapore. She went to their church service every Sunday and occasionally lunched with them. But she refrained from going out with them in the evenings.

As I went to the conference on my own, she would have stayed put and hence been alone for the three days I had been away. She would have been watching Chinese programmes on our television set.

I had never mastered any Chinese language, so if I had not attended the conference, I would in all probability have worked at home on a forthcoming publication. In effect, Pat and I had few interests in common. Each of us had continued to be immersed in the milieu of younger days. Pat had remained a typical Singaporean heartland Chinese. I had remained an ethnic mid-European Jew.

Our 20 years in New Zealand and Australia had not bridged the original gap. Neither did our return to Singapore. Pat had remained closer to her family than to me. I did go with her to family reunions during Chinese New Year and Christmas, but I did not enjoy these occasions.

In reality, I had developed a deep feeling of dislike for my in-laws. They purported to be Christian fundamentalists but, in reality, I had seen them acting unkindly and selfishly on many occasions. Pat, in turn, did not get on with my parents. They remained alien to her. I suspected she had a deep aversion for them. Naturally I visited my parents sporadically in Vienna, but preferred not to take Pat with me on these occasions.

As I was lying on my bed after supper, I kept dwelling on our family life. Eventually my eyes closed. But my sleep was interspersed with nightmares. It was not peaceful.

II

The next morning I had to get up early. My first teaching class was scheduled for 10 am and, of course, I had to prepare myself. On my arrival at the law school, I told my secretary Shamsia that if anyone rang, I was unavailable.

When I returned from my class, she told me that Raymond Bentley had asked me to join him for lunch at the Hilton Hotel in Orchard Road.

"I told him you had a departmental meeting at 2.30 pm, but he said that the matter was urgent. He wants to see you today."

I was about to reply when my telephone rang. Shamsia picked it up and, after a few seconds, whispered to me that Raymond Bentley was on the line. Unwillingly, I took the receiver.

"I gather you are very busy today, Peter."

"Quite so," I made an effort to hide my irritation.

"I must see you today. Can you come over for dinner?"

"We have something on! You can have coffee with me in our guild house at 4.30 pm. I'll have to leave by 5.15 pm."

"Oh, very well," he agreed. "Where is the guild house?"

"Right on the campus. Most taxi drivers know it."

Raymond was waiting for me in the guild house. His features, I thought, were unmistakably Jewish. The anglicised name-change could not mask his identity. I knew he was secular in his outlook but, at the very same time, regularly went to weekly services in the synagogue and was a leading member of the local community. I had met him sporadically during my Melbourne days, but had never been to his house.

Looking him over, I observed that he had put on weight, and that his once black hair was streaked with grey. I suspected that he was attending too many cocktail parties and business luncheons. Did he, at the very least, exercise?

"You wonder why I had to see you so urgently, Peter?"

"Quite."

"I came over at the request of a client and I thought it important to discuss the matter with you."

"Why don't you go to your correspondent firm? It is efficient."

"This is an unusual case. You must have heard about the drug arrest in the airport? Yesterday's?"

"Not the arrest made after the flight from Hong Kong?"

"That very one. A young Australian chap. His family uses our firm and so I came over. You see, the chap arrested is David Stone. He just carried parcels given to him by some fellow travellers. He is not an addict."

"I was on the same flight." As soon as I spoke, I wanted to bite my tongue off. In reality, I did not wish to have anything to do with such an affair. Further, during my days in Melbourne, the Jewish community did not show any hospitality to Pat and me. I knew that we had not made any effort to communicate. Still, in Wellington, where we had lived before moving to Melbourne, the community contacted us, had welcomed us and had remained in touch. In Melbourne, we should have taken the initiative to integrate, but we had failed to do so. In the circumstances, the mention of the offender's identity did not jar me. Naturally I was aware of the affiliation based on ethnic grounds, but I did not feel any personal involvement.

Raymond was quick to take up my remark. In the event, it seemed best to tell him the entire story. Raymond looked at me with concern.

"I can sense you have little sympathy. I understand that the group's caterwauling got on your nerves. But David is neither an addict nor a trafficker. You saw yourself how his friends gave him their parcels."

"True," I conceded. "But of course, I did not know what the contents were."

"I understand," he muttered. Raymond was too sound a lawyer to forget that any conclusions about the episode were the domain of a judge.

"You sound pessimistic, Peter. Surely the matter can be cleared up?"

"It is a serious matter, Raymond. Under our Misuse of Drugs Act, the trafficking, import or export of drugs can be a capital offence. Further, the act includes presumptions, which are not easy to rebut. And of course, the announcement by the plane's loudspeaker was clear. You get a rather similar broadcast when you fly to Australia. They tell you to dispose of any drugs, fruit or vegetables before you enter the country. I once had to throw away some lozenges for a sore throat. Fortunately I was able to buy similar ones when we got to Sydney's downtown."

"But this is different. In Australia you risk confiscation. In your town it is a capital offence."

"True. So why on earth didn't they flush the drugs down the toilet?" I wanted to know.

"I suspect they bought the drugs from the Chinese market and hoped to sell them in Oz to finance their holiday."

"So they didn't want to dispose of them. They knew all about the risk and so found a scapegoat. If the dogs hadn't been used that day, the holidaymakers' risk would have paid off!"

"Well, what is the best course, Peter?"

"Look here Raymond, neither of us is a courtroom advocate. You specialise in trusts and estates. I am a banking lawyer. Let me give you a list of the best criminal lawyers in Singapore. Some of them specialise in cases of this sort. They are also excellent in court. Each of them is quick on his feet."

"The family has asked Berry Lewis, QC, of Melbourne to be in charge."

"But he too specialises in commercial law and isn't really a top courtroom advocate. And he does not have a right of audience here. Why him?"

"He has handled the family's commercial litigation matters very successfully over the years!"

"But you are now talking about criminal law. And he may not be able to handle things outside Oz."

"We'll see," said Raymond.

Eventually he broke the ensuing silence by bluntly asking whether my patent lack of sympathy was due to my having distanced myself from the Jewish community in Melbourne.

"Not really," I assured him. "It only means that I am under no duty to assist. I am free to be guided by my attitude to matters concerning drugs. I have seen what their use can do to people. I am in support of any law that seeks to combat their availability. I am a hardliner. Still, I'll give you one piece of advice. Try to have the matter settled with the authorities through diplomatic channels before David is formally charged. If he is prosecuted, the outlook is dim."

"Can't you have a word with former students or old friends? Can't you ask for understanding on their part?"

"I am afraid I cannot. I am a guest in this country and am not prepared to step out of line. And Raymond, our system is clean."

Raymond did not take the matter further. After some small talk he took his leave. I was relieved to accompany him to the door. I realised that the severity of the matter had not dawned on him. He simply considered me unhelpful. In a way, he was right. I suspected that, unlike me, young David was born with a silver spoon in his mouth. Had he ever fought to secure his future?

III

For a few days all was quiet. The news media did not refer to the matter. I hoped that Raymond had taken my advice. Then, unexpectedly, he invited me for dinner at Raffles Hotel. David's mother, Ruth, and his grandfather, Jonathan Silver, had already arrived in Singapore, accompanied by Berry Lewis, QC. Apparently the authorities had decided to prosecute.

"I don't like going out in the evenings, Raymond," I prevaricated.

"But you do appreciate how serious this is. Surely, you do go out from time to time?"

"Why not have a quick meal in a less formal place and closer to where I live? In any event, what is the purpose?"

"You must explain to them that we are not dealing with a misdemeanour. Berry tried to talk to the people in charge and got nowhere!"

"Why on earth did you ask him? You should have gotten an experienced local lawyer."

"Ruth and Jonathan decided it would be best to leave the matter in Berry's hands. Ruth in particular thinks very highly of him."

"You ought to have made it clear to them that we are in Singapore, not in Melbourne!"

"That's why I want you to talk to them!"

"All right," I gave in. "There is a pleasant buffet in the Orchard Hotel, not far from where I live. I'll meet you there at 7.30 for a quick meal."

"Bring your wife with you."

"She normally watches her favourite television programme in the evening. I'll come on my own."

They arrived before me. Ruth, whom I had not met previously, was in her mid-40s. Her squat and heavily set figure suggested that she had not watched her diet. She enthusiastically dug into a dish of pork pâté and parma ham. In contrast, her father, Jonathan Silver, partook only in vegetarian dishes. It amused me to think that even in our community, everyone made his or her own principles. A strictly orthodox observer would, I suspect, have insisted on going to the eatery in the synagogue.

Despite his advanced age, Jonathan appeared vigorous and focused. He had the reputation of being a shrewd and principled businessman, and used Raymond's firm in all his business dealings. Before long, he started the conversation.

"Peter, I am sorry we remained worlds apart during your Melbourne days. But we feel we can rely on your advice. Raymond tells me you are uneasy about us engaging Berry. Why?"

"As I told Raymond, Lewis is a fine commercial lawyer, but he is not a renowned courtroom advocate. Why on earth did you contemplate bringing him over? We have a local bar."

"But is it any good?" interceded Ruth. "People who have lived in Singapore tell me they had bad experiences with your lawyers!"

"I suppose every lawyer in Melbourne is bound to outshine ours," I replied testily without the slightest attempt to suppress my chagrin. Ruth was about to retort when Jonathan stepped in.

"Look here, Peter, Berry is already here. You told Raymond that the first step was to talk to the authorities here. Well, Berry called on the fellow in charge of the file. As you know, they decided to press charges."

"Why on earth did you ask him? He has no experience or standing here."

"He is a great lawyer," interposed Ruth, "and we thought he would know how to talk to these people."

"Oh well," I retorted, trying hard to control my temper. "It isn't really my business."

Jonathan looked at me keenly. He sensed that I disapproved and, further, realised that I was pessimistic about the case and keen to be left alone. All the same, he felt the need to probe.

"Why do you think Berry was a bad choice?" he asked.

"You need a soft-spoken local who would know how to persuade the people in charge of prosecution. Actually, what did Berry tell them?"

"He told them all about human rights," snapped Ruth. "Someone has to enlighten them!"

I was about to retort in kind, when Berry made his appearance. My eyes widened when I saw that he was accompanied by Vardan Kilani. A few years earlier, Vardan had taken one of my courses. He received a good mark but did not shine. Further, although he built up a well-regarded boutique practice, dealing mainly with corporate matters, he was not an experienced or sought after litigator.

"Sorry to keep you waiting, I had a call from a client in Melbourne," explained Berry. As a few years had passed since our previous encounter, I was not surprised that his beer belly had grown out of all proportion and that he looked aged and worn out. He had the reputation of being a tough negotiator, but occasionally failed to pull his punches. From time to time, the counterparties were put off by his manner and the deal fell through.

"I understand. But I have to leave soon," I explained.

"Then let us get straight to business," said Berry. "Raymond tells me you saw how the drugs were passed on to my client."

"Have you already been admitted?" I asked him without answering his question.

"We shall see to that," explained Vardan.

"I did not realise that this was an issue," Jonathan spoke mildly, but I could sense he was bewildered.

"Only local practitioners have a right of audience. A foreign lawyer can be admitted in respect of a specific case if the judge is satisfied that his expertise is required."

"Surely there can be no doubt on this," snapped Ruth, ignoring her father's imploring expression.

Initially, I felt the need to take issue with her. Then I gave way to my strong dislike of contention. In any event, the family had placed the matter in the hand of a practitioner selected by them. Common sense prescribed a quick termination of the meeting.

"Look, I'll just have a cup of tea. Anything else I can do for you?"

"You can testify that the drugs were handed to David on the plane!"

"Surely, Vardan, you know I can't say that. All I saw was that some parcels were handed to him."

"But they contained the drugs," persisted Vardan. Berry nodded.

"Surely, I can't…"

"Or won't?" snapped Ruth.

"Let me finish," I lost my temper. "You know, Vardan, that I cannot testify about the contents of a bag or package not belonging to me, don't you? You have passed a course on evidence law, haven't you?"

"I too did law," snapped Ruth. "I know all about evidence!"

"Then you ought to know how things stand here." Having regained my temper, I added: "And I really must leave. Forget about the tea."

"How do you rate the chances, Prof?" asked Vardan.

"Now that the charges have been made?"

"Yes," muttered Vardan.

"Poor," I said after a short lapse of time. "Once the charges have been pressed, it is likely to be an open-and-shut case."

"Although David was not a drug user?" asked Jonathan mildly.

"In a sense it makes it worse. You have someone in possession of prohibited drugs. If he does not use them himself, why does he carry them?"

"How about the question of *mens rea*?" asked Berry. To my surprise, he spoke mildly and was not at all belligerent.

"Under our law, the carrier may be presumed to be a trafficker if the prosecution proves that the carrier is in possession of more than a prescribed quantity of drugs. You can call it a rebuttable presumption of *mens rea*."

"Surely *mens rea* needs to be proved and not presumed in all criminal proceedings," interspersed Ruth. "This is fundamental! Are you a criminal lawyer?"

"Of course not!" I snapped back. "Obviously my advice is irrelevant. Forget about it!"

As I got up to leave, Jonathan, who was viewing me keenly, stepped in firmly. "Really, Peter, what can we do? Don't you realise that, for us, this is a nightmare?"

"I know." Noting that Berry was watching me, I added: "Your best course of action is to put the matter in the hands of a competent local criminal lawyer. He may still be able to talk to the prosecution."

"We found Vardan Kilani excellent in all our dealings."

"I understand. But I'm sure they were all commercial in nature. Have you ever asked him to handle a criminal case?"

Shortly thereafter, I took my leave. All the same, the matter kept bothering me. I thought that David might be a mere scapegoat, who was unaware of the contents of the parcels belonging to his companions. The facts, though, brought him to the shadow of the gallows. And his family's bombast was unhelpful.

Pat looked at me with concern when I arrived home. She knew me well and realised that I was upset. After some prompting, I told her what had happened.

"But why do you care, Peter? If they want to prove that David did not know what was in the parcels, his own friends can tell this to the judge."

"Drug trafficking is an offence in Australia. Even if they get safe passage here, it becomes clear that they bought drugs for trading in Melbourne. The Australian authorities may prosecute them!"

"But what can happen to them?"

"Actually, no offence was committed in Australia. But even if they were charged and found guilty, they would be fined, or would have to serve a term or be granted probation."

"And your friend, David?"

"He is not my friend, darling. I've never met him. But I know that if he is convicted, capital punishment is mandatory. It will be rough on him and his family."

"But if his Australian friends do not want to help, why do you worry? You don't even know him! Peter, is it because he is a Jew?"

"That is one thing. But I feel sorry for his grandfather. He really wants to save his grandson."

"I understand. But did they care for us in Melbourne? I know you made contributions to a Jewish charity without telling me. I knew all the time. But this is really not your business. You better work on your new book."

I realised that Pat was right. Even if I had become a member of a local synagogue, the ethnical tie should not have led me to acts of folly. David's family had made their decision about the handling of the case. In my opinion, they were misguided. Both Berry and Vardan were out of their depths.

As my advice had been rejected, my only sensible course was to wash my hands off the entire affair. After all, I had never suggested that the law be reformed. I was known to be a hardliner and, in reality, did not experience a change of heart. My feelings were confined to sympathy for Jonathan and, to some extent, for David. But why had David agreed to carry his friends' parcels without verifying the contents?

Being unable to concentrate on the forthcoming publication, I induced Pat to switch on a television channel that showed *Don Giovanni*. Before long I was immersed in Mozart's uplifting music.

IV

Teaching, research and luncheons with colleagues kept me busy during the next few days. Then, unexpectedly, I received a telephone call from a former student who was in the government service.

"Prof, did you see today's paper?"

"No," I told him truthfully.

"They report that a university professor says that in Singapore, trial is by jury."

"What? I remember the long wrangling on the subject. Trial by jury was abolished quite a few years ago!"

"The lawyers of an Australian fellow accused of a drug trafficking offence claim that this reform was unconstitutional. And they say that a university professor is of the same view."

"Who is that?"

"They refer to a source 'that wished to remain anonymous'. I wanted to make sure that this 'source' wasn't you."

"You know I have no respect for juries!"

"I remember; you had expressed pretty strong views about the subject in seminars. I just wanted to be sure you haven't changed your mind."

Maybe a Swan Song: A Second Trip Down Memory Lane

For the next two hours, I concentrated on students' essays. I suspected that quite a few were ghostwritten. Some essays, though, evidenced careful research and fine analysis. As always, I had a few pleasant and some unsatisfactory surprises.

When I returned from lunch in the canteen, I found a voice message asking me to ring Raymond "as soon as convenient". Heaving a sigh, I called his number.

"What can I do for you, Raymond?"

"Look, Peter, Berry has decided to challenge the repeal of trial by jury. We were hoping to call you as expert witness."

"I am not a constitutional lawyer. And I don't believe in trial by jury."

"Haven't you watched *12 Angry Men*?"

"Actually I have, and the film convinced me that most jurors are guided by their prejudices and preconceptions."

"Berry has already dropped your name, confidentially, to a reporter."

"Without checking with me? He had no right to do this."

"He was in a hurry. And Jonathan gave him a free hand."

"Well, I did not. And I won't be implicated in this sort of nonsense."

"Peter, this is not nonsense. A man's life may depend on it! And Berry thinks that the death penalty is unconstitutional."

"I disagree! Berry acts like a bull in a china shop. Best of luck to both of you," I retorted and hung up.

Back at home, I related the episode to Pat. She was not pleased. She pointed out that, notwithstanding my efforts, I was being dragged into the case. She reiterated that it was not my affair.

"Any point in writing to *The Straits Times* to express disagreement with their 'confidential source'?"

"No," she replied promptly. "Just keep out of it. You already told the authorities you had nothing to do with it. You once told me that if reporters talk nonsense about you, you can sue them. Better wait and see."

In the event, I did not have to wait for long. That same evening, Raymond rang me to remonstrate. He thought that most lawyers in Western countries would agree that trial by jury was a fundamental human right and that the death penalty was improper. He agreed that Berry should have obtained my consent before dropping my name.

"But he has already done so!" he explained.

"Then let him retract his words. Handle the case in any manner you like. But leave me out!"

"We hoped to get some help or moral support from you!"

"Why from me? I opted out when I refused to carry that woman's hand luggage through the customs. Why doesn't she come forward and disclose her own role? And, come to think of it, has David withheld her name?"

"He says he is not a snitch! He doesn't want to implicate her. You may guess the reason."

"I suppose I can. But look here, Raymond, I am not involved and I intend to keep it this way."

V

For quite a while, I was left in peace. I gleaned from the media that Berry was not admitted and that the argument based on constitutional law — raised by Vardan, who remained in charge of the case — was rejected by the trial judge. His judgment was affirmed by our Court of

Appeal. The judges were neither deterred nor influenced by the hostile reports in the Australian media and by the clamour of international forums on human rights.

I was in agreement with the courts' approach but felt concerned about one aspect. Had David, the accused, agreed to his family's decision to put the matter in hands which, in my eyes, were unsuitable? The family and the counsel appointed by it were playing with David's neck! The thought disturbed me, but I told myself that this, too, was not my business.

An unexpected telephone call changed my attitude. Jonathan wanted to see me privately. We agreed to meet in a small coffee house in Holland Village.

"Look here, Peter," he told me. "David is my grandson. I want to be sure that he is getting the best defence available."

"Well," I prevaricated, "he is in the hands of a QC and a local counsel."

"But I want to be sure they are the right people."

"I understand, but how do I come into it? I am a banking lawyer and, actually, not in charge of the case. So why turn to me?"

"I want your advice. Look here, Peter, I believe that you are a Holocaust victim."

"My parents were but we escaped in time."

"Same here," he told me. "David is the last man in my line. You know very well what this means!"

"Yes, I know. I too am the last of my line. And I have no siblings. My closest relatives are first cousins and a very old uncle."

"That's the fate of many of those whose parents managed to escape. So, you know what I am talking about."

"I do. But what can I do to help?"

"Raymond tells me you have reservations about the lawyers."

"Actually, I do. Look, this is a criminal case. Our law in point is strict. I should really prefer a local criminal lawyer with a good track record in cases of this type."

"But I have a problem. You see, Ruth, David's mother, divorced her first husband. She has her eyes on Berry. He is a widower and is highly regarded at home. How can I discharge him? Ruth is bound to be furious. And how about Vardan?"

"Vardan is no problem. He would be happy to discharge himself and immerse himself again in his usual work. I suspect he took on the case simply so as not to lose your commercial business. And I don't think Berry is a real problem. The accused is David. He should decide whom he wants to defend him. Have a word with him. The prison authorities will allow you to visit David. I can give Raymond a list of the best local lawyers for cases of this type."

"But how about Berry?"

"If David does not want him, you must hint that you need Berry for some other matters at home. This way Ruth is unlikely to make a fuss."

"I would like to have your own assessment!"

"Okay. But remember, I have no experience in this field. In general, our law on forbidden drugs is strict. If a person is found in possession of more than a given quantity, he is presumed to be a trafficker. If the presumption is not rebutted, the death sentence is mandatory. The only way out is to satisfy the judge that the carrier did not know what he had in his possession. If the judge is not satisfied and has to convict, the only escape is a pardon."

"And your prognosis?"

"I am a pessimist, Jonathan."

Back at home, Pat felt that I had been too sentimental. David's family was wealthy and should remain in charge. We were not dealing with a poor devil who broke the law because he was hungry.

"I know," I told her. "But I think David agreed to carry the drugs because he was friendly with the girl. He probably wanted to please her."

"Then he is a fool! If she had the strength to carry the luggage up, she was also able to carry it down."

"You are right, but what do you think about the punishment?"

"But he broke the law, and he is an idiot. You better keep out of it."

Two weeks later, Vardan invited me for lunch at his club. We enjoyed some small talk — basically gossip about members of our legal fraternity. As soon as the main courses were served, Vardan told me that he decided to discharge himself from the case.

"I have made up my mind, Prof. But what do you think?"

"A good decision," I assured him. "You are not a litigator and, of course, not a criminal lawyer. I feel confident that Silver will continue to use your firm for his commercial affairs."

"I hope so. But even without the work he sends us, we are okay. What I cannot risk is my reputation. I don't want to lose my other clients. And of course, we have two problems in this case. To start with,

I prefer documentation to courtroom appearances. You said so yourself, Prof."

"And the other?"

"Berry Lewis. He has effectively remained in charge. He sends many messages, which suggest that he is not particularly good for this type of case. Look here, Prof, you offered to give Raymond a list of good local criminal lawyers. I have prepared my own list. Let us go through it."

Vardan's list of candidates coincided with my own choices. After some deliberation, we ruled two of them out. Neither of them would want to take the case at this stage. In the event, we settled on an Indian lawyer called Jack. He was quick on his feet and by and large imperturbable.

"I'll approach Jack. I've already hinted to Raymond that I wanted to pull out."

"If Jack agrees to take the case, insist that he take his instructions from the accused, not from his family."

"Because of Ruth?"

"That too, Vardan. But there is a more important reason. We are dealing with David's neck, and he is the client! Ruth is too set in her views and Jonathan does not have the guts to tell David what is involved. In my view, David must be consulted. And, between us, I am not particularly impressed with Raymond. He should have gotten rid of Berry as soon as admission was denied."

"That is more easily said than done," grinned Vardan. "But I agree with you. In any event, let us see if Jack is available."

"I suggest you approach him after a chat with David and, if necessary, Jonathan."

Maybe a Swan Song: A Second Trip Down Memory Lane

At home, Pat listened attentively to what had happened. To my surprise, she was not pleased. She thought that I should have clammed up. By talking to Vardan, I got even more deeply involved in the case.

"Look here, Peter, when my brothers want to talk to you about anything legal, you tell them their problem is not in your field."

"I did help your sister to find a divorce lawyer," I said defensively.

"Only after I pushed you. You let people from your own community bully you. This is not very nice of them."

"They are badly in need of help."

"But they are rich and can afford lawyers. I think, Peter, this is really not your business."

Pat's words convinced me. Further, I hoped that Jack would accept the brief. If he did, David's case would be in competent hands. I assumed that thereafter my advice would not be needed.

Initially, Jack was reluctant to take the case on at such a late stage. However, the fiscal arrangements proposed by Jonathan persuaded him. At the same time, he insisted that Berry Lewis be discharged. In the event, it turned out that Berry, too, thought it would be best to leave the case in the hands of another lawyer. He himself had failed on all preliminary issues. It was time for him to accept an honourable discharge and return to Melbourne.

Nonetheless, I remained involved. Berry wanted to have a final meeting with Jack and myself, with the objective of deciding whether I should be subpoenaed as a witness for the defence. I was informed about this development by Raymond, who invited me to a farewell lunch. He had concluded that his services were no longer required and decided to return to his more mundane, but highly remunerative, practice in Melbourne. However, before leaving the scene, he thought it would be good to solicit Berry's advice respecting my being called as a witness. Pat was not satisfied with the developments. She did not like the idea of my appearing.

"So you are not out, Peter. You may be called as a witness."

"Well, in any event, I may want to go down to court when the case is heard. I just want to watch it. But you are right. I may very well be called. In effect, the decision rests with Jack. I hope he recalls how dangerous it is to call a witness who is not in sympathy with his cause."

VI

My meeting with Raymond, Jack and Berry took place a few days later. It was clear that they had decided to collaborate. Both Jack and Berry conceded that my knowledge of the facts was limited. I could testify that some parcels had been handed to David. After some hesitation, both Berry and Jack decided that I ought to be served a subpoena. Raymond agreed.

My secretary at the university had jotted down the date of the trial and reminded me. After some hesitation, Pat agreed to accompany me to the courtroom and watch the proceedings. In the past, she had attended trials where I was called as an expert witness on banking practice. On reflection, she agreed it would be interesting to also attend a criminal trial. Further, as a potential witness for the defence, I would be barred from attending the hearing of the prosecution's case. Pat undertook to report.

To my initial surprise, the trial was poorly attended. On further reflection, it dawned on me that this was not a sensational trial and that most local residents would not be interested. Some had attended the earlier, unsuccessful, constitutional law applications. When these were settled, they lost their curiosity.

David was sitting between two wardens. Pat told me that he appeared ill at ease, although she sensed that he had been treated well during his life as a detainee. By and large, he left on her the impression of a youngster used to his comforts. She noticed that he was neatly dressed.

The prosecution was represented by just one lawyer, accompanied by her assistant. She had been one of my students a few years earlier, had written an excellent Masters of Laws dissertation and, following her graduation, had joined one of the best law firms in town. After completing her pupillage, she went for further studies overseas. She joined the legal service after returning to Singapore and, in due course, rose high in office.

The defence lawyer, Jack — a tall and imposing figure — was accompanied by two pupils. Jack's full Indian surname was tongue twisting, so that everybody used what had become known as his proper name.

Jack's record was impressive. He had graduated from Oxford and then passed the local practice course. For a while, he had joined one of the major law firms in town. Later on, he resigned from his post and launched his own successful practice. Many of his cases concerned white-collar crime, especially cases of employees and directors accused of a criminal breach of trust; but he also handled ordinary criminal cases. There was a general belief that "crime did not pay". Jack's lavish style of life showed that this maxim had its exceptions.

Jack was a fine courtroom advocate: methodical, quick on his feet and — the most important skill of an accomplished litigator — knew when to pull his punches. It pleased me that he had accepted the case. I knew his charges were on the high side, but Jonathan could afford them.

Pat had a comfortable seat on a neutral row. Having been subpoenaed as a witness, I sat with other witnesses on a bench just outside the courtroom. Pat told me that Justice Lam entered the virtually empty courtroom on time. I had met him on a number of occasions and wrote some opinions he had commissioned when he was still in practice. I knew he had an excellent grasp of even the finest points. He was one of the best legal minds I had encountered. Further, he had the ideal judicial temperament, involving firmness, detachment and objectivity.

The courtroom was constructed so that the judge's seat was elevated. Justice Lam had a stocky figure and was middle-aged. As was the custom, he wore a black robe and was formally dressed. Every judge was expected to be — and usually was — the master of his court. There could be no doubt about this issue in Justice Lam's case.

Justice Lam explained that he had been requested to take over the case after the constitutional issues were settled by the Court of Appeal. He then asked the prosecutor to present her first witness.

The first witness established that 550 grams of cannabis had been found in David's hand luggage. The drugs were placed in six small parcels. David had confessed that the hand luggage was his but claimed that the parcels did not belong to him. He alleged that he had been asked to carry them by other passengers. Still, he had not identified them.

Jack's cross-examination was brief. It shed no further light on the issue but affirmed that, right from the start, David had asserted that the drugs were not his. Throughout the investigation, he had insisted that the content of the parcels was unknown to him.

"Did you examine the fingerprints on the parcels?" asked Jack.

"We did," said the witness. "Each had the prints of the prisoner and also of others."

"Did your office identify these other fingerprints?"

"As far as I know, they weren't identified," answered the witness promptly.

"So you made no attempt to identify who had handled these parcels?"

"This issue will be the subject of the testimony of my second witness," interceded the prosecutor.

"No further questions," said Jack and resumed his seat.

"What was the objective of your test?" asked the prosecutor by way of re-examination.

"We had to establish that the prisoner had drugs in his possession."

"And did you?"

"We did!"

"No further questions," said the prosecutor.

The prosecution's second witness advised that he had conducted the laboratory tests. They established that the parcels contained cannabis. He had weighed the contents and affirmed that there were 550 grams.

"Did the parcels display only the prisoner's fingerprints?" asked Jack.

"No, Sir. They also had fingerprints of others and also some unidentifiable smudges."

"Did you identify the other fingerprints?"

"I tried and also consulted authorities overseas, who have their own records. But we were unable to identify them."

"But all parcels bore the prisoner's fingerprints?" asked the prosecutor by way of re-examination.

"They did."

Shadow of the Gallows

As soon as the prosecutor advised that she was not calling any further witnesses and was closing her case, Justice Lam announced a recess of 30 minutes. The recess enabled me to join Pat. We went to the canteen to have a coffee.

"Why did the judge call a recess?" asked Pat.

"You see, darling, in many cases the defence lawyer claims that the prosecution has not proved its case. We call this argument 'no case to answer'. Justice Lam wanted to give Jack the opportunity to consider raising this plea."

"Does it have any chance in this case?"

"I don't think so. The prosecution has established David's possession of the drugs. Once this is established, he is presumed to be a trafficker. His only chance is to rebut this presumption."

"So this plea, 'no case to answer', is out. But can a prisoner rebut the presumption?"

"He can — in rare cases. Suppose someone inserted the drugs into your luggage without your knowledge? But here the prosecution has proved that David had wilfully carried the parcels containing the drugs."

When the proceedings resumed, Justice Lam asked Jack to open his case. To my delight, I was invited to move to the witness stand. Jack thought it best to ask me to state what I had observed during the flight. The prosecutor's cross-examination was short and to the point. I willingly conceded that all I saw was that some parcels had been passed to the prisoner by other passengers.

"So you saw that some parcels were given to him and that he put them in his own hand luggage."

"Correct," I conceded willingly.

"You knew nothing about the contents of these parcels?"

"I did not," I affirmed.

"You cannot tell us anything about the general contents of the prisoner's hand luggage?"

"I cannot."

"Were all the items, including the parcels discovered in his hand luggage, handed to him?"

"I cannot be sure."

"Some of the parcels may have been in the hand luggage when the prisoner accepted the remaining ones?"

Instantly Jack rose and objected. The question called for my conclusions and as such ought not to be put to me. Justice Lam thought the matter over for a few seconds and then raised just one question: "Can you tell us whether the prisoner's hand luggage was empty when the first parcel was handed to him?"

"I cannot tell, Your Honour. His seat was too far from mine."

"I'll withdraw my question," announced the prosecutor. "And I have no further questions."

Jack did not raise any questions by way of re-examination. Justice Lam excused me. As neither counsel reserved the right to call me again, I was now free to take a seat in the courtroom. Naturally, I sat next to Pat.

Justice Lam turned back to Jack. Pronouncing his complex surname flawlessly, he asked him to present his next witness. Surreptitiously, the prosecutor grinned at me. A few years earlier, during a lunch party, we had a bet as to whether it was easier to pronounce Jack's long surname 10 times or to say (again 10 times) "She sells seashells by the seashore". In the event, we agreed it was a draw and went Dutch on the bill. Justice Lam, who had at that time still been in practice and had also attended that lunch, pretended not to see the exchange of glances. Jack, who had never been informed about the bet, looked at both of us bewildered.

As I shifted my eyes, I took in Pat's annoyed glance. "You, Peter, have many friends, ah?"

Keen to avoid a hissed explanation, I led her out of the courtroom, bowing politely to the judge. Sitting down on a nearby bench, I explained to Pat that the legal profession in Singapore was tight-knit. During appearances in court or in the course of negotiations, each of us had to take care of his or her client's interests and had to stick to formalities. Outside court and office, we generally enjoyed cordial relationships. Everyone knew everyone. I reminded Pat that I had told her all about that bet.

"But most Indians use a short name."

"Well, officially he is known as 'Mr. Jack'. But in informal gatherings we simply call him 'Jack'."

To my relief, Pat's strained expression relaxed. Still, she pointed out that very few practitioners had come to our house. Instantly, I felt remorse. I had kept my professional life quite apart from my personal life. That was also the position during our years in New Zealand and Australia. And I tended to avoid official functions.

When we sneaked back into the courtroom, Jack was completing his examination-in-chief of David. I soon realised that, basically, David had reaffirmed the details previously recorded. He had also insisted that the drugs sniffed out by the dogs were not his. The parcels had been handed to him by other passengers.

The prosecutor's cross-examination was short and to the point. Her last questions were pertinent:

"So, you say the narcotics were not yours?"

"They weren't!"

"No parcel belonged to you?"

"No; I owned none of them."

"So how come you cannot tell us who handed you the parcels?"

"I cannot remember!"

"So how would you have known to whom to return them?" interceded Justice Lam.

"I am sure each would have demanded his own parcel back."

"But how would they have identified them?"

When David hesitated, searching for an answer, Justice Lam asked: "And you cannot recall who was the first to hand you a parcel?"

"I am afraid I cannot. I cannot remember."

The prosecutor was quick-witted. "No further questions," she said and resumed her seat. All in court realised that David had taken a final stand. Jack, who was keenly aware of what had taken place, had but two questions by way of re-examination.

"So, the parcels were not your own?"

"They weren't," affirmed David. "I was just asked to take them through customs."

"And you did not know they contained cannabis?"

"I did not!"

Justice Lam announced that he would deliver judgment after hearing the counsels' argument following the lunch break. He then pressed a button. Instantly, a court attendant stepped in and asked all in court to rise. Justice Lam, too, rose, acknowledged the bows and retreated to his office.

All in attendance filed out of the courtroom. I saw how Jonathan and Ruth blocked Jack's way. I was certain they asked for his prognosis. Pat and I walked over to a popular restaurant in Raffles City.

"Peter, what do you think about the case?"

"The law is simple: the prosecution established that David carried 550 grams of cannabis. He had the right to show that he didn't know anything."

"But he didn't tell them who gave him the drugs. I thought he was just protecting somebody. How will the judge react?"

"We'll know when he comes back to court, darling. I am pessimistic. The only possible weakness in the case is that the authorities were unable to identify the other fingerprints on the parcels. Let us see how both parties handle this."

"And what do you think of Berry?"

"Actually, he tried to handle the matter as if we were in Australia." I replied, looking away. "This was unwise and narrow-minded. But he left when the case was taken over by Jack. I can understand Berry. He realised that he was simply not up to handling criminal cases in Singapore."

"But Peter, who made him a QC? I thought you had to be good..."

"... to take silk," I completed for her. "Yes, darling, this is the theory. But 'good' and 'experienced' can be interpreted in many ways. And of course, Berry has good standing and a captive audience in Melbourne. Many matters involving Jewish businessmen are referred to him for opinion. It was good that he went back home to handle commercial cases."

Maybe a Swan Song: A Second Trip Down Memory Lane

All of us returned to court punctually. Justice Lam did not keep us waiting. According to the local procedure, as David had given evidence, the prosecutor had the right to speak last. To my satisfaction, she waived the right and offered to speak first. Jack looked at her gratefully.

The prosecutor's address was short and to the point. She emphasised that David had been in possession of 550 grams of cannabis. Accordingly, he was presumed to be a drug trafficker. He had the right to rebut the presumption but, she argued, had failed to do so. His own fingerprints were displayed on the parcels and he had not denied that he had willingly agreed to take them down the plane as part of his hand luggage. The authorities had no duty to proceed to test the remaining fingerprints. They did not have to establish the ultimate source of the drugs. However, they had been extra careful, checked the other fingerprints but were unable to identify them. The net result was that David had failed to establish that the drugs, found in his possession, did not belong to him.

Jack's address was also concise. He did not dispute that drugs had been found in parcels which were in David's possession, but argued that, based on the evidence, David's testimony established that he was unfamiliar with the parcels' contents and therefore should not be held to be in possession of the drugs. His having taken some parcels during the flight had been corroborated. Undoubtedly, David had acted foolishly by agreeing to carry other people's luggage. But he established that he was not a courier or trafficker in narcotics.

"But why then does he not disclose the identity of the persons who, he claims, gave him the parcels?" interceded the judge.

"He cannot recall. And their identity could have been established by testing the remaining fingerprints. The police tried but came up with a blank; so David's testimony has not been seriously challenged," replied Jack.

"But you have not produced any witness confirming your client's allegation that the parcels handed to the prisoner during the flight were the only containers of the drugs in his possession."

"I am afraid we have not," confirmed Jack. "But the prisoner's testimony ought to be taken at its face value. It is believable." After a few more minutes, Jack concluded his address and sat down.

Justice Lam called a recess of 15 minutes. When he resumed his seat, he announced that he had decided to reserve judgment. True, the prosecution established that David had been caught whilst in possession of a forbidden quantity of narcotics. However, evidence had been produced to question David's knowledge.

Justice Lam decided to review the entire evidence again before reaching his conclusion. Regrettably, a lengthy case had been set for the next morning and the hearing would take at least 10 days. Justice Lam promised to deliver both an oral judgment and written grounds thereof within 20 days.

The prosecutor announced that David's passport would, in the meantime, be kept by the authorities. Justice Lam nodded and then rose.

VII

Back at home, Pat reminded me that we had to get ready for our annual holidays. I, too, was looking forward to our trip to Austria. I loved my birth town of Vienna and planned to drive us onwards via Salzburg to Liechtenstein. All the same, I had some misgivings. David's life was in jeopardy. Was this the right time to pull out?

Pat had no doubts. In her opinion, I had done my share. She was certain that David had not told the whole truth. If he sought to shelter the real culprits, he had decided to take the risk.

"This was never your business, Peter. And David has lawyers and family. And I want my holidays. And you need a break."

In the event, my dilemma was solved. Jack's assistant, Danny, rang to tell me that the other case, which was being heard by Justice Lam, was going to take longer than expected. Judgment in the prosecution against David would be delivered two days after my return from overseas.

Pat and I had a good holiday in Austria. I recall with pleasure the three days we spent in Salzburg. We attended two chamber music performances and went to an interesting puppet show. After three days in Vaduz, we took a train to Zurich. From there we flew back to Singapore.

Two days after I was back in my office, Danny rang me to remind me of the date set for the delivery of judgment in the prosecution brought against David. Both Pat and I decided to attend. So did Ruth, who had remained in Singapore.

Justice Lam's judgment was short and to the point. He held that the prosecution proved that David had been in the possession of 550 grams of cannabis. The accused's own evidence was that all the parcels containing the drugs were handed to him during the flight. On this point, there was some corroborative evidence. Further, the prosecution's own witnesses confirmed that each parcel had a second set of fingerprints. In the event, these did not lead to further identifications or arrests. All in all, despite David's failure to identify the parcels' owners, there was doubt respecting his knowledge that they contained prohibited substances. Justice Lam had, on this basis, decided to grant David the benefit of the doubt and entered a "not guilty" verdict.

Turning to the prosecution, he added: "You have 30 days to lodge an appeal. I suggest that Mr. Stone's passport be held by the authorities until this period expires. My written judgment is ready for collection."

Pat looked at me reproachfully as we left the court. "So, in the end you helped to save David's neck."

"I did, darling. But they were lucky: Lam is singularly conscientious and you can be sure he went through the evidence carefully. Some judges may have been annoyed by David's refusal to identify the real culprits."

"What would they have done?"

"Found David an evasive and unreliable witness. On this basis, they would have decided that David had not rebutted the presumption and would have held him guilty as charged."

"Would David then have been hanged?"

"He could have applied for a pardon. If it were granted, he might have been given a life sentence in substitution."

"Would he really have had to remain in prison for life?"

"Singapore does not have a lenient parole system. His sentence would only be reduced after 20 years."

"Then perhaps it was a good thing that the judge found him not guilty. I am only sorry they did not catch the others."

"Actually, so am I."

Two days later, I was surprised to receive a telephone call from Raymond. He was back in Singapore and wanted to catch up with me.

"You sure get around, Raymond. I thought you had flown back to Melbourne."

"Jonathan asked me to come to Singapore to take David back home. Can I please call on you?"

"Not today. I am busy. Tomorrow, I finish my morning classes at 11 am. But I must leave by 11.50 for a lunch appointment. Actually, what is this all about?"

"I'll discuss this with you tomorrow. But look here, you sure seem to be very busy!"

"Quite so. Some of us have to work to make a living!"

Startled by my rough reply, Raymond explained: "Look here, Peter. David has been acquitted. Still, we must decide what to do if the prosecution appeals."

"I would rely on Jack's judgment on such an issue. You can come over tomorrow by 11."

Back at home, Pat urged me to stay out of it. Further, she expressed doubts about the entire case. How could we be certain that David was clean? She had no doubt that he had been an evasive witness. Was it possible that, in reality, David had orchestrated the entire show? And was it also possible that some of the drugs were his own? As I reflected on the episode, I concluded that the entire matter was forced on me and that, in reality, I was keen not to get further involved.

The next morning, I finished my class early and was back in my office on time. By 11.20, I received Raymond's call advising me that he and a friend accompanying him were delayed.

"I told you I have to leave by 11.50, Raymond."

"Can't you reschedule the lunch?"

"No way!"

"We'll be there as soon as possible."

"You better hurry! I won't wait!"

"I only hope we get a taxi instantly."

I was getting ready to leave, when Raymond arrived. My eyes widened when I saw his companion. She was the very woman who had wanted to swap seats with me during the flight from Hong Kong, and who had asked me to take her hand luggage through the customs. Despite my attempt to keep a straight face, I tensed all over.

"I am sorry we are late, it took us a while to get a taxi," apologised Raymond, who was alarmed by my reaction.

"You could have booked one yesterday! And what is this woman doing here?" Turning to her, I gave way to my anger:

"You and your friends made a nuisance of yourselves during our flight! And then you tried to plant your filthy drugs on me. You then handed them to David and did not come forward to help him when your testimony was needed!"

"Don't you dare talk to me like this!" she yelled. "I came over here when I was told the verdict could be reversed on appeal!"

"I am not interested in the strategy to be adopted if the prosecution decided to appeal," I retorted.

"Our suggestions for such a strategy were planned by an experienced lawyer in Melbourne," advised Raymond. "Aren't you even going to look at his proposals? Helen brought them with her because she wanted to see David and try to help if needed, and Jonathan agreed to pay for the flight."

"And yours, undoubtedly. He sure has plenty of dough! And look here, Raymond, we had an appointment that you did not keep. I am not prepared to spend any more of my time on this issue."

I wanted to add a few stinging remarks, but sensed that the less said the better. All the same, for quite a few minutes I had to continue fighting for self-control. The appearance of the woman, whom I thought

David was trying to shelter, had shaken me. When at long last I regained my composure, I told Raymond flatly: "David has been acquitted. As far as I am concerned, this is the end of my role in the case."

"There may, of course, be no appeal. If there isn't, we want to celebrate the occasion. Wouldn't your wife and you join us?"

"No, Raymond. I am really beginning to wonder whether David, or perhaps the people behind him, financed the entire transaction. I suspect the group made a stop in Singapore because travellers who come back to Oz straight from China are more carefully examined than passengers coming from Singapore. And now you must excuse me, I do try to keep my appointments."

Back at home, I told Pat all about the episode. She did not hide her relief when I mentioned my decision. She added that even if I went to such a party, she would have stayed at home. She did not want to have anything to do "with that mob".

For the next few weeks, I was busy finalising the manuscript of a book to be published in London. The work was time-consuming. All the same, it was satisfying. Naturally, the royalties were bound to be a pittance. But there was a moral satisfaction in translating my thoughts into writing on a complex legal subject. In addition, I was revising the penultimate draft of a novel to be self-published. Somehow, the entire matter of David and the struggle to combat drug trafficking slipped into the background. It was the business of the authorities and, occasionally, of the judiciary. The university, the ivory tower, suited my temperament. My opinion work and occasional appearances as an expert witness were complementary to my academic work, which was far removed from criminal law.

After some three weeks, Danny rang to advise me that the prosecution had decided not to appeal. This meant that David was a free man and would get back his passport.

"The sooner they leave our Republic the better," I replied testily.

"You, Prof, are a real hard-liner. Jack told me that he would attend the farewell party, but was sorry to hear you have decided to give it a miss"

VIII

After some four years, I was surprised to receive an email from Berry. He was stopping in Singapore on his way to London and hoped we could have lunch in Orchard Hotel, where he was spending two days. Out of curiosity, I decided to accept.

To my surprise, Berry's beer belly had shrunk in size. He had lost weight and, notwithstanding his grey hair, looked fit. He led the way to the very same buffet we had attended years earlier.

"You look very fit, Berry. Congratulations."

"Ruth has taken charge ever since we married. And Peter, it is good to see you again. How are you? How is your wife?"

"We are fine, still living in the same flat."

"I understand your testimony had saved the day."

"I am not sure of this. A hanging judge would have held the evidence produced by the defence insufficient to rebut the presumption."

"You have a point there," he nodded. "Hanging judges are common all over the Commonwealth. I suspect the British judge, Henry Hawkins, remains the best known one. But even a sympathetic judge needs ammunition to support his decision to acquit."

"How did my testimony help? Everyone in court sensed that David was trying to shield the real culprits."

"True. But David claimed he did not know the contents of the parcels, and your testimony established that he did receive the parcels during the flight. You see, Justice Lam concluded that David did not know he was carrying prohibited substances and, hence, breaking the law."

"So, in a sense, Ruth was right. Indirectly the *mens rea* doctrine, or the accused's knowledge and intention, affected the judge's decision," I conceded.

"I think so," said Berry. "And Jack handled the case very well indeed."

Berry then explained that he and Ruth married shortly after the trial and that, under her influence, he decided to lose weight, drank less and, in addition, became a human rights campaigner.

"I still practise commercial law," he explained. "My heart, though, is in the campaign for human rights. In some African, South American and Asian countries, they are abused. Ruth reads all available sites and forwards them to me."

"How would you rate your chances on the human rights issues, Berry?"

"In terms of immediate results, the rate of success is poor. But, in the long run, we fight a winning war."

"I am not so sure," I told him openly. "Some politicians are evil, powerful and charismatic. You never know when your own life is at risk. Why don't you stick to your Melbourne practice, honestly."

"That's the easy way out, Peter. Many scions of Holocaust victims opt for it. You and others keep a low profile and avoid any political or sociological issues. All you want is to live your life in peace. And Peter, I suspect you really don't care too much about disasters that do not affect you."

"True!"

"Others, and I am now with them, want us to have a better world. Many opt for this way. Ruth has been one of them for a long time and has convinced me that hers is the right approach. Surely you do not approve of the Stalin or Pol Pot regimes?"

"I don't, and I do not approve of the harsh treatment Israel metes out to Palestinians. Israel's army can be unnecessarily brutal. I know this but, honestly, I am really keen to remain on the sidelines. Do you blame me?"

"Actually, I don't. But you, in turn, must accept that others may have a different life philosophy."

"I do. So, we have decided to disagree."

"Most governments prefer your philosophy to mine."

For a few minutes we remained silent. It then dawned on me that we had not touched on the subject which had led to our previous meeting.

"Berry, what has become of David?"

"That woman, Helen, whom you met on the flight, jilted him. Initially he was heartbroken. You know young men, don't you? Fortunately David is a presentable and good-looking man. Before long he found and married another girl. She is a qualified accountant and has a good job. So they are a two-income family. It will please you to know that they are happy and have two children. Incidentally, they travel only to destinations in Australia and New Zealand."

"What is David doing? I take it he has a job."

"He is employed by one of Jonathan Silver's firms."

"Wasn't he lucky to be born with a silver spoon?!"

A Matter of Compliance

I

It was late in the morning of a day in early 1990s when Norbert Schneider, Head of the Bad Loans Department of the X. Bank, called to tell me that he was coming over with Frederic Steiner (nicknamed Freddie), the bank's compliance officer.

The bank was an important client of our firm. Further, Norbert and Freddie were friends of mine. This, of course, did not mean they were in one another's good books. Despite their ostensibly amiable modus operandi, it was easy to spot the underlying antipathy. I had had pleasant luncheons with each. But never had they called on me together.

Our law firm had its premises in downtown Singapore. The walk from the bank to the firm would take about five minutes. Whilst Norbert and Freddie were on their way, I reflected on their backgrounds and their respective posts.

Before he became a banker, Norbert had been an antiques dealer in Frankfurt. He opened his business shortly after graduating from a well-known German university. He specialised in prints and ceramics.

Regrettably, the business did not thrive. In the early 70s, Norbert closed it down and joined a well-known German bank. Before long, he revealed a talent for recovering "bad loans".

In 1990, Norbert took up the post of Head of the Bad Loans Department of the X. Bank's Singapore office. We met shortly after I retired from my professorship at the Law School of the National University of Singapore and joined a law firm as a consultant.

The friendship between Norbert and myself was nourished by our common interest in ceramics and, odd to say, by an understanding based on our respective experiences during the Second World War. Norbert, who was partly Jewish, had remained with his parents in Frankfurt during the period of the Third Reich. I do not know how they managed to survive. My parents had fled from Vienna and, in due course, migrated to Palestine. I grew up as a predominantly Israeli youth. Still, my mother's influence had directed my mind to German culture, literature and philosophy. All in all, I liked the subjects. So did Norbert.

Unlike Norbert, Freddie came from pure Aryan stock. His parents, though, were persecuted on political grounds. After the end of the Second World War, they settled for a while in East Germany, but in due course migrated to Australia. Freddie grew up in Sydney but spoke German at home. After obtaining a law degree, he joined one of Australia's local banks as a trainee. In 1994, when he was in his early 30s, he joined the X. Bank in Singapore as their compliance officer.

Freddie's post made him an unpopular figure at the bank. In this regard, he suffered the fate of most compliance officers. Their task was to expose loopholes or technical errors in bargains, such as the absence of a required signature on a contractual document or a failure to comply with a local statute. In consequence, a compliance officer often frustrated deals on which an account officer had worked for months. When this occurred, the account office would lose his anticipated commission and would be unable to list the deal in his annual progress report.

Often a compliance officer was a thorn in the flesh of the staff dealing with the recovery of bad loans. Their task was to recover outstanding debts by legal means. Frequently, the compliance officer wrecked a settlement by discovering a loophole or an inadequacy. In such cases, the bad loans officer's inclination would be to proceed with the deal despite the irregularity. He hoped for the best. To do his job, the compliance officer had to exercise his veto.

These differences in tasks and business philosophy would have been an adequate ground for the constant tension between Norbert and Freddie. But there were additional reasons for their mutual dislike. Norbert had managed to stay put during the Holocaust. He had remained culturally German. To my delight, he had read Franz Kafka and Heinrich Böll. All in all, though, he remained a conservative and a believer.

Freddie had grown up as an Australian. His cultural ties with Germany were related to his parents' home. But there was also a German element in his orientation. He was attracted by German classical literature and, to my surprise, the literature of East Germany. He had, for instance, drawn my attention back to Lessing and Kleist — both early 19th-century playwrights I tended to ignore — and to Volker Braun, a modern East German writer. Ideologically, Freddie remained a left-winger and an agnostic.

These differences in outlook were, I suspect, of limited significance. Both Norbert and Freddie were tolerant men. The main problem related to my two friends' characters and life philosophy. Norbert was a shrewd conformist. He knew how to handle difficult situations and was always in control of his temper. Freddie, in contrast, was a rebel. Quite often he spoke his mind even when common sense dictated silence. On such occasions, Norbert was put off by Freddie's plain words. Freddie, in turn, was repulsed by Norbert's "live and let live" philosophy.

Their mutual differences did not affect their respective friendships with me. I was about 20 years older than Norbert. Freddie was my junior by some 35 years. Despite these age gaps, both found it easy to communicate with me. Lunch or morning coffee with either was never dull. Years of experience at universities and in law practice had taught me tolerance, discretion and, most importantly, to have low expectations in everyday life. I was, for instance, pleasantly surprised when Freddie lent me a rare edition of Kleist's plays. A fine illustrated edition of Böll's short stories, given to me by Norbert, has continued to grace my collection. So did a porcelain piece he sneaked out of Dresden before the fall of the iron curtain.

II

When Norbert and Freddie arrived, the former was out of breath. Notwithstanding his energetic and imposing bulk, he found it difficult to keep up with Freddie's youthful speed. In addition, Norbert was badly shaken. I suspected the two had had a row. My fears, though, were allayed when Freddie asked Norbert to raise the problem they had encountered. My heart sank when Freddie said, impulsively, "Curse that bastard Hendra; what a *Schweinehund*!"

"You'd better tell me all about his latest misdeed. That fellow is the limit!"

"He is. On this point, Freddie and I are in agreement," muttered Norbert.

I concurred. Hendra, whose real surname was one of those Indonesian tongue-twisting titular tags, was a man of about my own age. The nature of his business has remained unclear to me ever since we first met. I suspected he was a financial jack of all trades but, alas, never a master of his fortune. He kept hitting the jackpot only to squander his gains.

Like many wealthy Indonesians, Hendra used Singapore as a base for his dealings. Over the years, the bank lent him a substantial amount of money under the guise of shell companies and straw men. All in all, Hendra and his nominees had some 20 accounts with the bank. Each, except an account in his wife's name, was heavily overdrawn.

Most facilities had been granted before Norbert took over the bank's bad loans portfolio. He was flabbergasted when he familiarised himself with the file. All his attempts to reason with Hendra failed. So did a visit to Hendra's hometown of Surabaya. Hendra was not only a glib talker, but also an excellent host. Norbert added two kilograms to his bulk; but the accounts remained in debt. On a few occasions, Norbert was even talked into sanctioning further credit facilities. No attempt was made to consolidate the accounts.

The situation changed when Freddie took up his position. Some of the facilities had been granted without the formal approval of one of the members of the bank's credit committee. When this deficiency was brought to the new compliance officer's attention, he went through the entire history of Hendra's accounts.

Freddie was outraged by the facts emerging from the file. Practically, a firm word with Norbert would have sufficed. Instead, Freddie referred the matter to the bank's head office in Germany.

The directors of the bank reviewed the file. In the event, Norbert was instructed to pursue the matter "energetically and diligently" and

Maybe a Swan Song: A Second Trip Down Memory Lane

to report back within three months. As always, he controlled his temper. Freddie's name, though, had been entered in bold letters in Norbert's bad books. Norbert did not like snitchers.

Shortly after that incident, Norbert decided to refer the file to me. Having discussed the details with Freddie, I concluded that the first step was to consolidate the accounts. To do so, we required a document known as a "set-off letter" authorising the bank to "combine". In theory, it was a simple step. Practically, we faced a quagmire. As was to be expected, Hendra had the right to transact any business in respect of any account. Legally, though, the ownership was vested in different parties. We needed the consent of all of them.

I used a rough draft prepared by Freddie. Each party whose name appeared in the bank's ledger as co-owner or as joint holder of any account was required to execute it.

The final document comprised two pages. One spelt out the set-off agreement and was executed by Norbert on behalf of the bank. The second page was a schedule, which bore the signatures of all required parties. Attached to this were powers of attorney executed in Jakarta by all relevant parties. Hendra was given the authority to sign on behalf of each of them. Once executed, the agreement would be airtight.

Initially, Hendra refused to execute the document. Two days later, he caved in. The bank remained the only financial institution prepared to deal with him, and Hendra required "further accommodation" of S$55,000. Norbert, who oversaw the file, refused to consider any further advance prior to the execution of the set-off letter. Reluctantly, Hendra agreed to sign on the dotted line.

Freddie perused all the documents for regularity prior to the date of execution. After two hours of meticulous perusal, Freddie confirmed that all was well.

Norbert summoned Hendra so as to proceed with the formal execution. Hendra, though, had many questions to ask. As Norbert was not prepared to invite Freddie to attend, he asked me to come over to the bank.

It took me a while to allay Hendra's feelings of unease. His main concern, I sensed, was his fear of the Indonesian tax authorities. Further, he advised that his wife was not prepared to consolidate "her account" with his. Norbert yielded and, to avoid difficulties, sent various documents for re-typing. When they were properly typed out, it was time for a break.

Norbert and I accepted Hendra's invitation to have lunch with him in a nearby Indonesian restaurant. Seeing that spicy food did not agree with me, Hendra ordered various dishes suitable for my unsophisticated European palate. Following the repast, I had to return to my office. Hendra and Norbert walked back to the bank.

During the next few months, Hendra asked for several extensions and for extra credit facilities. Notwithstanding Freddie's misgiving, Norbert approved them. The total indebtedness in the consolidated account stood at S$650,000. Despite the constant memorandums from the head office, Norbert refused to take action. Sooner or later Hendra was going to settle his debts voluntarily.

Freddie disagreed. He feared that Hendra might declare bankruptcy. I shared his misgivings. Norbert, in contrast, remained confident. He was certain that "his client" would not seek refuge in insolvency

Maybe a Swan Song: A Second Trip Down Memory Lane

proceedings. Hendra's main objective was to keep going. Bankruptcy would cripple him for at least three years.

III

"Well, what has Hendra done now?" I wanted to know.

"It all relates back to the consolidation of his accounts. You see, Peter, we have just received a remittance of S$500,000."

"Why not set the amount off against his debt?"

"He has further instructed that S$400,000 be remitted to a numbered Swiss bank account. If we do so, the debt remaining after the consolidation and the remittance to Zurich will be some S$250,000," advised Freddie.

"Better than a debt of S$650,000," noted Norbert.

"I agree. But Peter, can we set-off?" asked Freddie.

"Whyever not? Surely, the set-off letter is airtight. I have a copy on file!"

"Have a look at the original."

When Norbert produced the original, which had been kept in the bank's vaults, my eyes widened. The text typed on the X.bank's premises had remained fresh and clear. The signatures, in contrast, had vanished. Hendra, Norbert explained, had used his own pen to sign the document. The bank's secretaries, who had witnessed his signature, had used the same pen. Mesmerised, I breathed on the blank paper, held it up against the light, and let my fingers travel over it, all to no avail. The signatures did not reappear.

"We tried all that, Peter. We even summoned a specialist. He was prepared to give it a try. But the outcome is questionable. There are too

A Matter of Compliance

many types of disappearing ink around. The signatures might be obliterated altogether if he went ahead."

"How did this trick happen?" I asked, bewildered.

"I offered Hendra my own pen. He declined and insisted on using his which — so he said — was the pen used by Sukarno when he executed the Treaty of Independence. I fell for it!"

"I, too, would have fallen for it," admitted Freddie. "The question is, what shall we do?"

For a few minutes I was lost in thoughts. To clear the picture, I asked Norbert whether he had been present when Hendra had signed. When he nodded, I wanted to know whether he could identify the secretaries who had witnessed the signatures. It turned out that both had left the bank. Still, their signatures as witnesses were displayed in full in the copies.

When I had digested the facts, I advised them to effect the set-off. If Hendra wanted them to remit any funds out, he would have to apply for a fresh overdraft. Norbert would know how to handle him.

"But how about the blank original?" asked Norbert.

"Freddie, what do you do when a document is lost or destroyed by accident, say, by fire?"

"Under Australian law, we can ask for the court's leave to prove it by submitting a copy verified by us as true."

"Our law is the same. I have a photocopy and Norbert can confirm its authenticity. So go ahead and set-off!"

"And if Hendra makes a fuss?" asked Freddie.

"Surely the bank sent him monthly 'statements of account'. I'm sure they include a 'verification clause'."

"They do. The clause is spelt out in the terms and conditions executed by him."

"If the worst comes to the worst, we can rely on them," I assured them.

The verification clause referred to was a standard term and condition used by most banks in Singapore. Under it, the customer was given a period of 7 or 10 days to object to any incorrect or false entry. If he failed to do so, the statement would become conclusive evidence of the existing balance. The validity of the clause had been upheld by local courts.

"I think Peter's right, Norbert. In any event, do you think Hendra would dare to unveil the nature of his business practices? Nobody would touch him with a bargepole if he became known as a conman. Unfortunately, there is a separate problem. We have discussed it. And you, Norbert, can't ask a compliance officer to close his eyes to it."

"Another problem?" I wailed.

IV

Heaving a sigh, Freddie raised the issue of the funds remitted and Hendra's order to pay out a substantial part forthwith. Bearing in mind Hendra's nefarious conduct, Freddie suspected that the case might involve money laundering.

A few years earlier, the issue would not have been a cause for concern. A bank's function was to receive amounts payable to its customer and to execute his payment instructions as long as he had the requisite balance. The position changed in the wake of terrorist activities in the United States. Under American pressure, many governments in the Western world passed laws under which a bank was expected to freeze amounts suspected of coming from dubious sources and to notify the reserve bank. The funds would be unfrozen only if cleared by it.

The Republic of Singapore passed the required regulations in 2002. The money laundering provisions required a bank to advise the "authority" when the bank had "reasonable grounds" to suspect that funds remitted to the credit of a customer could be traced to, or linked to, terrorist activities or laundering of illegal funds. If a bank reported the receipt of such contraband funds to the authority, the funds had to be frozen, and the customer could not be advised or "tipped off". In consequence, the customer would not even know that the money involved was no longer available to him.

"Freddie, do you suspect Hendra is involved in terrorist activities or is a money launderer?"

"Surely that's not the question, Peter!"

"What is it then?" asked Norbert.

"Freddie is telling us that the issue is the source of the money. If it's black money, its payment to a numbered account in Switzerland would complete the laundering cycle."

"Precisely!" Freddie spoke firmly. "And look, I can understand why Hendra arranged for the remittance of the money to his account in Singapore. If he had asked his 'payer', or 'remitter', to credit part of the sum directly to the payee's Swiss numbered account, the payer could work out how much money Hendra was making."

"So what?" I asked innocently.

"In future transactions, the remitter might manage to discover the payee's identity and deal directly with him."

"So why is the transaction suspicious?" asked Norbert.

"The remittance is coupled with an instruction to pay a similar amount out. That is suspicious. Further, I'm sure that Hendra would not care too much about the source of money paid to him! In his eyes, money doesn't stink," Freddie said vehemently.

"You are right about him," conceded Norbert. "But Hendra told me that he had purchased some mobile phones cheaply and sold them at a huge profit. He rang me this morning to ask if his purchaser had paid up."

"What did you tell him, Norbert?" I asked anxiously.

"I said I'd let him know as soon as the money comes in. I should ring him back before 4 o'clock. Up to now we haven't credited his account. But look here Peter, suppose we credit his account. Where is the risk? His balance will be short of the amount he wants us to pay out?"

"But the very crediting of the money is prohibited," interjected Freddie before I had a chance to answer.

"Should we send it back then?"

"You can't do that. There is case law in point, Norbert," I interceded.

"So, what should we do?"

"Credit the money to a temporary account — I mean a 'suspense account' — which includes a reference to the transaction. It's the only thing to do," insisted Freddie.

"Is it that simple?" asked Norbert.

"I am not certain," I warned. "If the suspense account is then frozen until the matter is cleared up, Hendra could get a court order diverting the money to another bank as soon as it's unfrozen by the authority. It could then be too late to exercise a set-off."

"So what should we do?"

"Why not contact the authority and ask for a direction?"

"I did so earlier today. They advised me to refer the matter to our legal advisers," chuckled Freddie. "Norbert rang you as soon as I showed him their email!"

"So we are back at square one," I muttered unhappily.

We continued to discuss the matter over coffee. In point of fact, the bank faced an impasse. In an attempt to sort out the matter, I volunteered to to think it over further.

V

Initially, my intention was to have a discreet chat with individuals at the authority, who had been my students or whom I met over the years. On further reflection, I decided to tackle the issue on my own. The reason was clear: discretion dictated that any officer with whom the matter was raised, would suggest that we freeze the amount received and ask that the authority give its ruling. The process, though, could take a few days. Commercially, this would be unsound because, in the instant case, time was the essence. The X Bank could end up with 'an omelette on its face' – that is to say, might end up in an embarrassing situation – if Hendra's supplier seized the goods 'in transitu' or, in other words, stopped their delivery.

If this happened, a commercial transaction would be defeated: Hendra would fail to make his profit and the 'goods' (that is, the phones) may be sold directly and more cheaply to the ultimate buyer. Was this really the purpose of the regulations?

To clear my mind I arranged to have lunch with, S., a fellow banking lawyer and discussed the case with him. He pointed out that, in essence, the entire Western World – and even the Eastern – thrived on free trade. The object of the relevant Regulations was to combat money laundering and the receipt of funds by terrorists. The aim was, accordingly, to target transactions of an illegal nature.

"What, then, are you telling me?" I asked.

"In my opinion, whether or not a remittance is suspicious has to decided by the bank. If the bank believes that a transaction is above board, the freezing of the funds would be counterproductive."

"Right you are," I replied. "But who in the bank has to take the decision? Surely, not the CEO!"

"Of course not. That worthy is most unlikely to be familiar with the transaction. Referring the matter to him would be bound to lead to delay. He would have to take some time to study the nature of the transaction."

"This is bound to take at least 24 hours; perhaps even longer than that! Who then must take a stand? The compliance officer?"

"How does he come into the picture?" asked my colleague.

"He would notice that a large amount is remitted to an existing account and that a comparable amount is withdrawn by means of an instantaneous subsequent remittance. From his point of view this is a 'red flag'."

"Which means that he has the duty to query the case. In a way, he has a right akin to a veto, doesn't he?"

"A right and also a duty. He must be vigilant. This is his very function," I augmented.

"Quite so. But if the employee in charge of the account involved is in a position to allay the compliance officer's misgivings, the sums need not be frozen.

I found myself in full agreement. Neither the United States nor the Republic of Singapore sought to interfere with free trade. If Hendra's transaction was genuine, then there was no need to freeze the amount received. It could be credited to the designated account and the X Bank was entitled to exercise its right of set-off and 'combine the accounts'. The person familiar with the transaction was, of course, Norbert. He alone could shed light on its legitimacy.

VI

Back at the X. Bank's premises, Norbert told us that he had examined the transaction and was satisfied it was an ordinary trade deal. In the circumstances, we decided he could go ahead. Both Freddie and I felt relieved.

At 4pm, Norbert rang up Hendra. He confirmed the receipt of the funds but added that the bank had exercised its set-off. In consequence, the account balance was well below the amount Hendra had ordered the bank to remit.

Hendra exploded but, after some empty threats, fixed an appointment to discuss the matter. When he arrived, Norbert and I were ready to face him. At this stage, our compliance officer Freddie thought it best to keep out of the picture.

To my relief, Hendra did not question the bank's right of set-off. He did not ask us to produce the original of the set-off agreement. Further, Hendra acknowledged that he had received his monthly statements. Without any tussle, he asked Norbert to approve the ensuing overdraft.

"I can't grant you such an amount. S$250,000 is well above my authorised margin. And you know your account has been the subject of concern."

"But if I don't pay up, the supplier of the phones may try to seize them before they are unloaded. I must pay!"

"But then, Bang Bang," Norbert addressed his client informally, "why don't you remit the money from your wife's account? You have moved it to another bank. But we know you have a substantial credit balance there."

Hendra didn't claim that the money belonged to his wife rather than to himself. He knew we were familiar with his trading patterns. Instead, he told Norbert candidly that this money was required for his ongoing dealings. If he lost control over these funds he would be "commercially finished".

"I understand, Bang Bang. And you know I always try to help you. But the head office would chop my head off if I authorised the remittance. Why don't you give us a cheque for, say, S$200,000?"

"I can't, Norbert, honestly. It would be my ruin. You can't let this happen, my friend. How about a cheque for S$75,000?"

For a while they haggled. Hendra tore his hair and pretended to break down. Norbert did his best to appear supportive and understanding, but the twinkle in his eye remained unchanged throughout the scene. I was relieved when, after some 20 minutes of pantomime, Hendra agreed to give us a cheque for S$125,000. Norbert promised to order the remittance of the funds as soon as the cheque had cleared. Smiling supportively, he proffered Hendra his own pen.

"This was used to sign the ASEAN Treaty, Bang Bang," he advised proudly.

"Can I have it?" asked Hendra eagerly.

"Of course!" said Norbert magnanimously, whilst I hid my face in a sheaf of papers and did my best to suppress a fit of laughter.

To my relief, Freddie was happy with the arrangement. All in all, it meant that Hendra's overdraft was reduced to some S$125,000. Like the rest of us, Freddie knew that to win some, you could not help losing others. In this case, the loss was moderate. The head office, too, was satisfied.

VII

The Hendra affair did not disrupt my good relations with Norbert and Freddie. And strangely enough, the tension between them eased. In a sense, the affair brought them together.

Hendra remained a thorn in the bank's side. On quite a few occasions, as I passed by the building housing the bank, I saw Hendra proceeding happily on to Collyer Quay. I had no doubt that, on each occasion, he had managed either to extend or to replenish his overdraft.

Bang Bang Hendra greeted me warmly whenever our paths crossed. On two occasions he invited me to have lunch with him, assuring me that he had just discovered a restaurant with "suitable dishes". I reciprocated. In due course, we became acquainted with one another. As was to be expected, informality replaced the cold business protocol.

Bang Bang manifested an interest in my obsession with 18th-century porcelain. I, in turn, was impressed by his activities as a breeder of exotic fish. When he discussed his hobby, he shed his image of a questionable business entrepreneur and talked about his subject with a fervour verging on devotion. It was difficult to associate this aficionado with the financial charlatan who used disappearing ink in his contractual transactions.

Soon it became clear to me that he wished to shed that unsavoury image. One morning he came over to my office and asked me to help him in his latest dealings with the bank. His overdraft at that time stood at S$180,000. He wanted the bank to accept payment of part of the amount in full settlement. Effectively, he was asking the bank to waive part of his indebtedness.

"But how can I help you in this matter? As you know, I am one of their legal advisers. I can't take a position that conflicts with their interests."

"Oh, I know this, Peter. But you see, Norbert is prepared to settle. His main fear is that Freddie will make a fuss."

"But surely, Bang Bang, this matter is up to the Head of the Bad Loans Department. It has nothing to do with compliance."

"Norbert and I know this. But Freddie was involved in some... earlier dealings. Norbert wants to forestall any further unpleasantness."

"So how do I fit into it?"

"Norbert says you are Freddie's good friend. He thinks that a gentle word from you might do the trick."

"I think, Bang Bang, that the best way is to have a frank word with Freddie. I suggest you call on him in person. But you know, Freddie will ask why they should accept part payment."

Hendra was aware of the need to show cause. To explain his position, he produced a memorandum prepared by his accountant. It showed that, over the years, Hendra had paid a great deal of money by way of penalty interest and bank charges. He would have been better off if a rate of 8.5 per cent had been charged on his median debit balance over the period.

"But surely penalties and charges are not part of a bank's profit?" I averred.

"Not in theory. But all in all, the total amount is paid out of my own pocket and is received by the bank! What I am saying, Peter, may be wrong in theory. But commercially it's sound. After all, I am poorer by the total sum paid by me for obtaining banking facilities and their extensions."

"You may find it difficult to convince Freddie. But Bang Bang, I take your point."

To my relief Freddie, too, was impressed by the figures. They demonstrated that if the bank accepted payment of some S$90,000 in full settlement, it would end up with a small profit. True, it would have been accrued through the imposition of penalty interest and charges. All in all, though, the bank would not have lost money.

VIII

A few days later, Hendra advised that a settlement had been reached. He had met Norbert and Freddie and, after some haggling, gave them a cheque for S$100,000. He was pleased with the arrangement. A chat with Freddie confirmed that the bank, too, was satisfied.

In due course, I invited Hendra for lunch. My objective was to find out what had induced him to settle. After all, the bank was unlikely to issue a writ as long as the balance remained steady.

"I have my pride, Peter. I am not prepared to escape through the back door. And you see, I have decided to quit the financial markets. I'm fed up with them and, honestly, I've made too many mistakes."

"But you are younger than your age. How will you occupy yourself, Bang Bang? You can't give up like this. I can't see you just sitting at home."

"I won't. Don't you worry."

"What will you do?"

"I'll devote the time left to me to the breeding of tropical fish. I'm good at it, much better than with currencies and shares."

"How splendid!" I replied.

Bang Bang Hendra smiled with satisfaction. He then gave me a copy of a book on fish breeding he had published in Jakarta. As I had no command of Indonesian, I was unable to read it. Nevertheless, I knew I was viewing a magnum opus. The colour plates, which I perused with fascination, demonstrated Hendra's love of and devotion to his hobby.

I had no doubt the publication had cost him a fortune. He would, of course, be unable to recover his investment. The photography alone had taken many hours of patient observation, good planning and time spent studying techniques for taking pictures of this type. I was also certain that he had spent a great deal of money on the acquisition of cameras and various other pieces of equipment.

Obviously, Hendra had changed his focus. He had left his unsavoury dealings behind him. It might have been a narrow escape. All the same, he had managed to break away. After many a fall, he had finally landed on his feet and had resolved to devote himself to an activity he found interesting. In this sense, he had been smiled upon by fortuna.

An Ageing Gourmet

I

The Oxford Dictionary defines a *gourmand* as "a person who enjoys eating and eats large quantities"; a *gourmet* is "a person who knows a lot about good food ... and who enjoys ... eating". In plain English, the former is a glutton; the latter is a connoisseur. During my long life I fell, I hope, into this refined group, although I always tended to pay attention to the price. "'Good food' had to be 'good value'"; if it was unreasonably expensive, consuming it would be extravagant. Thereupon, it became too dear for my purse.

Nowadays, when I recollect events triggered by my enthusiasm, I tend to break into a smile. Good food was not my only hobby. During my school days, I was an avid reader. This hobby stood me in good stead throughout my life. Later on, I collected porcelain. All in all, books, porcelain and food kept me going. Recently, though, I had to stop collecting books and porcelain. My house is full of them. But, from time to time, I leave home and go to a moderately priced food outlet. In more than one way, each occasion takes me back to my long-gone youth in Israel, to my first spell in Singapore, to my years in Australasia and, finally, to the period following my return to the Lion City.

Today, I propose to tell my gourmet story or, in other words, my food-loving odyssey.

II

During my years in primary school, I used to stray to my grandparents' home on Dizengoff Street in Tel Aviv. Like my parents, they had fled from Vienna in 1938 and settled for a while in Palestine. Walking from our flat to their place took some 20 minutes, but anticipation cut it short.

Grandmother — my Babbe — was an outstanding chef. The recollection of her stuffed chicken neck (Helzel), stuffed beef intestines (Kishke), roast goose and eggplant dishes makes my mouth water. She had the magic gift of turning even the most common ingredients into delicacies. My love of good food can be traced back to her culinary skills.

Shortly after Grandfather decided to move back to Vienna and relaunch his wholesale business, I was enrolled in Tichon Ironi A, my splendid secondary school. Before long, the Israeli delicacy known as pita-falafel became a common and beloved treat.

The pita-falafel is made of small chickpea dumplings, deep fried in vegetable oil and placed in a "pita", that is, unleavened bread sliced so that it opens like a small bag. Cumin seed and coriander are the spices that give the dish its flavour.

I tasted this Israeli delicacy for the first time when I was still in primary school. Dad took me to watch a soccer match between Maccabi

Tel Aviv and a team from "that other city" — Haifa. The loud cheers for our home team fell on deaf ears. The Haifa "upstarts" kicked the decisive goal.

When my deflated Dad and I left the stadium, we spotted a tricycle with an attached wok — a huge frying pan — of piping oil. The hawker dipped a gadget into a pan filled with a white-looking mass, used it to form dumplings and tossed them into the oil. The deep-fried browning dumplings looked delicious. Dad, who liked to try everything, bought one pita-falafel. We shared it, enjoyed it and went back for another. The hawker bestowed on us a knowing smile and treated us to an extra portion. There and then, I became hooked.

My class at Tichon was sociable. In the evening, some of us went out for walks. More often than not our legs took us to a small yard in which a hawker sold pita-falafel. When we first visited, he called himself "The Desperado." Over the years, he acquired a substantial clientele. We had to queue in order to get our treat. Eventually, he changed his nickname to "The Happy Prince".

Most of us made do with just one portion of the delicacy. One member of our group, good old Pilkin (which means the "little elephant"), was tall and massive. Usually all of us looked tolerantly as he ordered a double portion. The real trouble was that one of us — Fair Shosh — had a ravenous appetite. Usually she ordered one portion but, within the next few minutes, took "bites" from all others. Poor Pilkin ended up with just one portion; the other half was gobbled up by her. Unsurprisingly, by the time we finished secondary school, Shosh had become bulky. Pilkin remained a heavy weight but did not acquire fat. To my mind, Shosh demonstrated that gluttony was risky.

III

In 1951, I enrolled as a student at the Faculty of Law of the Hebrew University of Jerusalem. Good pita-falafel outlets were far from both our lecture hall and my lodgings. Usually I joined fellow students and had meals at the eatery in Rehavia, known as the Menza cafeteria. The food was plain yet nourishing.

I then discovered a small café, which served excellent Turkish coffee with a piece of baklava — an oriental cake: excellent for a tea break. When Mother came up to Jerusalem for a visit, she commended the place and enjoyed the treat. Neither of us was concerned or even aware that the place was run by an Arab.

Lectures at the university were uninspiring. When it dawned on me that I could pass the examinations by studying notes taken by conscientious students, I accepted the post of a cadet at a well-known law firm in Tel Aviv and went up to Jerusalem only from time to time. The law firm was far from the falafel outlet. In due course, I discovered a small eatery run by a Yemenite. Oriental delicacies, like humus and kebabs, appealed to me. Before long, I went there for my daily lunch.

Shortly after graduating and doing my pupillage, I proceeded for further studies to Oxford. There were, of course, quite a number of fish and chips joints, but this British staple did not agree with my sensitive digestive system and my "sophisticated" palate. Pita-falafel, humus and kebabs were obtainable in restaurants in London, but these were too expensive and, of course, out of daily reach.

Most students went to an inexpensive outlet, known as Crawfords, in Carfax, Oxford's centre. Before long, I learned to relish the steak and kidney and the mushroom pies. They were wholesome and good. Their fame explained the fact that the eatery was patronised by some of the legendary Oxford luminaries. One of the postgraduate students, whose table I joined from time to time, became, in due course, the senior legal adviser of a prestigious United Nations body.

During my second year in the university town, I discovered that a filling slice of buttered bread and coffee were available in the Covered Market near the library in which I spent most of my time. The chap who took me to "Gorgi" became a well-known barrister and later on a highly respected High Court Judge. During my last visit to London, he invited me to his club. The food was gorgeous. It reminded me of my single extravagance in Oxford. Once a week, usually on Saturday evening, I went to "The Elizabeth" and ordered a Dover sole. It was excellent and quite affordable. Later in life, I enjoyed the treat in Amsterdam and in Hamburg.

IV

When I ran out of money in 1961, I accepted the post of a junior lecturer at the University of Malaya in Singapore. Shortly after my arrival in Singapore, I discovered the G.H. Café on Battery Road. This eatery was spacious and homely, though not posh. The best dish it boasted was a gado-gado, an assortment of potatoes and vegetables covered with a tangy sauce of peanuts and spices. There were, of course, some other local delicacies like laksa, a coconut-based spicy soup with prawns and scallops, and hor fun made of broad rice noodles. I, though, stuck to the gado-gado.

Practising lawyers came over during the lunch break and enjoyed the local treats. Our group occupied at least one table. Frequently, the conversation turned to leading cases, which the attendees used to dissect. In due course, though, the discussion turned to tittle-tattle.

The assemblage then listened open-mouthed to the antics which lawyer X. (usually a Mister but from time to time a Missus or Miss) performed with a member of the opposite (rarely of the same) sex. In due course, it dawned on me that saints were just as rare amongst the ranks of our fraternity as, indeed, they were in legal circles in other places.

Most of the cases discussed by us were mundane. Two of them, though, were out of the ordinary. I recall them with a smile. The first took place in the courtroom of Justice T., who was universally admired for his cordial demeanour and pleasant disposition. In the lawsuit I recall, his tolerance might have gone too far. Counsel for the plaintiffs opened his case with a detailed and thorough analysis of a doctrine known as the constructive trust. When counsel finished, Justice T. (who had not interrupted the flow) observed that this was an excellent discussion. Counsel replied that it was his privilege to have pleased "Your Honour". Looking slightly bewildered, Justice T. then pointed out that he failed to see why the points made were relevant. The case before him involved breach of contract. It then turned out that counsel had picked up the wrong file when he had left his office.

The second noteworthy case involved a prosecution. The "prisoner at the bar" was accused of assault and battery that took place in a nightclub. His counsel, Lawyer M., was a fine courtroom advocate who knew how to address both the judge and the jury. I pause to add that, in those days, the verdict was pronounced by the jury, who had to determine all points of fact but was guided by the judge's summing up.

Lawyer M.'s "demonstration tactics" were well-known. Many of us hoped that in a suitable contested divorce, he might ask the correspondent to demonstrate how "she" (or "he") kissed the errant defendant. Lawyer M., however, did not appear in cases involving matrimonial disputes.

In the case in question, the defences included "provocation" and the contention that the accused merely "pushed" the victim, whose injuries were allegedly sustained in the ensuing fall. To substantiate the validity of this well-trodden plea, Lawyer M. asked the accused to demonstrate how he had "pushed" the complainant and asked his junior to step forward as the "subject of the demonstration". To the amazement of all present, the accused delivered a mighty punch. One of the spectators, a boxing aficionado, counted the young lawyer out.

The case was hotly debated in the café. One of the attendants, whose shirt was stained with traces of sauce, argued that Lawyer M. was "vicariously liable" for the accused's "assault" on the young lawyer. Another lawyer pointed out (over a dish of hor fun) that, under the doctrine in question, a master would be liable for a tort committed by his servant. In the instant matter, though, Lawyer M. was the accused's (the client's) servant. Accordingly, the doctrine would be inapplicable because an agent was not liable for the principal's act.

Just for once, I took an active part in the discussion, asserting that as Lawyer M. had initiated the "demonstration", he was a "joint tortfeasor". He was as liable as if he had delivered the punch himself. One of our crowd, who purported to be a good friend, asked whether my argumentation was reflected in the courses I was teaching "up there in the ivory tower". He added that, in his opinion, I ought to take a walk into the "real world", that is, practice.

The discussion was getting heated when, unexpectedly, Lawyer M. made his appearance and ordered a laksa. It must have been excellent because he smacked his lips and relaxed. In response to our questions, Lawyer M. advised that he had paid the young lawyer "damages" for the injury and humiliation suffered. He added that the case had taught him a lesson: prior to the embarkation on a "demonstration", an advocate ought to familiarise himself not only with the facts of the case but also with "related circumstances". In the instant matter, it turned out that the accused was married to an attractive girl, who had all the virtues of a good wife except fidelity. And it so happened that on the very day preceding the hearing, the accused had discovered that she was carrying on with none other than the young lawyer. Was it then surprising that when asked to "demonstrate", the accused delivered a mighty punch so as to avenge his loss of "honour"?

Some two years after this memorable case, I met my future wife. During the months of courtship and also after we tied the knot, we used to patronise a food court known as Quek Lane (pronounced Cook Lane). One stall served a splendid curry puff. Another hawker had fine satay, that is, thin and short sticks of wood on which the hawker skewed lamb, beef or chicken meat pieces and grilled them over charcoal. They were served with a spicy sauce, into which you dipped the skewers. I enjoyed satay just as much as the falafel I used to take in Tel Aviv. There were also some modestly priced Chinese restaurants. Occasionally, we went to them and enjoyed a square meal.

V

In 1967, we migrated to New Zealand, settling in Wellington. Within walking distance of our house we found a fishmonger who used vegetable oil in his wok. Unlike in England, his "fish and chips" were tasty. Oysters, too, were good and cheap. When taken home and consumed with a slice of bread and butter, they were a fine starter of a meal.

Occasionally, I got a dozen and consumed them during faculty luncheons. These were usually dominated by vivid arguments of applicable issues between two colleagues: J.T. and G.P. Although the latter was usually outsmarted, he later became the country's prime minister. I still believe that J.T. would have ousted him, had he chosen a political career.

During our second year in this picturesque town, we discovered a farm which sold chicken livers and fat — not popular on the home market — for a token. Pat, who had mastered Jewish cooking, prepared excellent pates. The faces of local guests expressed sheer delight when they consumed the delicacies. Little did they know that they were enjoying traditional East European delights.

Another treat was black boy peaches, which were plentiful (and inexpensive) during the summer. We bottled them and usually consumed them with whipped cream during the winter. Today, as a diabetic, I am not permitted to take such sweets. All I can do is to recall them.

During my last years in New Zealand's capital, I found additional entertainment. During lunch time, the university's cafeteria served strongly brewed coffee and good cakes. Frequently, I went to it and joined a table of bridge players. In this way, I met colleagues from different disciplines who, like myself, liked to get away from the humdrum of lecturing and administrative work and get immersed in the "multi-discipline" game. It would be wrong to pretend that this type of session involved a gourmand's treat. Nevertheless, it was fun.

After a few years we moved to Melbourne. Excellent and moderately priced restaurants were available to patrons in all parts of town. Many of them operated on a "bring your own" basis. This meant that you could order a fine meal and have a bottle of wine, acquired at a supermarket, uncorked by the restaurant's staff and consumed during a meal.

Then we found a doner kebab outlet. I had enjoyed the dish years earlier, on a trip to Turkey taken during my long-gone youth. It was a pleasure to watch the lamb shawarma cooked by rotating it around a heated element. The stall-keeper cut a few slices, placed them in unleavened bread, added tahini and chili, and enveloped the wrap in plastic. This was an excellent lunch. Getting to the stall required a 10 minutes' drive, which was time well-rewarded.

VI

In 1986 we returned to the Lion City. My employers had changed their name to the National University of Singapore. A food court adjacent to the premises, known as "the canteen", served excellent chicken rice and a wonton soup. Whilst some of my colleagues liked to drive to Holland Village, I usually took my lunch on site.

Before long I got addicted to Hainanese chicken rice, which had not been available in Melbourne's Chinatown. In a way, this was perplexing. The dish simply comprises cooked or roast chicken slices and a bowl of rice steamed in chicken broth. Served with a few pieces of cucumber and soup, the dish constitutes an excellent lunch. I am uncertain why I had not come across it earlier, and wonder why it was not offered in Australasia.

My brothers-in-law, too, liked the dish. I recall how one of them took a holiday in the Hainan province in Mainland China, only to return with a sad expression. When asked what the matter was, he explained that chicken rice was not available there. It then dawned on me that the dish was a creation of Hainanese settlers of Singapore. It was, I concluded, a national delicacy.

One bright morning I drove to town. To my disappointment, the G.H. Café had disappeared. Lawyers tended to congregate in the

Supreme Court's cafeteria. It was far from our campus and very few academics took the time to drive over. Further, I gathered that the lively discussions of old had ceased. The younger generation of lawyers was far more serious-minded and less adventurous than their predecessors.

Shortly before my 65th birthday, a former student asked me to join his firm. I accepted and became a full-time practitioner. My office was in Battery Road, in the very street in which the G.H. Café used to be. As this lovely spot was no longer in existence, I had to find another suitable outlet. For a while, I kept searching. Then I spotted an Italian restaurant in the basement of a nearby building. I went almost daily to my new den, which was not frequented by colleagues and clients. I used to order a calzone — a pizza turned onto itself (creating a large puff) and stuffed with cheese, butter and ham. Consumed with a glass of red wine, it was a lunch befitting a king. I recall how, on one occasion, my physician came over for a meal and joined my table. As he had prescribed a strict diet, I watched with unease as he took note of my glass of red wine.

"Don't look so sheepish," he told me. "One glass of wine a day is okay for your sugar levels."

"It uplifts my spirit," I replied.

"Then go ahead with it; but don't overdo it."

Practice was fun. Before long I gathered that most clients thought they knew more about the law than their legal advisers. Frequently, prudence dictated falling in with their plans. In due course, I started to draft oppressive clauses that bankers wanted to include in the "general terms and conditions" imposed on their customers. I knew that courts might set them aside. Still, it was best to comply with my clients' whims. To guard my rear, I highlighted the risk.

I also learned that some bank customers could be tricky. One of them had signed documents with fading ink. On one occasion we had to apply for a court order, validating a copy I was lucky to have made before the signature had vanished. In another instance, a customer invited the bank's officer and me for lunch in an Indonesian restaurant and ordered dishes so spicy that we needed soda bicarbonate tablets to alleviate our sufferings. Still, to please the client, we had to consume the food.

Later on, a friend took me over to the Fullerton Hotel. It turned out that an Indian food buffet was served at lunchtime. The tandoori dishes were outstanding. There was also a cafeteria, which served tolerable chicken rice. After a few weeks of shuttling between this cafeteria and my den, I stopped missing the G. H. Café.

VII

During my last few years of practice, my wife had her fatal struggle with an incurable disease. Shortly after her demise, I retired from both practice and teaching and moved into a flat on the East Coast, which we had acquired after my move downtown. It had a splendid view. On pleasant days, I could even see the Riau Islands of Indonesia.

Regrettably, the apartment was far from the city. To start with, I hankered after the eateries I had become used to. Fortunately, I discovered an excellent food court nearby. Here, too, I was able to get my chicken rice and dumpling soups. Some stalls offered duck and beef noodles.

The Thai restaurant on the premises was initially disappointing. Then the place changed hands. The new Indian restaurant was exceptional. The chef came from Gujarat, and his dishes were genuine.

Before long I came to appreciate his tandoori dishes, the tasty spinach with cottage cheese and the dahl. After a while I started to place orders for luncheons and dinners.

An excellent restaurant within a short driving distance became another outlet. The beef carpaccio was reasonably priced and accommodated my weakening teeth. Occasionally I went to a nearby steakhouse and tackled a tenderloin slowly and gingerly. I have become an old man. Still, my memories keep me going. It dawned on me that being of an advanced age could be comfortable, and that my existence was enjoyable.

Through the Glasses
of My Cabinets

Sitting in the black easy chair in my sitting room late one evening, I watched the skyline with the hope of spotting an aeroplane descending gracefully to Singapore's Changi Airport. I knew that my own travelling days were over. At the ripe age of 90, when living in full and comfortable retirement, my only option was to stay put. The very thought of queuing in an airport's departure hall made me shiver.

Prior to sitting down, I had viewed with pride and satisfaction my vast collection of European porcelain pieces. Some came from Europe's first porcelain factory, Meissen, which was launched in the early 18th century. Over the years, I also acquired many pieces produced in other German firms or in other countries.

The bulk of those manufactured during the 20th century were housed in a cabinet adjacent to my television set. Another cabinet, at the other end of my sitting room, displayed my musical apes — an entire orchestra — and some other treasures. A magnificent three-tiered centrepiece produced by Meissen, which used to grace the dining table in a Prussian mansion, was amongst them. My other trophies — mainly pieces modelled and fired in the 18th and 19th centuries — were displayed in the study. Some were of museum quality. More recently, I kept buying attractive pieces put up for sale in auctions or on eBay. To display them, I had turned a bookshelf in my master bedroom into yet another porcelain cabinet.

Most of my pieces were figurines. But I also had some urns, plates, cups and saucers, and some decorative dishes. It was one of the largest collections in our region. As I thought about them, I mused: "Won't it be nice if some of my treasures were animated?"

Suddenly, I heard a bark. "It must be the neighbour's dog," I told myself. I knew the animal was complaining. It wanted its master to take it for a stroll on the grounds of our spacious condominium. The sound, though, came from the opposite direction.

When I turned to face one of my trophy cabinets, I saw to my utter surprise that a porcelain dog, modelled by Theodor Karner after he had moved to the Rosenthal factory in 1947, had come to life. To start with I could not believe my eyes. I then realised that my hidden wish had been fulfilled.

Even so, I asked myself: "Am I dreaming?"

"Not at all, Peter'le," said the voice I knew so well. "You have many faults, but hallucinating is not one of them!"

"That's not fair, Maestro," I told my lifelong friend. "Why did you animate this dog? You know I am always happy to talk with you; so why the go-between?"

"It seemed reasonable to fulfil your hidden wish. Further, I wanted to remind you that things are not always what they appear. And you, Peter'le, did you really think that this black-and-red-dressed figurine is a good representation of myself?"

The porcelain figurine, which was meant to be "the devil", was no longer in my cabinet. Mephisto, whom I had dubbed Theophil out of veneration, assumed the guise of a grown-up man. He was sitting in a chair adjacent to mine.

"You have a good taste in porcelain, Peter'le," he told me.

"I love it," I conceded. "I still have pieces which my mother bought in Vienna in her teens."

"But she bought only Viennese pieces. You bought many pieces made in Germany, including the musical apes. Come, let us walk over to see and enjoy them."

His friendly grin convinced me. Some of my 21 musical monkeys were fakes — and I had acquired them with full knowledge of this — but just one was a Johann Joachim Kändler original, modelled and fired in Meisen in 1753. This feminine ape (dubbed Liz), holding her notes in front of her whilst singing, had cost a fair penny. But then, she was special.

"Would you like your orchestra to perform?" he asked genially.

"That would be lovely," I assured him. "But they are apes, not real musicians!"

"Sometimes the distinction is hard to fathom," he replied, grinning. Then, seeing my awkward expression, he asked me to name a composition I would like to listen to.

"*Rhapsody in Blue*," I told him, adding as an afterthought, "but it does not make provision for vocal participation. So how about Liz?"

"Don't worry about this," he let his generosity show. "We'll turn her into a clarinet virtuoso. This way, she won't feel left out!"

"But how about the piano? My monkey has a keyboard, which is not adequate for such a performance."

"That's easily fixed."

As he spoke, the keyboard transformed itself into a miniature fortepiano. The monkey sitting on the stool in front of it had a human face. It looked familiar.

"Don't tell me you emulated Gershwin," I muttered.

"For you, Peter'le, only the best."

"But he died years ago!" I exclaimed.

"What do you know about death, Peter'le?"

"Not much, Maestro. I know that when a person dies his physical remains are left motionless."

"And the spirit?"

"Is there such a thing?"

"You tell me," he replied sternly. His response was true to character. Theophil kept his secret knowledge to himself. He left research and speculation to mankind.

"There is some power or energy that propels us. And I know the law of the preservation of energy. So this power cannot be lost. It must be absorbed somewhere."

"But where?" He asked laconically.

As often when talking with him, I was out of my depth. In my spare time — and I had plenty of it during my life as a retiree — I watched many programmes dealing with cosmology. These told me that the universe was vast, perhaps even infinite. One difficult point, though, remained unanswered: how did it begin? Could something be created from "nothing"? The three monotheistic religions sought to provide an answer by postulating "creation" by divinity. Polytheistic religions attributed the task to one of several deities. Agnostics and atheists were unable to come up with a reasonable reply.

"Why don't you tell me, Maestro? I am sure you know the answer!"

Through the Glasses of My Cabinets

"We better turn back to your concert," he grinned. "Let the scientists do their work."

At that very moment one of my musical apes stepped forward. He looked distressed and his next few words threw light on the subject: "I am a clarinettist. Peter'le bought me as such. So why do you want to turn Liz into one? I can perform!"

"Let us not argue," suggested Theophil. "We can next play Mozart's clarinet concerto and you can perform."

"But I don't like Mozart; his music is not to my taste!"

To my relief, Liz stepped in. Acting like a real lady, she told us that she liked Mozart and would be thrilled to participate as soloist of his concerto; and she wouldn't mind giving noisy George Gershwin a miss. Accordingly, the roles could be swapped.

For just a moment I thought we were all set. Then Liz raised a point. She thought it would be futile to carry on without an audience. Magnanimously, Theophil animated a mandolin player, a guitarist, a hurdy-gurdy player, an elegant lady and three pedlars. My two replicas of the Greeting Harlequin — modelled by Kändler at Meissen but copied or faked by many factories — waved connoisseurs into the sitting room, which turned itself into an auditorium. The last to come through the door were my hunter and a fish thief. The latter, who remained true to the character given to him by Kändler, looked carefully around, hoping to pickpocket some sleepy patrons.

"This is a small audience but a discerning one, not musical critics who think they know everything. As far as they are concerned, the ordinary listener is superfluous!"

"Should we perhaps also invite the lady bowler and the attractive tennis player?" I asked my ephemeral friend.

"I don't think so," he concluded after a momentary reflection. "Both of them were modelled in the 20th century. You acquired them because they looked good. You, Peter'le, had an eye for attractive women, but did not reflect on human rights. Both of them demonstrate the role of modern women in social gatherings and in sports. But there is no reason to suggest that they liked music. There is no need to invite them to a concert."

It was an exciting performance. The conductor, one of the apes acquired by me and animated by Theophil, was an excellent timekeeper. Then, to my surprise, there was a knock on my entrance door. The neighbour's son, a pleasant chap in his early 30s, came to deliver his mother's message: could we kindly be less noisy? She wanted to sleep peacefully.

"But how about your dog, doesn't he bark?" I wanted to know.

"We have trained him to keep quiet at night," was the sanguine reply.

Suddenly, a fine Meissen bulldog, modelled by non eother than Kändler, left the cabinet, grew to his life-like size and barked threateningly.

"I didn't know you kept a dog," said the startled lad.

"He is a porcelain dog," I advised.

"I must be seeing things," muttered the frightened youngster. "I better seek medical advice."

To aggravate the situation, another acquisition of mine, the Geisha, came to life and looked invitingly at our guest. The fellow, still a bachelor, viewed her with alarm.

"I have never seen this lady before!" he exclaimed. "Are you a married man?"

"He's a widower and she's of porcelain," Theophil told him dryly, whilst the animated figurine resumed its place in the porcelain cabinet. He then added: "You are seeing things! A GP may be unable to help!"

"Psychiatrists, too, must make a living," averred Theophil after our visitor's hasty departure. "But we better turn to Mozart; less loud."

My monkey band rose to the occasion. When they metamorphosed back into figurines, I decided to raise a question that had been troubling me for years.

"Maestro, what is the real world? The one in which they performed or my peaceful existence as an ageing retiree on Singapore's East Coast?"

"Why do you ask me?"

"I thought you might be able to tell me."

"But suppose I might — would I want to?"

"Whyever not?"

"Mankind doesn't know! And I am not an interventionist."

"You helped scientists to find some speculative answers," I told him firmly. "Why not take the next step?"

"Perhaps one day — a suitable day! When there is a real need for a breakthrough!"

"So you nudged Newton and Einstein on previous occasions!"

"Quite so. But, as you know, even Einstein failed to come up with a final theorem!"

"And many scientists have started to doubt him," I summed up. Theophil nodded but did not say a word.

"I'm thirsty," I told him. "Usually I take a nightcap before getting ready to switch off."

"We can do better than that," he averred. The elegant lady who graced one of my cabinets, and who had been in the audience, metamorphosed once again to a human being. She sat on my comfortable sofa and sipped coffee from a fine cup produced in Meissen in the early 20th century. It was trimmed with real gold, as was the saucer that accompanied it.

"One of your best acquisitions, Peter'le."

"I first got the cup and two years later the saucer." Turning to my elegant guest, I observed: "It's getting late. Drinking coffee in the evening is a bad idea."

"Here, have a port," suggested my friend. At that very moment a bottle materialised in front of us.

"I think I'll have a glass," she smiled and looked bemused as a conservatively dressed waiter appeared in my sitting room and poured out the dessert wine. He did not look familiar and so I raised my eyebrows.

"One of the figurines which was sold for a price higher than your final bid," grinned Theophil. "You, Peter'le, were the underbidder."

"So how did he appear here?"

"Surely you don't expect my powers to be limited. I brought him over from another collector's display case."

"*Bothe moi*," I muttered. Then, swiftly, I corrected myself, saying: "Good grief!"

"Why not simply say Good Satan?"

"I never use that word, Maestro," I assured my friend. "In any event, the Old Testament is ambivalent about him. He appears in a favourable light in Job and as a mere observer in Zechariah. He is regarded as a source of evil only in post-exilic Judaism and in the New Testament!"

"Some theologians maintain that the Snake of Genesis is none other than him," pointed out my friend in an irritated tone.

"They would come up with any statement that supports their dogma," I told him feelingly.

"But they may have a point," averred my protagonist. "If I can animate porcelain pieces or assume a human form, I can also transform myself into a snake. You, Peter'le, must cultivate tolerance!"

At that moment, the elegant lady rose from her comfortable chair, gave me a stern look and announced that she was tired. Instantly, Theophil transmuted her back into a porcelain figurine.

"And you, Peter'le, have remained a slow operator!"

"Oh well," I muttered, "I hate headaches. Life is easier without them!"

"I better draw you to the geisha's attention. She knows how to take charge when necessary. Or I might decide to bring out your bowling lady. She might ram a ball at you if you keep staying put."

"Come off it, Maestro. I prefer the status quo," I assured him. "I am too comfortable to seek a change."

"Very well," he replied and moved the geisha back into my show cabinet. At that very moment, another figurine stepped forward.

"I gather that some drink is available," said the drunken peasant. Initially, I was unable to understand him. Taking in my bewildered expression, Theophil explained that the language used was German spoken in the 17th century.

"You know, Peter'le," he chided, "languages undergo an evolutionary process. Think about Hebrew. Do you really know how Jeremiah or Amos pronounced vowels? But don't you fret, I'll endow you with an extra linguistic facility."

Thereupon, I was able to understand my guest. But one aspect puzzled me. Kändler, who had modelled the figurine, was active in the

18th century. Why then did my ephemeral guest converse in 17th-century German? Theophil, who read my mind, explained that the prototype used by Kändler was a 17th-century peasant. The drunkard used the tongue prevailing during his days.

"Makes sense," I had to agree. "But does language change according to a linear process?"

"Not really. Frequently the change is triggered by a mutation. It is, therefore, unpredictable."

"Can't it be induced?"

"I can trigger the mood for a change. Its effect remains unpredictable. This is one argument against intervention."

As often before, I looked at my friend with admiration. I knew that observing human development was one of his hobbies. His objective, though, was to discern rather than to influence. Frequently he was tempted to intervene but, in the event, decided to refrain. It was, therefore, unreasonable to regard him as the source of evil. His stand was clear: he kept aloof and detached. One question, though, bothered me whenever I read the Book of Job.

"We are told, in Chapter 1 of Job, that when the Good Lord asked you from where you came, you replied that you were wandering throughout the earth and walking across it. Is this correct? Surely you aren't confined to our globe."

"Of course not. I told him that I came from wandering through his universe. The scribe misquoted me. But the vast size of the cosmos was unknown to him."

"But are you able to visit domains other than our universe?"

"Come, come, Peter'le, you know better than to ask such questions. You appreciate that there may be other universes but remain unable to define them. And I do not intend to enlighten you. Come, let us attend to your ephemeral guest."

The inebriated peasant looked at me sombrely. His only desire was to quench his thirst. Accordingly, I watched him as he gulped down the liquid in his mug. His next words threw light on his feelings: "You condemn me because I'm a drunkard!"

"I want to be fair. I'm not prepared to pass judgment before I hear you."

"Alright, listen. I was a farmer. Then the great war broke out. And they burnt down my barn."

"Who?" I wanted to know.

"How do I know? They emerged from the woods, slaughtered my entire entourage and then set everything on fire. So, what do you think remained for me?"

"So now you begin to understand, Peter'le," said the archfiend. "He has told you all about his lot. Let us have a word with another fellow."

A war cripple stepped out of one of my cabinets. He, too, conversed in 17th-century German. He had been modelled and fired at Frankenthal in Germany in the 18th century, but depicted a victim of the Thirty Years' War (1618–1648). One of his legs had been replaced by an ill-fitting wooden prosthesis.

"Alms for the poor," he begged, holding out a worn-out hat.

"What happened to you? How did you lose your leg?" I asked him.

"They pressed me into the army. I lost my leg at the Battle of Nördlingen."

"On which side were you fighting?"

"I don't have the foggiest idea. They told us it was a noble cause." Pausing for a moment, he added: "You know, I was lucky. Many were left behind and perished."

Gently, Theophil transferred him back into my cabinet. For a while, both of us remained silent.

"So they fought for an unknown cause," I muttered.

"A novelty?" asked my friend.

"War and mayhem have been part and parcel of human history. I know that much. I gleaned this from our history courses in secondary school."

"How about your extracurricular readings? You studied the history of ancient Egypt."

"The unification of Upper and Lower Egypt at the dawn of civilisation was the end result of skirmishes ... of early warfare."

"Quite so," he confirmed. "Mankind's history tells you all about wars and conquests."

"Is this then part of our nature? Is it ingrained in us?"

"It is, rather," he affirmed and went on to explain: "Homo sapiens has a compelling survival instinct. It aided him to defeat and annihilate other humanoids. Later on, it triggered territorial struggles amongst factions of the group. Frequently, the real cause of warfare was camouflaged. People fell for propaganda or simply did as they were told."

"Was the Thirty Years' War the worst?"

"Far from it; it was deadly but so were many others. The Battle of Borodino (1812) was sheer butchery, as were all other campaigns of the Corsican upstart."

"Is sexual drive related to our survival instinct?"

"Of course. It assures the survival of the species."

Through the Glasses of My Cabinets

"Maestro, I find all this a bit confusing. Most religions and legal systems have firm provisions against murder and homicide, but killing the opponents' fighters becomes a task of soldiers. And most societies expect fidelity in marriage. Some even apply the death sentence to adultery, but rape and rapine prevail during wars. Isn't there some inconsistency here?"

"Not really. The survival instinct postulates law and order in society during periods of peace. Human life has to be treated accordingly as sacrosanct. Society also seeks to entrench stability in families. This way nations prosper. At first glance, the order of peace conflicts with the tenets applicable during wars. On a more careful consideration, all is dictated by the ever-prevalent survival instinct."

His words made sense: he was a keen observer. But did he empathise with humanity? Could he really have remained detached all these years?

"Yes, Peter'le," he replied to my unuttered thoughts. "To form an objective conclusion, you have to be aloof — an alien. Occasionally, though, we form attachments. As you know, I liked Job although I had to inflict him."

"You won that bet with Him (the Almighty). When overtaken by malady, Job cursed God! Your prediction was accurate. Why didn't He perceive this?"

"Perhaps he didn't want to see the obvious. We, too, have our vanities!"

For a while we sat together in harmony. I had known him for years and learned to appreciate his insights. I also knew that his objectivity remained intact even in stressful situations. Quite frequently, what appeared a tough spot to us did not sway him.

After a while, he offered to produce yet another show. The neatly dressed ballet dancers of my collection started to get ready.

"Any ballet you like in particular?"

"How about *Coppélia*? But who would assume the role of Dr. Coppelius?"

A neatly modelled and fired middle-aged Pantalone, with a lamp in his hand, stepped out of one of my trophy cabinets.

"I think he is suitable," observed Theophil. "Coppelius searched for a way to blow life into a manikin, hence his lamp. Agreed?"

"Of course," I replied. "I suspect that the modeller, Wenzel Neu of Kloster Veilsdorf, did not expect that his porcelain figurine would come to life."

"His soul might have anticipated or hoped for the experience," grinned Theophil. "That is, if there is such a thing as a soul."

"You do not intend to tell me if there is."

"Of course not. Remember, curiosity killed the cat."

"But I'm not a cat!"

"True. And so you do not have nine lives, and even the one you have keeps its secrets."

It was a graceful ballet. The mazurka was impressive, as indeed was the setting. Once again, I wondered which was the real world. The one I was watching or my plain existence as an aged retiree. Asking Theophil was pointless. He would keep his detached silence.

As I kept watching, my eye caught sight of a porcelain boy. He was lying down in a relaxed manner and playing the flute.

"Care to animate him?"

"If you please," I replied willingly. Initially, the boy retained his posture. He then grew in size and in age. Before long he became a horn player in an orchestra: a musician.

"You see," observed my friend. "As a child he played the flute. It was a game. Later in life, it became his career. He was not a high-flyer. Orchestras from around the world did not seek to engage him as a soloist. But he held on to his chair at the local ensemble until his retirement; and he had students. All in all, a happy career and a good life."

"Commencing with his boyish game," I put in.

"Precisely! Children must learn how to play. Their future often depends on it. Many chess champions had humble beginnings in a local club. Later on they would develop into grand masters."

"Nowadays children are often pressed by their parents into endless strife in their schools; they do not learn how to play or to relax," I grumbled.

"Quite so! And the rate of suicide amongst youngsters continues to climb."

The ballet dancers had finished their performance and went back into my cabinets. As they took their place, I recalled my attempts to collect during my days as a postgraduate student at Oxford. Frequently, I went to porcelain auctions. Many good pieces were snapped up for a price I was unable to outbid.

An old recollection made me smile. The field research respecting my studies at Oxford required lengthy spells in London. During these I stayed in a students' dormitory. In the evenings, I usually watched (in the company of other residents) films or programmes displayed on the television set in the spacious hall thereof. To my chagrin, in many an evening the hall was occupied by political discussions led by distinguished guests. When these were on, the use of the set was precluded.

Initially I tried to participate with the hope of bringing the heated arguments to an early end, but soon discovered that my intervention simply added fuel to the fire and prolonged the debates. In the end, I acquired a stink bomb (encapsulated in a small glass ball) and activated it during the height of one session. Before long the spacious hall was vacated and, after ventilation, the television set could, once again, be activated.

"No wonder that later in life, when you had money, you developed a liking for the Harlequin and purchased porcelain pieces depicting him. He too played childish pranks, which often served his needs and which he considered funny," observed Theophil dryly.

Even as he spoke, a harlequin — modelled and fired in a German factory of the 18th century — came to life and looked daggers at me.

"Why did you give a miss in that auction to Columbine?" Harlequin wanted to know.

"I was outbid," I replied.

"And I remained lonely, just as in real life. So I had to play practical jokes!"

"You see, Peter'le, this is cause and effect, even if the latter is unpredictable."

"Please elaborate."

"Very well. At the dawn of history, humans gathered around a fire ignited by lightning in order to warm up. Then, one bright day, a naughty boy picked up a burning branch and scared others with it. Another humanoid who was present got the notion of transporting fire from place to place."

"Any other examples?"

"The first stone tool was crafted by a boy who sharpened a stone for fun. The idea, though, caught on. Man became a tool maker."

"Any examples of modern times?"

"Of course. Do you recall one of your friends in secondary school, who drew caricatures of your teachers and also of you yourself?"

"How could I possibly forget. But why is this relevant?"

"His sketches exploited dents in his subjects' armour. For instance, he magnified your principal's bald head. Later in life, he became a leading plastic surgeon, who shortened protruding chins or unduly long noses: dents in his patients' make up. His boyhood hobby became a professional asset."

"Neither his father nor his mother was a caricaturist."

"True," Theophil talked slowly and deliberately, "but the observation gene might have been present yet failed to materialise."

"I hear you. Effectively you are telling me that evolution proceeds at random?"

"I don't think so, but mutations do! And we don't know when or whether they would materialise. And they played their role in the rise of humanity!"

"Is it possible that, but for a mutation, our long voyage to supremacy would not have eventuated?"

"I think so, but the point is obscure. The data is subject to varying constructions."

"So even you can't be certain?"

"I can't. I observed the slow evolutionary rise. But I remained an observer — a theoretician. I am unable to predict haphazard events. I don't even try."

"Occasionally you produce them by nudging!"

"I do so rarely. And this applies even to Him. Remember: theologians tell you that He grated humanity free choice. And we adhere to this. For instance, both of us watched the two world wars but let them take their course. We did not intervene!"

"In a strange way, the persecution of the Jews by Hitler led to the foundation of a sovereign Israel," I observed.

"Quite so; and I don't think this development was foreseeable!"

"Right you are! What would have been the 'Führer's' reaction if the point had been raised with him?"

"Probably a shrug of the shoulders. He wanted to massacre all European Jews. What happened to them elsewhere was immaterial to him."

"Why did he hate us so much?"

"I'm not sure he did. Antisemitism was a ticket to power. He capitalised on it and drove it to its extreme, until he came to believe in it."

"Was the outcome predictable?"

"In hindsight it was; during Hitler's reign it wasn't."

"So it was a mutation."

"You could treat it as such!"

At this stage a commotion took place in one of my cabinets. An advocate figurine, dated to the 18th century, vied for animation with a young girl having a chat with her teddy bears. Graciously, Theophil asked me to whom he should give priority. After a short discussion, we settled on the man of the law.

The advocate donned 18th-century clothes. He wore a reddish sort of suit and a heavy black gown. As he became alive, he looked critically at my sitting room. Was he accustomed to a more luxurious environment? All the same, he settled down and looked at us inquisitively: "What can I do for you, Gentlemen?"

"Well," I ventured, "please tell us how you handle expert witnesses."

"Expert what?" he asked, astounded.

Through the Glasses of My Cabinets

"Sometimes in a trial you seek to establish a point, which is in the domain of an expert, like a medical man. In such a case, don't you call expert witnesses?"

"He practised law in the 18th century," interceded Theophil. "The rules of procedure and of evidence were not as developed as later on."

"Didn't they need expert opinion?" I wanted to know.

"Sometimes we needed experts. Like in the trial of witches. Experts were able to tell a court whether the accused had the attributes," volunteered *Avocato*.

"Witchcraft trials — that sort of nonsense," I muttered in disgust.

"He and many of his contemporaries believed in witchcraft," pointed out Theophil. "And are you sure this was 'nonsense'? Future generations may take a similar attitude to some of the scientific principles you accept, like the Big Bang theory!"

"How about legal principles applicable nowadays, like fingerprints and DNA evidence?" I asked after a contemplative lull.

"Don't forget that fingerprints can be faked. This has been proved in some cases; and DNA evidence became acceptable only a few decades ago. Frequently, the accepted dogma of one age is dismissed with the passage of time. Prior to Galileo, the earth was considered the centre of the universe." For a few minutes he kept his silence, then returned to the issue under consideration. "Come, let us hear what modern lawyers tell us about expert evidence."

As he spoke, *Avocato* transmuted into a 20th-century barrister. He felt quite at home in my sitting room, discarded his wig and accepted a drink proffered by Theophil.

"We wanted to have your views about expert evidence," explained Theophil.

"A hornets' nest!" exclaimed the man of the law. "You summon an expert witness because the judge must not rely on his own knowledge of a discipline other than the law. Occasionally, this is ridiculous. A judge, who also has a medical degree, often knows more about an issue arising in a case involving personal injuries than an 'expert'. Still, we have to call an expert on the subject. Similarly, we call a psychiatrist to advise the court about issues respecting a person's psychological makeup, such as the cognitive capacity of a testator."

"How do you handle an expert witness?" I wanted to know.

"Well, you know that you cannot match his expertise. We usually read the report of the other party's expert, call a witness of our own and seek to combat the effect of evidence given against our case. For instance, we call a psychiatrist to refute the other's view."

"Don't you have a method, or tactics, for such instances?"

"Well, our courtroom training assists us to detect weak points in any theory or conclusion of the other party's witnesses. This experience can help us to defeat a shaky stand of witnesses you cross-examine."

"So, in reality, it is a battle of wits?"

"You can call it that. But remember, the judge is familiar with courtroom tactics. Prior to his elevation to the bench he was, in all probability, a courtroom advocate."

"So, in the end, he decides what to accept and what to reject?"

"He is supposed to know. But mistakes can take place. Want me to elaborate?"

"No need," observed Theophi. "The point has been covered many times".

When *Avocato* was back in the cabinet, we turned to the next supplicant: the young girl delivering a lecture, or some teachings, to three teddy bears. Noticing my expression, Theophil spoke firmly: "Don't you feel superior, Peter'le! Try to recall your childhood. Who taught you the basics — good behaviour and things like brushing teeth and washing hands?"

"Mother, of course! So?"

"Well, isn't this exactly what your girl figurine tries to teach her teddy bears? Let's hear what she has to tell us."

The young girl — she was about 10 years old — faced us with self-assurance. She knew her mind. In response to my question, she explained: "I'm trying to teach them what Mother taught me. I'm a good girl."

"And they?" I asked.

"I hope they learn. I sure try."

"Is this so different from your own role as an academic?" asked Theophil. "Didn't you try to impart to your students the skills that you had acquired from your own teachers?"

"I tried to teach my students how to reason and argue!"

"But isn't that exactly what your teachers aimed to impart when you were a student?"

"Actually, you are right, Maestro."

"I'm glad you see the point. And please tell me, what would happen if all adults were exterminated or died out before the youngsters matured? And suppose, further, that all their acquired knowledge died with them. Would their successors be able to retrieve it?"

"I doubt it," I conceded following some reflection. "I suspect that a new evolutionary cycle would have to start, and its direction would remain unpredictable."

"And how about language, Peter'le?"

"We learn it by osmosis. If there is nobody to convey speech, languages may die out and be replaced by other dialog forms or means of communication."

"And, as is well known, some tongues disappeared!" he summed up.

"Some had to be revived. Middle Egyptian is a case in point. And, you know, the pronunciation remains uncertain."

"And how about your beloved Hebrew? Do you know how Job was voiced?"

"Nobody knows. It isn't even certain where and when the Book was composed. People use the Sephardic intonation; but the point is contestable."

I needed to digest the knowledge imparted to me. Even prior to this evening, I had realised that the development of mankind involved a winding evolutionary process. Theophil rubbed the conclusions in. It dawned on me that knowledge, like science, underwent a process involving periodic revitalisation. Our age gave priority to gender equality and human rights. Previous ones adhered to religious dogmatism. Often, though, those who came to power forgot all about the doctrines they had supported during their years of struggle.

"Darwin hit the nail on its head when he postulated the survival of the fittest," I ventured. I knew that I was digressing but thought that the issue under discussion led to this, the second one.

"Didn't he ever," consented Theophil.

"Our own society embraces it," I persevered.

"Not just your society, Peter'le. It is an attribute of mankind as a whole."

"Religions tried to circumvent it, I believe," I tried to step in for the defence.

Through the Glasses of My Cabinets

"And frequently the priests — the preachers — ruled the population with an iron fist."

His words made sense. Knowing that I was exhausted, Theophil animated a violin player modelled in Meissen late in the 20th century. To my delight, he played the last movement of Jean Sibelius' violin concerto. Before long I felt revived and was ready for further encounters.

"On what basis do you make your acquisitions, Peter'le?"

"Basically I bid for a piece (or acquire it through the net) if I like it. Usually I like it if it has a meaning or if it appeals to my aesthetic sense, Maestro. Also, I tend to get pieces modelled by artists I admire like Kändler of Meissen or Wenzel Neu of Kloster Veilsdorf."

"Why did you get that piece depicting me as a man wearing black and red? Did you really think that I look like that?"

"Of course not. The seller advertised it as a depiction of Tyl Eulenspiegel — the German jester. I knew better than that. I knew the modeller tried to portray you, Maestro."

"Oh well," he shrugged. "And how about that piece which seeks to show 'the devil' dancing with a nude? Did you think I was more likely to dance with such a being than you yourself with an attractive female chimpanzee or gorilla?"

"Of course not. I liked the piece because I found it beautiful."

"Because it depicted an attractive nude?"

"No, Maestro. I liked the rhythm and harmony it displayed. Mankind has always tried to treat you as sort of an honorary human. So did the composer of Job, when he told us about your wandering from place to place. I know that you exist in another dimension and that observing humanity is just one of your hobbies."

"Well spoken, my objective onlooker. And why did you acquire that other nude?"

"I intended to place her next to my Rabbi, either to discard or to tempt him!"

"As good an excuse as any. I think that she simply appealed to you, didn't she?"

"You may be right," I had to concede. "Please don't blame me."

"I don't. After all, buying her was less dangerous than infatuation with a tramp or slut. And you, Peter'le, like to play it safe! But come, let us see what your Rabbi has to tell us."

The Rabbi, who stepped out of my cabinet, looked bewildered. To start with, he wanted to know where he was. The location of my place — on Singapore's East Coast — baffled him. His usual abode had been in Lvov in Eastern Europe. The Far East was unknown to him; and he had no wish to familiarise himself with it. His main objective was to control the lives of members of his own cluster. Proselytising to adherents of another creed was not on his agenda.

"What can I do for you, Gentlemen," he asked in Yiddish which — under Theophil's ministration — I comprehended better than ever before.

"Tell us a bit about the book from which you read," suggested Theophil. "When was it written and what does it tell us?"

"It is the Book of Psalms. King David, who composed many of its chapters, praised and aggrandises the Good Lord!"

"Do you really believe that King David wrote the chapters attributed to him?" I interceded. "Modern scholarship takes the view that they were written and used during the period of the Second Temple, especially throughout the reign of the Maccabees."

"This is heresy!" exclaimed the Rabbi. "Sheer rubbish and nonsense!"

"Come, come, Rabbi," I countered. "Don't you realise that religion must adapt itself with the passage of time in order to remain relevant? Here in Singapore, we have a vibrant community spread all over town. To go to the synagogue — the Schul — on Shabbat (Saturday), members have to drive to the city or take a taxi. Driving is considered 'work' and hence is precluded on Shabbat and on holidays. But can you really expect members of the congregation to walk? For some of them this would entail a two-hour march from home to the prayer hall and back. So the Chief Rabbi sanctioned driving. Was he wrong? And in some reform communities, women are ordained as Rabbis."

"This reform movement is risky. Once you modernise, you don't know where to stop," replied the Rabbi. Theophil nodded supportively but remained silent. I, too, intended to keep my peace. The Rabbi was bound to know that orthodox believers were becoming a minority. Secular Jews were the norm in the diaspora. Furthermore, in cities like Singapore it was difficult to adhere to the dietary laws. The only kosher restaurant in town was attached to the synagogue. Going there every day was burdensome. In addition, some religious tenets led to absurdities. When one of my orthodox friends went to a lecture scheduled for Saturday afternoon, she climbed seven flights of stairs to the designated location only to find out that the talk had been cancelled. She did not take the lift because touching the call button was regarded as work and hence proscribed on the Shabbat. To me, a secular Jew through and through, the walk up the stairs appeared harder work than pressing a call knob.

"But Rabbi, don't you realise that modernisation was the aim of Saint Paul?" I asked eventually.

"This may be so. But look at the outcome: he helped to lay the foundation of a new religion, which rejected Judaism as a whole."

I realised that argument was futile. Theophil, who appeared to be of the same view, catapulted the Rabbi back to his stand.

"You are tired, Peter'le."

"I am, Maestro. But you know, this wonderful display is unique! Please carry on."

Giving me a searching glance, Theophil animated my organ grinder. We were standing with him on Waterloo Bridge in London, just prior to the outbreak of the First World War, and listened to the somewhat monotonous tune being played. Noting my disapproving glance, Theophil pointed out that the street organ, a watered-down version of the barrel organ, could play just one tune. The grinder's monkey danced to it and held out a hat, into which listeners dropped pennies. One generous onlooker dropped in a tuppence piece — which was a handsome tip in those remote golden days.

"You look bored, Peter'le. Shall I animate your flute and accordion players?"

"Please do. But would they be more versatile?"

To my delight, the duo embarked on a Bach sonata followed by a toccata and fugue, and then by the Goldberg variations. I listened with admiration how the accordionist played the music on the keyboard, situated on the right side of the instrument, and accompanied himself on the left-hand buttons. The flute player chimed in at the right moment. It was a splendid performance.

"Maestro, why not make them play contemporary music?"

Through the Glasses of My Cabinets

"Willingly! Remember, the accordion was invented at the beginning of the 19th century. It took a while before it became 'respectable'. Musicians did not compose for it. But it was embraced by popularisers. Listen!"

As he spoke, the accordionist played *La Paloma*. His art mesmerised me. He then played dancing music and, to my delight, performed Dmitri Shostakovich's second waltz. One of my figurines, a guitarist, came to life and accompanied him. Soon thereafter, a drummer and a horn player joined in the performance of Frédéric Chopin's *Grande Polonaise*. It was not as good as its performance on a piano but, at the same time, was impressive. The *Lara's Theme* from *Doctor Zhivago* followed. I enjoyed myself.

A gentle knock on my entrance door brought me back to my ordinary existence. Another neighbour, a girl who lived in a flat opposite mine, explained that she and her girlfriend had enjoyed the performance. She wondered if they might join me. She also wanted to know how I had acquired these splendid performances.

Instantly, Theophil metamorphosed into a salesman and explained that he had been trying to persuade me to acquire a new type of DVD player. He had been playing some new CDs.

"I'm here after office hours because I want to clinch a sale. I offered Mr. Berger a discount. If he purchases the player and one CD, he gets another CD free of charge."

"Why don't you give one to her? I'll buy the player and a CD. They are excellent."

Magnanimously, Theophil gave her a CD and assured her that it could be played on an ordinary player. Thanking both of us profusely, she accepted the CD and returned to her own abode.

"You wonder whether she would have accepted it if she had known the giver's real identity, don't you, Peter'le?"

"I do," I conceded. "Please enlighten me."

"Actually, you know the answer."

His assertion made me think. I was aware that my neighbour and her partner were not deeply religious persons. If they were, they would not have lived together openly. I also knew that each of them was able to shrug off snubs. This meant that their decision to accept a gift would not be affected by pious considerations. I then recalled a song by Tom Lehrer, in which he told listeners that the old dope peddler "gives the kids free samples [of drugs] because he knows full well that today's young innocent faces will be tomorrow's clientele".

"Quite so, Peter'le. Mankind's inclination is to take whatever is available, unless a looming danger or hazard is patent. People like your neighbours do not believe in the devil's existence. So why should they be afraid of accepting a gift proffered by him?"

His words triggered further thoughts. I recalled how children occasionally grabbed a shining surface, like an electric bulb or neon light, only to receive a mild shock. Thereafter they were careful. Their initial instinct, though, was clear. They were curious and, in addition, wanted to possess.

"Yes Peter'le, mankind is inquisitive and acquisitive. It's all based on the survival instinct. Many a drug addict or alcoholic got hooked because they wanted to try and to acquire a new thing: curiosity and the wish to possess."

"Are we a weak lot?"

"Of course not, Peter'le. Instincts enabled humanity to overcome many hurdles. Your planet is mankind's, not the planet of the apes."

"I hear you," I conceded.

Sensing my ever-increasing fatigue, Theophil suggested we have a refreshing drink. He knew I craved for a cup of hot chocolate, but feared to partake because of the heavy sugar content of the coveted drink.

"Don't worry about the sugar, Peter'le. I'll take care of it this time," he assured me.

Instantly the liquid in a chocolate pot, produced in Meissen early in the 18th century and acquired by me in an auction, started to bubble. A narrow but lengthy spoon, inserted through a hole meant for the purpose, enabled us to stir the crust emerging at the top of the drink back into the substance. Theophil poured the delicious creamy drink into two trembleuse cups and handed me one of them.

"These cups were fired in Vienna, Maestro, and I acquired only one."

"I know. You were too mean to bid for the second one."

"The reserve was high. I couldn't really afford to continue," I pleaded, crestfallen.

"Let me then present the second one to you," he consoled.

"How did you get it?"

"I bought it when they first hit the market. I knew the piece could be handy one day."

For a while we sat together. I was both sleepy and tired. Theophil, who was aware of what was taking place, remained quiet. It is also possible that he sensed that it would be difficult for me to absorb any additional points. He was aware of my limitations and did not wish to disrupt.

I watched him with admiration. He had assumed the role of an observer. Affecting changes was within his power. But he had decided to use it sparingly. Mankind's progress interested him. But he knew that any mutation, especially when initiated by outside influence, might lead to unexpected outcomes.

"You better retire, Peter'le. A good night's sleep will do you good and restore your spirits. You feel low at the moment. But this is a temporary phase. Tomorrow you will be as energetic as ever."

"Will you visit me again soon?"

"I'll materialise again when the time is ripe for it," he promised. Then, unexpectedly he added: "Today is a special occasion and I'm in a generous mood. Would you like an extraordinary gift? It is within my power to restore you to your youth. You would be back in the past; the clock would be rewound. Well, what do you say?"

"It is a generous offer, Maestro. But does it mean that I would have to start once again?"

"Precisely. You will revert to your youth but retain your old age wisdom. Still, you would have to embark on a fresh voyage."

"Do we know where it would lead to? Would mutations or random events be controlled?"

"No Peter'le, you cannot have the cake and eat it. You would be well-equipped for the new trip but, just as before, the outcome would depend on your reactions. These are akin to mutations. I do not seek to affect them."

"I understand. And it is a gracious offer. But, if you don't mind, I prefer to stick to the present. I am ready to cede. A new trip sounds formidable!"

"I thought this would be your answer; and it is a wise one. In your own way you overcame obstacles placed in your original journey. And all in all, you have arrived."

"Quite so. The 'top' is far away, but so is the 'bottom'. A new journey may lead to a less satisfactory endgame."

"Couldn't it ever? Suppose you had opted for the safe job in an Israeli bank that was open to you and had given postgraduate studies at Oxford a miss. What would have been the outcome?"

"Difficult to tell. I would have had a secure desk job and might have married an Israeli girl and built up a family in Tel Aviv."

"Quite possible. But then you might not have travelled so much, might have experienced a messy divorce and have ended up a bitter nonagenarian chanting 'if only'."

"In other words, an old '*chrek*' (crank) full of regrets about his past!"

"True. So, it is safe and sound to stick to the status quo."

When I rubbed my eyes, the sitting room appeared as peaceful and as solemn as ever. The chocolate pot, and all other porcelain pieces, were back on the shelves. Still, two trembleuse vases now occupied one of them. Did I acquire the second during a European excursion? My carefully maintained catalogue of porcelain acquisitions would enable me to come up with a conclusive answer. But I did not feel inclined to browse.

For a while, I stared at the skyline and, to my delight, spotted an aeroplane descending to Changi Airport. Could it be the very plane which a friend had boarded in London with the objective of breaking his return flight to Australia for a few days in our city? I was looking forward to his visit and had booked a table in a restaurant to which I planned to take him for lunch the next day.

The forthcoming visit uplifted my spirits. I then realised that I was extremely tired and sleepy. It was time to retire.

Essays by a Non-Specialist

Love and Friendship*

In *A Painful Case* (one of the short stories narrated by James Joyce in *Dubliners*), the hero opines: "Love between man and man is impossible because there must not be sexual intercourse and friendship between man and woman is impossible because there must be sexual intercourse." It is not clear from the text whether this statement is made by Joyce's hero as a consequence of a personal disappointment or is meant to be the author's statement of a universal truth. This essay sets out to establish that, in general, the statement is a fallacy.

The difficulty in construing and applying Joyce's statement stems from the fact that the two seminal words — "love" and "friendship" — are inadequately defined and are hence often misleading when used in everyday language. The confusion that may arise from imprecision in language is masterfully discussed by Wittgenstein (*Tractatus Logico-Philosophicus*, 1921). More often than not, a misunderstanding or conflict results from semantics.

---

*written in 2012; revised in 2024

The word "love" is a prime example. The *Oxford Advanced Learner's Dictionary* (7th ed., p. 913) distinguishes between three types: (i) "love" in the sense of affection; (ii) romantic "love"; and (iii) the "love" of doing a certain act, like watching an opera. In all these cases, "love" is a noun. However, similar differences in meanings apply when "love" is used as a verb. "I love [a given author]" conveys a meaning very different from the phrase: "I love [my wife]."

The confusion respecting the word "love" is not confined to English. In Hebrew, for instance, "love" may describe a person's feeling for a deity (Schema: Deut. 6:4), for a friend (like the love of David and Jonathan[1]) or for a spouse. Thus, in the modern translation to English, Isaiah (41:8) refers to the people of Israel as "the seed of Abraham my friend." Notably, in the Hebrew original, Abraham is described as "my lover". The translators conveyed the meaning of "love" in the context of the relationship of Abraham with God by substituting "friend" for "lover". In this way, the translators transliterated the Bard's intended message.

In another Biblical book [Jeremiah (31:2)], the Lord tells the people of Israel: "I have loved thee with an everlasting love...." In a different context, the Prophet Malachi (1:2–3) tells us that God "loves" Jacob and hates Esau. Another example is to be found in Genesis 25:28, in which the reader is told that Isaac "loves" Esau and Rivka "loves" Jacob. It is clear that, in all these instances, the world "love" does not have a carnal implication. The point was understood by the Biblical Bard.

---

[1] Samuel I (18:1) relates "that the soul of Yehonatan [King Saul's son] was knit with the soul of David, and Yehonatan loved him as his own soul". The traditional construction treats the passage as referring to brotherly love. Some Bible critics do, however, raise their eyebrows when, in his lament, known as the Song of the Bow, David says: (Samuel II, 1:26): "I am distressed for thee my brother Yehonatan ... your love for me was wonderful, more than the love of women."

The same ambiguity respecting the word "love" exists in German.[2] In particular, the "love" of the fatherland has a completely different meaning from a man's declaration of love to a woman. Notably, even Wolfgang Mozart's middle name, viz. "Amadeus" (beloved by God) is devoid of any physical connotation.

It is feasible that this ambiguity respecting the word "love" relates to the difficulty in using a word to express an emotion. Ideally, different words ought to be used to describe separate emotions. For instance, it would be useful to employ one word to express "love" for a deity or a dogma and another word to describe feelings between persons. However, the analysis of the meaning of an emotion may be of a later date than the introduction of a generic word used to express emotions of a similar nature but of separate types.

In the words quoted from Joyce's work, the speaker uses the word "love" as a synonym of "lust" (or physical love). The questionability of the statement emerges if we think about filial love, such as Isaac's feelings for Esau, described earlier. Is such "love" proscribed because father and son (or daughter) ought not to have intercourse? Further, is a person proscribed from loving a friend, be he of the same or of the opposite sex, because the issue of intercourse should not (and need not) arise in the mind of either?

It is important to add that languages — including English — metamorphose. Here the word "house" is of interest. Emily Brontë (in *Wuthering Heights*) uses "house" for what would be called in modern English "the sitting room". A similar ambiguity exists in Singlish. "House" describes a person's dwelling (or home), regardless of whether it is an apartment or a unit such as a bungalow or a semi-detached building.

---

[2] It is understood that the same ambiguity arises in other tongues, but it appears advisable to confine this discussion to languages commanded by me.

The metamorphosis of language is a well-known phenomenon. By way of illustration, take parts of a motorcar, such as "clutch", "brakes", "gears" and "tank". Each phrase is an adaptation of an early and well-established word to the mechanics of the motorcar, which is a relatively modern invention.

On occasions the modern — or innovative — sense of a word replaces the older meaning. Thus, in the days of wind-propelled ships, the words "topgallant" described the uppermost sail. In the 21st century, it is a satirical expression referring to an overdressed, extravagant and often condescending man (a dandy).

This analysis is relevant as regards "love". Originally, it may have been used as a word describing a well-recognised, all-embracing emotion confined to feelings within an extended family or tribe. Later on, it was applied to other emotions, such as loyalty to a nation or a deity. In a sense, the ramifications of "love" metamorphosed as mankind's structure underwent changes.

Friendship — the other seminal word in the quote from Joyce's story — is also ambiguous. According to the *Oxford Advanced Learner's Dictionary* (supra, p. 622) "friendship" means a relationship between friends. The word "friend", though, has different connotations. To start with it may refer to a person you know well and like (id.). In some other cases it refers to a supporter of an organisation or cause, such as a charity. In still other cases — and this in all probability is the traditional meaning — a "friend" is somebody you are close to and are prepared to make sacrifices for him (or her) when in need.[3] Undoubtedly, this is the sense in which the word is used to describe Hushai as David's "friend" (Sam. II, 16:17). Similarly, the element of loyalty and the notion

---

[3] But note that in some cases, the word is used so as to negate a relationship, e.g., "they are just friends".

Love and Friendship*

of brotherhood is emphasised in respect of the bond of David and Jonathan (Sam. I, 18:1–5).

It must, at the same time, be noted that in recent times, the distinction between a friend and a mere acquaintance has eroded. Thus, according to *The Collins Paperback English Dictionary* (1986, p. 339) the word "friend" encompasses both "a person known well and regarded with liking, affection, and loyalty" and "an acquaintance or associate".

Indeed, the news media and websites tend to use the word "friend" as a synonym of an acquaintance. Thus, one site enables entrepreneurs to place their résumés on it with a view to meeting professional "friends" with a similar focus. Other websites enable a person to search for individuals with a similar interest, e.g., art collecting. Undoubtedly, such an acquaintance may, in due course, develop into a friend in the classic connotation of the word. Their getting in contact through the Internet is, however, best regarded as a first step.[4]

A discussion of "friendship" is bound to remain incomplete if it fails to refer to platonic love, discussed by Plato in *Symposium*. It has been succinctly defined as "an affectionate relationship into which the sexual element does not enter, especially in cases where one might easily assume otherwise. A simple example of platonic relationships is a deep, non-sexual friendship between two heterosexual people of the opposite sexes" (*Science Daily*).

It has to be pointed out that Socrates, who in many of Plato's dialogues assumes the principal speaker's role, does not rule out the development of a sexual relationship between platonic lovers, even if they are of the same gender. Notably, the Greek attitude to physical

---

[4] As a member of a bridge club, I have become a "friend" of some other players. This means that we are prepared to have matches against each other or join efforts as a team. But none of us expect this friendship to stretch to areas other than bridge.

relationships — including homosexual intercourse — is more lenient than the approach of societies based on Judeo/Christian philosophy.

Plato's emphasis in *Symposium* is on the bond that exists between friends. In the antique culture of the Levant, such a bond often took the form of blood brotherhood. All in all, a platonic friendship is geared in loyalty which, notwithstanding the language of the Internet, is not to be expected from a mere acquaintance.

An overview of platonic friendship leads to a further seminal conclusion. It will be recalled that love encompasses, inter alia, a "sense of affection". In that sense, "love" is an ingredient of a platonic friendship; intercourse need not form a component of it. The assumption is that a physical affair does involve love. But do the parties always have a "sense of affection" for one another?

To further develop the point just made, it is best to turn to famous illustrations from human history and from literature which, all in all, is an expression of human experience. Reference has already been made to the friendship of David and Jonathan. There is no evidence to suggest that it involved intercourse. Further, sagas of the Levant abound with instances of platonic friendships. The bond between Gilgamesh and Enkidu (the *Epic of Gilgamesh*; ca. 2600 BC) is one of them. The friendship between Abraham and Lot is another (Genesis, 13:8–13).

Turning to more recent experiences, the bond between Genghis Khan and his main strategist Subutai was anchored in mutual trust and affection. There is, of course, no suggestion of any physical nexus between them. All the same, the bond between the two did constitute a genuine friendship.

The friendship between Clara Schumann and Johannes Brahms is a 19th century example. The two were loyal to one another and certainly had mutual affection. There is, at the same time, no sound suggestion of the existence of an affair.

In the early 20th century, Hermann Hesse described the deep friendship of *Narcissus and Goldmund* (1930). Narcis, who has taken orders and is committed to a monastic life, befriends Goldmund, a novice, who leaves the monastery before long. The bond though is lasting. When Goldmund's life is in danger, Narcis — who had by then been elected Abbott — saves him from captivity. There is, of course, no intercourse involved.

The discussion leads to the conclusion that "love" is not restricted to relationships involving intercourse. The same applies in a "friendship". "Love" may not be present at all where the "friends" are not united by a bond but are acquaintances. In contrast, where the friendship is close, be it by affection or out of loyalty, the fact that the friends care for one another entails love regardless of whether or not there is intercourse.

What then had induced Joyce to put the words I had quoted earlier in the mouth of his hero?

Contextually, it is possible that the hero jotted these words in his diary in consequence of an unsuccessful attempt to form a platonic relationship with a married woman. When she sought to proceed to an affair, he withdrew and resumed his reclusive existence. However, even as a personal outcry, the quoted words are objectionable. Joyce's hero seems to reach a general conclusion on the basis of a personal — unsuccessful and hence painful — experience.

If the words quoted were meant to imply a broader concept, i.e., meant to state a universal truth, they are fallacious. A friendship or bond of loyalty can be real and meaningful even in the absence of intercourse.

Maybe a Swan Song: A Second Trip Down Memory Lane

To further clinch the argument, it is useful to turn to Euler's diagrams (circles). According to the theorem (of 1768),[5] matters are divided into zones. There can be a complete overlap where each subset is covered by the larger zone. For instance, the zone "mammals" encompasses each variety of the species. "Elephants" would, accordingly, constitute a subset of "mammals". In other cases, the zones merely intersect. For instance, "feet" intersect with "hands" to the extent that both are used in "movement". In the third type of case, the zones are disjointed or, in other words, do not intersect at all. "Eye" and "thunder" provide an illustration.

The words quoted from Joyce's story treat "intercourse", "love" and "friendship" as subsets. Once the diagram is invoked, the absurdity becomes clear. The "intercourse" that takes place in a brothel may be without any "love". Similarly, "friendship" and "love" are separate concepts. They may intersect but neither is a subset of the other.

It is, therefore, sound to dismiss the quoted words as a fallacy. They are expressed pugnaciously but without an analysis of their soundness.

---

[5] I wish to acknowledge my debt to Professor Hugo Bergman of the Hebrew University of Jerusalem, whose excellent course on logic has remained fresh in my mind.

Job: A Reassessment*,[1]

I. Sources and Background

Before turning to the discussion of the *Book of Job* (hereafter referred to as "*Job*"; the hero's name is spelt as "Job" [in Roman letters]), it is important to refer to the extant texts available to us. The one usually cited is the Masoretic Text (MT) version.

Scholars believe that it was composed during the 5th or early 4th century BCE, that is, before the Hasmonean period. The book is unlikely to have been composed earlier than that. It is true that the issue discussed in it — the theodicy issue — was raised by Jeremiah [Jer. 12:1–3]. However, the 6th century — covering this prophet's long ministry — witnessed the struggle of Judah with Babylon and the final destruction of Jerusalem by Nebuchadnezzar, followed by the exile.

---

*written in 2023; revised 2024

[1] This paper is dedicated to the memory of my Biblical Studies Master in secondary school, Old Frank, who taught all his pupils how to analyse the Bible and love it. My thanks are due to Professor E.L. Greenstein for his searching comments on a draft hereof. All mistakes are, of course, mine. The issue of the *Book of Job's* authorship is discussed in detail in a paper available on Amazon's Kindle Direct https://www.amazon.com/Author-Book-Job-Who-Wrote-ebook/dp/B0CWJSNRP5

During the next century, Nehemiah was active in Jerusalem, which was a small and under-populated town at that time.[2] It is unlikely that *Job* was written there during that century. At the same time, philological evidence indicates that the book was written before Greek became the lingua franca of the Levant or, in other words, before the advent of Alexander the Great and the struggle of his successors. Further, *Job* is renowned for words unique to it. Many of these hapax legomena ("hapaxes" for short) are derived from Aramaic or other Semitic languages but not borrowed from Greek.[3] This circumstantial evidence suggests that the MT version was composed when Aramaic was the principal language of the Orient but prior to the advent of Greek. In turn, this supports the view that *Job* was composed either late in the 5th century or early in the 4th BCE.

It is questionable whether the MT version is the very first text of *Job*.[4] It is plausible that a previous version was circulated to a limited group. To date, though, no such earlier version has materialised. Further, scraps of the MT's Hebrew version were discovered amongst the Dead Sea Scrolls in Qumran.[5]

There are also ancient translations of *Job* into Aramaic and into Greek. The earliest is a translation into Aramaic discovered amongst

---

[2] See I. Finkelstein, *Hasmonean Realities behind Ezra, Nehemiah and Chronicles* (Atlanta, 2018), at p. 15.

[3] For a list of hapaxes and of words borrowed from Semitic languages, mainly from Aramaic, see S.J. Vicchio, *The Book of Job — A History of Interpretation and Commentary* (Oregon, 2020), at pp. 298–307.

[4] See B. Jongeling, C.J. Labuschagne and A.S. Van Der Woude, *Aramaic Texts from Qumran* (Leiden, 1976), ("Jongeling"), at p. 7.

[5] Set out in Ulrich, *The Biblical Qumran Scrolls* (Leiden, 2010), at pp. 727–731.

the Dead Sea Scrolls.[6] As this settlement in Qumran was destroyed in 70 CE, the "Qumran Scroll" predates the later Aramaic translation, colloquially referred to as Onkelos.[7] Scholars have concluded that the Qumran Scroll's script is of the Herodian period.[8] Regrettably, the Qumran Scroll comprises only about 15 per cent of the book. The later translation into Aramaic, sometimes printed in current Hebrew bibles, was promulgated after the destruction of Jerusalem by Rome (the "late Targum").[9] It is possible that some other translations were composed but were suppressed by Rabban Gamliel.[10] Presumably, all these translations were made so as to make *Job* available to Jews, who were not conversant in Hebrew.[11] The same can be said about the Septuagint ("the LXX"), that is, the translation of the Old Testament into Greek, which had by then become the lingua franca throughout the Levant. The date of the compilation of the LXX is outside the scope of this investigation. However, the scholarly consensus[12] is that it was

---

[6] 11Q10, also included in *Discoveries of the Judean Desert*, Vol. 23 ("DJD23"), pp. 78–180. It is reproduced in Jongeling. The Dead Sea Scrolls were composed between ca. 200 BCE and 70 CE. I thank Emeritus Professor Emanuel Tov for giving me access to this text. For a fine analysis, see M. Sokoloff, *The Targum to Job from Qumran Cave XI* (Ramat Gan, 1974).

[7] Who lived during the period of Hadrian Caesar (reigned from 117 to 138 CE) and translated the Old Testament into Aramaic? Some sources claim that Onkelos lived some 70 years earlier, viz. during the reign of Titus (reigned 79 to 81 CE).

[8] JDJ23, at p. 87. And see Jongeling, op. cit., at pp. 4–5 (suggesting a date around 50 BCE).

[9] It is *The Targum of Job, by Céline Mangan* (Minnesota, 1991). This valuable targum is based on all the manuscripts available to the editors of the *Aramaic Bible,* which includes the late targum in its Vol. 15.

[10] By Rabbi Gamliel (active ca. 25–50 CE) and by his grandson of similar name (90–110 CE.): see Shabb. 115a.

[11] For the deterioration in the command of Hebrew, see Nehem. 13:24.

[12] The LXX is dated from the 3rd to the 1st century BCE. See L.C.L. Brenton, *The Septuagint with Apocrypha* (Peabody, 1987), at pp. i–iii.

completed by the end of the 1st century CE. This is later than the presumed date of the MT version of *Job*.

In the MT, *Job* is included in the last part, known as the Scriptures — the Ketuvim (כתובים). In some canons,[13] *Job* is treated as a prophet or as a historical book. In the LXX, *Job* appears after the narrative parts but prior to the prophets.

As *Job* deals with a specific question, viz., divine justice (the "theodicy issue"), rather than with adherence to faith (which is dealt with by the prophets), the MT's classification is the soundest one. Further, the Scriptures encompass books promulgated later than those of the first two parts of the MT: the Pentateuch and the Prophets. In this way, the MT gives us an indication about a work's age.

Job is a difficult book to read.[14] Writing in the 12th century,[15] Abraham ibn Ezra suggested that *Job* might have been composed in some other Semitic language and that the MT version was, itself, a translation. Notably, a separate text, entitled the *Testament of Job*, is included in the apocrypha,[16] which means that, in all probability, it was written well after the compilation of the MT. The *Testament* manifests a belief in the immortality of the soul and reward in the afterlife.[17]

---

[13] For a detailed positioning of *Job* in different systems, see L.M. McDonald and J.A. Sanders, *The Canon Debates* (Michigan, 2019), at Appendix C.

[14] For an encyclopaedic text covering all sources, see S.J. Vicchio, op. cit.; for the best translation into English, see E.L. Greenstein, *Job — A New Translation* (2019). An attempt to preserve the meter is made by C.K. Chesterton, *The Book of Job*, (2022 [reprint]).

[15] Referred to by Vicchio, op. cit., at p. 30; and see Baruch Spinoza, *Tractatus Theologico-Philisophicus*, Chapter 7.

[16] The apocrypha comprises ancient books that did not find their way into the MT. They encompass Maccabees I and II.

[17] Vicchio, op. cit., at p. 2 referred to other differences between *Testament* and *Job* of the MT. He also referred to the apocryphal *Life of Job*, written in Greek by Aristeas.

Many books and papers have been written[18] with the objective of coming to grips with *Job's* meaning. The views of Greenstein are of particular guidance. This paper is written because a new overview and ideas based on it is timely.

As already noted, the MT version is the only complete Hebrew text that has come down to us. Some variations appear in the LXX and in the late Targum.[19] The extant manuscripts used for the rendering of the MT date to the 10th century CE and are known as the Codex Vaticanus, the Aleppo Codex and the Leningradus Codex.[20] Obviously they are late and, of course, may contain technical copying errors.

Before turning to *Job's* structure, it is important to consider whether or not it constitutes a historical record. The point is controversial. Some sages concluded that the book was an allegory.[21] This view appears realistic and finds support in the writing of Maimonides.[22] *Job's* residence, in the country of Uz (Utz), is thus not to be taken more literally than the reference to *Utopia* by Thomas More. Still, the reference to Uz shows that the writer thought to place the tome in the Middle East (Kedem קדם). This may also explain his attempt to use archaic phrases.

Notably, this very setting supports the view that *Job* is a late book. When Jeremiah referred (in the 6th century BCE) to the Babylonian threat, he described it as emanating from the North, that is, the route

---

[18] For essays on *Job* in Hebrew, see, e.g., Z. Adar, *The Book of Job*, in הספריה של מטח III, pp. 1 et seq.; דור-שב, תכלת .א 32, 2008. For a detailed bibliography of books and articles dealing with *Job* see Vicchio, op. cit., pp. 403 et seq.

[19] On the problems faced by translators of *Job* and the frequent attempt to depart from the meaning of the original, see Greenstein, op. cit., at pp. xxxiv–xxxvii.

[20] Parts of the Codex Aleppo were destroyed in 1947; the intact pages are preserved in the Shrine of the Book in Jerusalem. The Codex Leningradus may be based on the Codex Aleppo.

[21] Baba Batra: 15, at pp. 1–2.

[22] *Guide to the Bewildered,* Part III, Chapter 22.

showing Mesopotamian armies as traveling along the Euphrates and, accordingly, attacking southwards. The correct location of Mesopotamia (in the East) is not mentioned by him.

II. The Structure

At first glance, *Job's* structure appears straightforward. Chapter 1 and 2 — the prologue — are complemented by the epilogue — Chapter 42 (verses 7–end). They are written in easy to comprehend prose, like that of Esther.[23] They were, it is generally believed, written by the very hand which added captions or introductory statements to the ensuing text. By way of illustration, take verse 1 and the first words of verse 2 of Chapter 3, which read: "After this Iyyov [Job] opened his mouth and cursed his day. And [Job] spoke and said...." The remaining part of verse 2 and the rest of the chapter are poetic and differ from the explanatory caption preceding them.

The prologue is followed by the exchanges between Job and his three friends Elifaz (Eliphaz) the Temanite (Yemenite), Bildad the Shuhite and Zofar (Zophar) the Naamatite. These encompass Chapters 3 to 27. They are expressed in fine poetry. In essence, Job questions divine justice, maintaining his being innocent. His friends argue that God is just and that Job's sufferings must be due to his having sinned. Job disputes their stand and protests his innocence in a final monologue — Chapters 29 to 31.

Next come the words of Elihu, a young outsider who is not referred to either in the prologue or in the epilogue. Elihu's arguments cover Chapters 32 to 37. Elihu's speeches differ in style and vocabulary from the earlier chapters of *Job*. Notably, scraps of them were found in

---

[23] See, in particular, Esther: 2:5, introducing Mordechai.

Qumran and they are also included in the Qumran Scroll, in the late Targum and in the LXX. They, too, will be discussed subsequently, including the issue as to whether they constitute an integral part of *Job*.

The penultimate part of the book — Chapters 38 to 42: 1–6 — is God's replies from the whirlwind (Storm: סערה) and Job's response. They assert God's greatness (which has not been doubted by Job) and imply that His justice is unquestionable. All the same, they do not explain why in some instances wrongdoers or villains are not penalised. *Job* is included in the MT on the basis of these chapters. Regrettably, they raise difficult issues especially in respect of Job's apparent acquiescence.

Before turning to the different parts of *Job*, it is important to stress that the poetry is outstanding. This is the case as regards the speeches of Job and his friends and the replies of God from the whirlwind. Doubtless, some other books of the MT encompass fine poetry. Deuteronomy Chapter 32 (Ha'azinu [האזינו]), Jeremiah 31, Psalms 104 and Isaiah 40 are amongst them. Job's last monologue [Chapters 29–31] surpasses even these.

III. The Framework or Setting

The prologue and epilogue are expressed in readable and elegant prose. The first chapter describes Job's piety and orthodoxy and then refers to the day on which "the sons of god" congregated in His front. "Satan" came with them and questioned the motive of Job's piety, alleging that it was due to the protection and prosperity conferred on him by divinity. Satan says that if these were taken from Job, he would curse God "to [His] face".

In this manner, Satan challenges God to a bet respecting Job's motivation. This, though, ought really to have been clear to God!

Another passage of the MT advises that "a man looks on the outward appearance, but the Lord looks on the heart" [Sam. I. 16:7].

All the same — and notwithstanding the ensuing misery that would follow — God accepts the bet. He permits Satan to try Job, whereupon a series of disasters destroy Job's prosperity. Notably, his sons and daughters also perish. Job withstands these calamities and actually praises the Lord.

In the next chapter, the sons of God and Satan present themselves again before the Almighty, who tells Satan that Job has remained pious notwithstanding his misfortune, and says to Satan that "thou did move me against him, to destroy him without cause" [2:3].[24] Satan replies that Job's stand would change if God touched his bone and flesh. In this manner, Satan seeks to extend the bet he made with God. The latter grants Satan the required permission but orders Satan to spare Job's soul (meaning life). Satan thereupon smites Job "with vile soars from the sole of his foot to his crown" [2:7]. At this stage, Job's wife counsels him to curse God and die. Job refuses and scoldes her. We are told that "[i]n all this [Job] did not sin with his lips" [2:10].

Thereafter, Job's three friends Elifaz (Eliphas), Bildad and Zofar "come to mourn with him and to comfort him" [2:11]. The ensuing debates between Job and his friends about divine justice take place in his house or, in other words, *inter partem*.

These debates (and Elihu's speeches) are followed by God's replies from the whirlwind [Chapters 38–42:6]. In the epilogue, which is expressed in the same prose style as the prologue, God tells Elifaz that the three comrades "have not spoken of me the thing that is right, like

---

[24] Unless otherwise indicated, quotations are taken from the version of Harold Fisch appearing in Koren, *The Jerusalem Bible* (Jerusalem, 2008).

Job: A Reassessment*,

my servant" [42:7] Job, and instructs them to entreat Job to "pray for" them, viz. to induce God to forgive them. The epilogue ends with God restoring Job to his wealth and position. Job lives to a ripe old age and is blessed to see four generations of offspring.

The prologue and epilogue give rise to a number of issues. First and foremost, they do not make any reference to Elihu who is, thus, not foreshadowed in the setting of the work. Second, Job's sons and daughters are considered part and parcel of Job's prosperity. God sanctions their demise at the hand of Satan, although there is no hint that they deserve this harsh treatment. It is true that, when Job is restored to his erstwhile position, he is blessed with fresh sons and daughters. It is, at the same time, noteworthy that those who perished were not brought back to life. In reality, the harsh fate of Job's original sons and daughters would be condemned by Jeremiah and Ezekiel,[25] who took the view that the sins of the fathers ought not to be visited on their sons. A fortiori, they would be perplexed by the demise of Job's offspring in a mere attempt to test his piety.

Third, the MT version does not describe Satan as "evil". He is an accuser and doubter, who ascribes mean motives to people.[26] He acts only when granted permission by the Almighty. Still, the LXX and the late Targum refer to him as a source of evil. In this manner, these texts accommodate the view taken of Satan by Orthodox Judaism during the height of the Second Temple period.

Fourth, the MT version refers to the sons of God. Such an anthropomorphic designation was not acceptable to later Jewish Orthodoxy. Accordingly, the late Targum refers to the sons of the angels.

---

[25] Jer. 32:2–3; Ezek., 18:2–3.

[26] This is also the role ascribed to him when mentioned elsewhere in the MT. See Zech. 3:1–3.

The LXX simply refers to the Lord's angels, whose presence appears also in books of the prophets.[27]

Regrettably, the extant portion of the Qumran Scroll does not comprise the prologue. In contrast, part of the epilogue has survived.[28] All in all, it may be surmised that right from the beginning, the "setting" has been part of *Job*. This assumption leads to the next question, viz. when was the setting composed: was it written prior to the composition of the MT version or was it composed by the anonymous author of the debates?

The prevailing view is that the legend, in which Job remains patient and penitent throughout his ordeal, is antique and was used by the anonymous author of the MT version. Presumably in the fable Job speaks about the greatness of the Lord and his friends express doubts.

Professors Greenstein and Newsom refer to some legends reminiscent of *Job*.[29] Indeed, the story of the penitent Job, narrated in the prologue, has been found in Mesopotamian sources.[30] However, when looked at carefully, no text is *in pari materia* with the MT version. The ancient texts discuss the theodicy issue from the viewpoint of a society with a polytheistic religion. The hero (akin to Job) often

---

[27] See, e.g., Isai. 6:2.

[28] See Jongeling, op. cit., at pp. 72–73; DJD23, at p. 170.

[29] Greenstein, op cit., at pp. xxi et seq.; C.A. Newsom, *The Book of Job* (2003), at p. 5. The narration of the patient Job of the prologue is to be found in Mesopotamian texts. As to the issue of a monotheistic belief by Jews in a diaspora which often required tolerance of other faiths, see C.A. Newsom, *Daniel — A Commentary* (Louisville 2014), at pp. 108–109.

[30] See, in particular, E.L. Greenstein, "Wisdom in Mesopotamia in Relation to von Rad's *Wisdom in Israel*" in T.J. Sandivar and B. Schipper (eds.), *Fifty Years of Wisdom: Gerhard von Rad and the Study of Wisdom Literature* (2022), at pp. 287–320 ("Greenstein, art., op. cit.) and the neat summary in the article by J.J. Mark, *Ludlue-Bel-Nemeki*, published in *World History Encyclopedia*.

wondered which deity he had offended. This issue does not arise in *Job*. Here the hero believes in a single God. In reality, the Mesopotamian sources do not include an analysis of the theodicy issue against a monotheistic background. Admittedly, Job is mentioned as praiseworthy by Ezekiel [14:14, 20], who likens him to Noah. There is, at the same time, no basis for the suggestion that Ezekiel was familiar with the highly articulated text here considered.

This analysis demonstrates that another explanation needs to be considered, viz. that the anonymous author, who composed the speeches, was familiar with Job of the Mesopotamian tales. He used the legend when composing the setting, but embarked on a detailed discussion of the theodicy issue. In support of this argument, it is strongly arguable that the epilogue was meant to appear after Chapter 31, which concludes with the words: "*tamu divrei Iyyov* (תמו דברי איוב)", meaning "The words of [Job] are concluded" [31:40].

If this construction is accepted, then Chapters 32–37 (Elihu's speeches) and 38–42:1–6 (God's reply from the whirlwind) are late additions. Actually, the epilogue is an appropriate sequel to the debate between Job and his three friends. It clarifies that the Almighty prefers Job's honest attestations of his innocence — which is the gamut of the book — to the false accusations and the dogmatic stance of Elifaz, Bildad and Zofar.

In support of this construction, it is to be noted that God tells Elifaz that the speeches of the three friends were not נכונה[31] ("*nechona*" viz.,

---

[31] The verses are not preserved in the Qumran Scroll. The LXX read "anything true" and "the truth", respectively. The only other place in the MT which uses the word in the same sense is Psalms 5:10. But note that נכחים (nechochim) is used in the same sense in Sam. II: 15:3; Prov. 24:26.

"the thing that is right" [42:7,8]). The sins the friends attributed to Job were, of course, never committed by him whilst Job's manifestation of his innocence was, as is clear from the setting, factual.

IV. The Debate

The prologue is followed by the debate between Job and his three friends. It would be tedious to go through each cycle of the debate because in essence, only two points of view are set out: Job's stand and the opposite outlook.

Job's position is clear, commencing with his lament: "I had no repose, nor had I rest, nor was I quiet yet trouble came" [3:25] and his bitter question: "[W]hy is light (meaning 'life') given to him that is in misery…" [3:20].[32] Job accepts the existence of an underworld, She'ol,[33] which is the destination of all mortals.

In subsequent speeches, Job emphasises his innocence and states that he has not "denied [concealed] the words of the Holy one" [6:10]. He then exclaims: "I am fed up; I shall not live forever; leave me alone for my days are meaningless" (7:16; my translation). He then points out that his sins, if any, do not affect God and enquires why he is denied forgiveness and a peaceful death.[34]

Job continus in the same vein. In Chapter 9, he describes God's greatness and refers to him as the creator of "Hyades (the Bear), Orion, the Pleiades and the South Wind Chambers" [9:9].[35]

---

[32] For a similar lament, see Jer. 20:14 till the end, esp. verse 18.

[33] See Part VIII and see Job 3:15, 7:9 and 14:13.

[34] For an analysis of Job' first speech, see J. Hartley, *The Book of Job* (2nd ed., 1988), at pp. 165 et seq.

[35] See Greenstein, op. cit., at p. 39, who explained the significance of these constellations.

This reference supports the view, to be discussed later, that the anonymous writer of *Job* was a Diaspora Jew.

Job then voices his complaints, asserting that God crushes him "with a tempest, and multiplies [his] wounds without cause" [9:17]. In sheer bitterness he adds: "It is all the same. And so I declare: The innocent and the guilty he brings to [the same] end. While his scourge brings death to fools, He laughs [mocks] at the trials [sufferings] of the spotless" [9:22–23].[36]

Job points out that there is no entity capable of acting as a judge,[37] to whom he may complain, and amplifies his bitter speeches by saying: "Oh that I had perished and no eye had seen me ... I should have been carried from the womb to the grave" (10:19). He adds that his days are numbered and that, in due course, he is to end up in Sheol from whence he would never return.

Conceding God's omnipotence,[38] Job disputes His being just (the "theodicy issue"). In Job's opinion, "the tents of the robbers prosper, and they who provoke God are secure" [12:5]. "He [God] leads counselors away [astray] bereft of counsel, and makes judges fools" [12:17]. Emphasising his innocence [13:18], Job asks God to tell him where he sinned and to enable Job to contend without being afraid of retribution [13:21]. Subsequently, Job expresses doubt about his three friends' motives. "Will you speak wickedly [*contextually: incorrectly or wrongfully*] for God? And talk deceitfully for him? Will you show him

---

[36] Greenstein's translation, op. cit., at p. 41, which is believed to be correct. Note that the word "shot"(שוט) appears also in Isaiah (10:27) where it ought to be correctly translated as "disaster".

[37] For the traditional construction see *Rashi*.

[38] And see F. Delitzsch, *Biblical Commentary on the Book of Job* (1876), Vol. 1, at p. 111.

partiality?" [13:7–8]. Asking his friends to remain loyal to himself, he says: "Have pity upon me, have pity upon me, O my friends: for the hand of God has touched [torched] me. Why do you, like God, persecute me ..." [19:20–21].[39]

It is difficult to translate Job's bitter words. The tendency of translators is to soften Job's pronouncements. The climax is in Chapter 14, where he exclaims: "Who can tell the pure from the impure [tainted]. No one [can]" [14:4].[40] It has to be conceded that this translation is based on rendering the word יתן (*yiten*) as "tell". Traditionally, the words are understood as indicating that no one can **produce** pure humans from tainted ones.[41] יתן is, however, closer to "tell" than to "produce".[42]

With these pungent words, echoed by the Ecclesiastes [9:2], Job reiterates his doubts about divine justice and, further, questions God's capacity to tell observant disciples from transgressors.[43]

Notably, God's fallibility emerges from the prologue. Just as Satan questions Job's motivations, so Job questions God's justice and sympathy for the fallen. We also know from the prologue that Job's misfortunes were not a retribution for sins but the fruit of a bet between the Almighty and Satan!

---

[39] For a further rebuke of the friends, see 21:27–28.

[40] My translation. *Ct.* Greenstein, op. cit., at p. 60; the late Targum at p. 44 and the LXX at p. 675 differ. Regrettably Chapter 14 was not preserved in the Qumran Scroll. Cave 11 of Qumran includes a scrap which follows the MT's text (Ulrich, op. cit., at p. 728).

[41] See, e.g., the late Targum and the LXX. The real meaning of these words was conveyed to me (and my classmates) by our teacher in Tichon Ironi A, Old Frank.

[42] Generally, all words based on נתן (and יתן is its "future" third-person declination) mean "give". Contextually, though, the word means "tell" in the present instance.

[43] For a detailed analysis, see Vicchio, op. cit., at pp. 111 et seq.

Job's bitterness is emphasises in subsequent speeches in which he treats God as being both unjust and merciless. He complains that God "has filled me with wrinkles, which is a witness against me" [16:8] and adds that He "tears me in his wrath, and hates me: he gnashes at me with his teeth" [16:9]. Seeking support for his unjust sufferings, Job exclaims: "O earth, cover not my blood ... Even now, behold, my witness is in heaven and my testimony is on high" [16:18–19].[44] Here Job calls on earth to be witness his having been wronged. His words may be an outcry. It is also possible to discern in them the influence of polytheistic creeds, which rank divine beings and which regard "earth" as superior.[45] Job also expresses his having been deserted by all who were close to him and berates his three friends. In desperation he exclaims: "Why do you, like God, persecute me, and are not satisfied with my flesh" [19:21].[46]

Job adds [Chapters 23, 24] that his sufferings would prevent him from pleading his cause. In a sense he argues that an adversarial hearing is ruled out by his having been penalised before his guilt was established.[47] He concludes this part of his addresses by affirming his innocence and his having been penalised unjustly [27:1–12].

The Qumran Scroll lends support to this analysis. It indicates that Chapter 26 commences with an attribution of it to Job but does not

---

[44] And see Greenstein's elegant translation in op. cit., at p. 73.

[45] It has been suggested that these words allude to Cain's murder of Abel; A Clarke, *Commentary on the Book of Job* (2015), at p. 70.

[46] See also 21:27–28 and Chapters 23–24, in which Job reaffirmed his innocence and complained about his sufferings. *Cf.* Greenstein's translation and comment, op. cit., at p. 85.

[47] An issue arises in respect of Chapter 26. The editor's caption attributes it to Job. Greenstein, op. cit., at pp. 113 et seq. treats most verses of faith as forming part of Bildad's third speech.

comprise the first verse of Chapter 27, which advises that the words that follow are further (or supplementary) words uttered by him.[48] In this manner, the Qumran Scrolls treats the first verses of Chapter 27 as spoken by Job and as being a clear sequel to what he says in Chapter 26.[49]

Indeed, Job's stand is crystallised in Chapter 27, where he says: "Far is it from me that I should justify you: till I die I will not put away my integrity [innocence] from me. My righteousness I hold fast, and I will not let it go: my heart shall not reproach me as long as I live. Let my enemy be as wicked, and he who rises against me as the unrighteous" [27:5–7]. These are not the words of a patient and penitent Job.

An interesting issue arises from Job's statement "ותטפול על-עוני" (translated as: "though dost daub my iniquity with wax"). It may be argued that in these words he averred that even if he sinned, the loss of his property, offspring and health is unjust. In other words, Job averred that the "punishment" or "sentence" did not fit any transgression attributed to him. This point is not raised in any other book of the Bible.

The approach of the three friends — Elifaz, Bildad and Zofar — differs. Although the prologue tells the reader that they came to comfort Job [2:11–13], they turn out to be accusers. Their attitude is best captured in William Blake's illustrations[50] and is neatly expressed by Elifaz, who set the tone for the ensuing speeches of the trio.

To start with, Elifaz rebukes Job for his doubts and asks "who that was innocent ever perished?" [4:7]. By saying this he hints that those

---

[48] DJD23, pp. 104–105, which indicates that the speech of Chapter 26 is Job's but omits the first line of Chapter 27 of the MT, which reads: "and [Job] continued his discourse and said…"; see ibid. at p. 107.

[49] For a different construction, see Greenstein, op. cit., at pp. 113 et seq.

[50] Published in 1812.

who suffer (as does Job) are not innocent. Elifaz goes on and emphasises that God is just and raises the rhetorical question of can "mortal man be more just than God?[51] Can a man be more pure than his maker?" [4:17].[52] Praising God's justice and might, Elifaz opines that "man is born to trouble as the sparks fly upward" [5:6]. He urges Job "not to despise the chastising of the Almighty; for he makes sore, and binds up: he wounds but his hands make whole" [5:18].

Bildad's opinion is similar. He observes that "God will not cast away an innocent man, nor will he uphold evil doers" [8:20]. In his opinion, Job's only hope is to supplicate for divine help, for "... does the Almighty pervert justice?" [8:3]. He maintains that "if thy children have sinned against him, he has cast them out for their transgressions" [8:4].[53]

Notably, Bildad does not treat Job's offspring merely as a facet of Job's property. He suggests that they perished because of sins. The prologue indicates that he is wrong. Bildad's stance does not undergo any change in his second (Chapter 18) and third (Chapter 25)[54] speeches.[55] Likewise,

---

[51] Cp. Greenstein's translation, op. cit., at pp. 19 et seq.

[52] Most translations use "shall" rather than "can". I disagree. Greenstein, op cit., at p. 16 suggests that the words just cited constitute part of Job's first discourse. Again, I disagree. Both contextually and as regards points of argument, the phrase expresses Elifaz's stand. Note that Greenstein, op. cit., at p. 17 also reads "can".

[53] For a comprehensive analysis of Bildad's approach, of his view being geared in theodicy and in the firm belief that Job's sufferings evidenced his having sinned, see R. Cordis, *The Book of Job: a Commentary* (New York, 1978,) at pp. 100–105, 140.

[54] And see Vicchio, op. cit., at pp. 134–135; T. Aquinas, *Commentary on the Book of Job* (Steubenville 2016 ed.), at p. 92.

[55] It has been argued that Chapter 26:5–14 complete Bildad third speech which commences in Chapter 25:1. See Vicchio, op. cit., at pp. 185–186 and authorities there cited.

the third friend — Zofar (Chapters 11 and 20)[56] — delivers speeches reminiscent of Elifaz's original stand. Both of them refrain from accusing Job of any specific transgression but take the view that only the guilty are penalised.

In the same way, Elifaz restricts himself, in his second speech (Chapter 15), to imply that Job's words manifest his guilt and tells us: "What is man, that he should be clean? And ... that he should be righteous?" [15:14]. He concludes his speech by saying that evil people come to a bad end,[57] and that God alone can determine a human's purity.

Elifaz' tone changes in his third speech. He is irked by Job's firm rebuke: "Behold, I [Job] know your thoughts and the device you wrongfully imagine against me. For you say: Where is the house of the prince? And where is the tent in which the wicked dwelt?" [21:27–28]. Elifaz's retort is equally harsh. He accuses Job of oppressing the poor and the helpless (the widows and orphans) [22:5 et seq.]. This is a shift in Elifaz's language, though not in his stand. In his earlier speeches he hinted that Job was guilty. He now raises the accusations which, as is known from the prologue, are unfounded.

By now it is clear that the friends' stand is diametrically opposed to Job's. The latter maintains his innocence and his having been wrongfully penalised. The friends' approach is neatly summarised by Bildad, who asked: "How can man be justified with God?" [25:4].

V. Analysis of Chapters 26 & 27 and the Debate

It will be recalled that Chapter 26 commences with the caption: "And [Job] answered and said" [26:1]. The verses that follow express Job's

---

[56] For an analysis of his words, see Hartley, op. cit., at p. 70; Vicchio, op cit., at pp. 92–93.

[57] Vicchio, op. cit., at pp. 117 et seq. *Cf.* Rashi.

viewpoint. He completes his discourse in this chapter by observing: "...the thunder of [H]is power who can understand?" [26:14]. The compiler then advises, at the very beginning of Chapter 27: "And [Job] continued his discourse and said, 'As God lives, who has taken away my right ..." [27:1, 2] and reaffirms his innocence. Subsequently, in the last 10 verses, namely 13 till the end, *Job* expresses the view taken by Job's three friends. These words cannot be ascribed to Job the sufferer. The conclusion is that the first 12 verses of Chapter 27 are rightly attributed to Job but that they should have been followed by a caption indicating that the remaining verses are part of Zofar's final retort.[58] Regrettably the opening words of Zofar's last speech have not come down to us.

In support of this construction, it is to be noted that it is in tandem with *Job's* structure, which constitutes an exchange of the views held by Job with those of his three friends. To this end, every speech of Job is followed by the response of one of his friends. Thus, Job expresses his views in Chapters 3, 6–7, 9–10, 12–14, 16–17, 19, 21, 23–24 and 26–27:1–12. Elifaz delivers his three speeches in Chapters 4–5, 15 and 22. Bildad speaks in Chapters 8, 18 and 25.[59] The only two chapters expressly attributed to Zofar are 11 and 20. The construction proposed here would give Zofar a third speech, namely 27:13 till the end, and some sentences that have not come down to us. In this manner, Job's nine speeches are contested nine times by the retorts of his three friends.

Regrettably, the Qumran Scroll does not shed light on this issue. Both Chapters 26 and 27 are mutilated in it.[60] The late Targum and the LXX follow the MT without significant variation.

---

[58] Contrast Vicchio, op. cit., at p. 187, who regarded the absence of a third speech by Zophar as "the silence of the vanquished".

[59] And possibly parts of Chapters 26 and 27: see Vicchio, op cit., at p. 187.

[60] Jongeling, op. cit., pp. 24–15 (reproducing and translating the extant parts); DJD23, at pp. 106–107; Sokoloff, op. cit., pp. 46–49.

Numerous attempts have been made to draw a distinction between the speeches of the three friends. In reality, there are only two basic theses in Chapters 3 to 27 (inclusive), namely: (i) Job's viewpoint and (ii) the opposite concept manifested in the addresses of the three friends. Undoubtedly, there is progression in the words and metaphors used for the expression of the two views. Both Job and his three friends crystallised their opinions in the course of the debates. There are, nonetheless, only two basic philosophical approaches.

A point frequently raised is that in the course of these lengthy debates, concluding at the end of Chapter 27, ideas are repeated again and again. In a tome expressed in prose, this would be a stylistically and methodically unforgivable blemish. The relevant chapters of *Job* are, however, poetic. Whilst the basic notions are repeated, the imagery and the metaphors differ.

By way of comparison, take Edward Fitzgerald's translation of Omar Khayyam's *Rubaiyats* (quatrains). The basic idea of enjoying life is repeated many times. Nonetheless, nobody would levy the redundancy complaint because each poem has its own thrust. Another illustration is presented by the Psalms. Many of them praise God. But are they redundant? In a similar manner, *Job* is not repetitive. The two opposing viewpoints are developed and effectively crystallised. Further, the arguments are presented in poetry at its best. In my opinion, the redundancy plea is misguided.

VI. The Mysterious Chapter 28

Sandwiched between the three cycles of debates and Job's final and seminal monologue (Chapters 29–31, discussed subsequently) is the enigmatic Chapter 28. It is neatly divided into two parts: (i) verses

Job: A Reassessment*,

1–11 and (ii) verses 12–28. The first part commences with the word ki (כי). Greenstein[61] rightly points out that a poetic work does not commence with this word, which — literally translated — means "for". Regrettably, the ensuing words do not constitute a meaningful succession to Chapter 27. Indeed, it is difficult to fit them into the contents and the matrix of *Job*. The book deals with the theodicy issue.

The first part of Chapter 28 deals with the origin of metals and then proclaims the reign of cause and effect in our planet. It does not add any new nuance about the greatness and the invincibility of God. The second part of Chapter 28 is a eulogy of wisdom. The concluding words advise that "the fear of the Lord, that is wisdom: and to depart from evil is understanding" [28:28].

Just as the first part of the chapter, this eulogy of wisdom does not accord with the theological discourse of *Job*. In the words of Terrien: "There can be little doubt that this magnificent poem [Chapter 28: 12–28] on the accessibility of wisdom does not belong to the discourse of Job. It is not written in his style; it is not connected with the Joban context."[62] Greenstein argues[63] that the chapter constitutes part of Elihu's discourse (discussed subsequently). Notwithstanding its elegance and authority, this specific analysis is subject to argument. Elihu's thesis, to the effect that God is just, is not supported by Chapter 28.

This leads to the conclusion that Chapter 28, as a whole, does not form an integral part of *Job*. It has been included *per incuriam*.

---

[61] Op. cit., at p. 160.

[62] S. Terrien, *Job: Poet of Existence* (2004), at p. 979; Vicchio, op. cit., at pp. 190–194 and authorities there cited.

[63] Loc cit.

The error, though, is of considerable antiquity. Parts of Chapter 28 are preserved in the Qumran Scroll.[64]

Two points support the conclusion that Chapter 28 is not part of *Job*. First, the MT versions of *Job* and *Proverbs* (that have come down to us) are contemporaneous.[65] They are an integral part of the wisdom literature of the Old Testament and, in the MT, *Job* is placed immediately after *Proverbs*.[66] The feasibility of errors made in the copying process of biblical books is well known.[67] There can be no doubt that the second part of Chapter 28, that is the hymn to wisdom, can be neatly read together with *Proverbs*. It is in harmony with the sentiments expressed in Chapter 8 thereof.[68]

Admittedly, the first part of Chapter 28 does not mash neatly with *Proverbs;* but it might have been meant as a lead-up to the notion that wisdom is akin to worship. The reason the compiler placed the hymn of wisdom in *Job* is because *Proverbs* deals with points made in it succinctly; a lengthy discourse appeared more in line with *Job* than with *Proverbs*. There are, of course, lengthy passages in *Proverbs* like the praise of a "worthy [diligent] wife" [Prov. 31:10–31]. A lengthy eulogy of wisdom does not militate against that book's structure.

---

[64] DJD23. The LXX adhered to the MT version. The scraps of the Hebrew text discovered in Qumran do not include any verse of Chapter 28. This, though, is of no significance as the scraps are haphazard.

[65] Although *Proverbs* incorporates parables attributed to King Solomon, the MT version, which has come down to us, was compiled in the 4th century BCE: R.N. Whybray, *The Book of Proverbs: A Survey of Modern Study: 1* (Hall, 1995), at pp. 33 et seq.

[66] But note that in the Leningrad manuscript *Job* is placed before *Proverbs*.

[67] See, e.g., Greenstein, op. cit., at p. 16.

[68] And note also Prov. 1:7; 2:1–4.

Job: A Reassessment*,

The second point which highlights the alien nature of Chapter 28 in the context of *Job* is in that it breaks the continuity of the main discourse. Chapter 29, which is the first part of Job's closing monologue, follows naturally after the conclusion of the debates in Chapter 27. Chapter 28 simply derogates from the lucidity of the Jobian discourse. The inescapable conclusion is that it does not form part of *Job* and, in all probability, was inserted in it after the promulgation of an original version which has not come down to us.

VII. Job's Closing Monologue

Job's seminal monologue, comprising Chapters 29–31, follows the conclusion of the three-cycle debate that ends with Chapter 27. In this monologue, Job narrated his tragic story. In Chapter 29, he expounds his standing prior to the bet of God and Satan. The first part of the second verse, correctly translated "oh that I be restored to my heyday",[69] has become a phrase in use in modern Hebrew. Job then tells us all about his uprightness and his exalted status before his fall. He says: "I put on righteousness, and my justice clothed me, as a robe and diadem" [29:14]. He sums up by stating: "I ... sat as chief, and dwelt as king in the army ..." [29:25]. This assertion is borne out by the prologue which describes him, inter alia, as "... the greatest [wealthiest] of all men of the East [1:3]."[70]

In Chapter 30, Job describes his fall. In the first verse he tells us that he is being mocked by younger people "whose fathers I would have

---

[69] Usually translated as "Oh that I were as in months past"; in Hebrew: "מי יתנני כירחי-קדם".
[70] There is here a play on words. "Men of the East [קדם]" can also mean: "men of antiquity".

disdained to have set with dogs of my flock". He adds that even these people abhor him and spit in his face [30:10]. Addressing God, he complains: "I cry to thee, and thou dost not answer me. I stand up, dost thou then regard me? Thou art become cruel to me: with thy strong hands thou opposest thyself against me" [30:20–21].[71] By way of contrast, Job refers to his own virtue. He says: "Did I not weep for him that was in trouble? Was not my soul grieved for the poor? But when I looked for good then evil came…" [30:25–26]. He concludes: "I am a brother to jackals, and a companion to owls. My skin hangs down black from me, and my bones are burned with heat. Therefore my lyre is turned to mourning and my pipe[72] to the voice of those who weep" [30:29–31].

His decency and strict observance of good behaviour are expanded in Chapter 31. To start with, he affirms his veracity and exclaims: "If I have walked with vanity, or if my foot has hasted to deceit; let me be weighed in an even balance, that God may know my integrity" [31:6].[73] He gives details of his caring attitude to widows, orphans and the fallen and concludes "if my land cry against me or its furrows complain together; if I have eaten its fruits without money, or have caused its owners to sigh: let thistles grow instead of wheat, and cockle instead of barley" [31:38–39].

Here Job affirms his innocence by way of oath and pleads his case. From a legal viewpoint, his concluding monologue resembles a "case stated". In essence, he maintains that he has been wronged and avers that he is entitled to a reply. To this end, he says: "Oh that one would hear me! Here is my mark, let the Almighty answer me! And would

---

[71] Cp. Greenstein's translation, op. cit., at p. 127.

[72] Greenstein, op. cit., at p. 128 uses "flute".

[73] See the Vicchio's analysis, op. cit., at pp. 204 et. seq.

that my adversary would pen his writ" [31:35].[74] Job does not deny God's superiority and omnipotence but asserts his right to question His justice (the "theodicy issue"). On this point, he is, of course, borne out by the prologue.

The last verse of the chapter reads: "The words of [Job] are ended" [31:40]. They differ from the monologue, in which Job speaks and, accordingly, his words are expressed in first person. The concluding phrase, in contrast, is an editorial comment, expressed in third person. Here the compiler/editor tells the reader that Job has completed his discourse. Notably, a portion of it is preserved in the Qumran Scroll.[75]

The epilogue [42:7–end] is in harmony with the poetic part ending in Chapter 31. It does not refer to Elihu's speeches (Chapters 32–37) or to God's replies from the whirlwind (Chapters 38–42:1–6).

This leads to the conclusion that in the original version of *Job*, which has not come down to us, Job's bitter reproaches are not favoured with an answer. If this analysis is correct, this original version would have had to be suppressed as being apostate. Nonetheless, this conclusion is appropriate: it will be recalled that Job's sufferings do not constitute a befitting punishment for his sins. They are the outcome of a mere bet between God and Satan, a bet won by the latter. Is it possible that the translations destroyed by Gamliel were copies (or translations) of this original version?

Contextually, too, the proposed analysis is sound. It will be shown that neither Elihu nor God's replies from the whirlwind came up with an answer to the main query raised in *Job*: the theodicy issue. Job's concept of Sheol (the afterlife) is discussed hereafter.

---

[74] *Cf.* Greenstein's translation, op. cit., at p. 132.
[75] DJD23, at p. 125 (line 2 of Col. XX Figure 17 ii). See also Jongeling, op. cit., at pp. 38–39; Sokoloff, op. cit., at pp. 66–67.

VIII. Job's Concept of She'ol

Belief in the afterlife was common to the cultures of antiquity. That these had a major influence on Judah is beyond doubt. In a thesis examining such influences, we are told: "Even though the Hebrews had wanted to remain aloof from the world they could not have done so with the alien caravans and armies consistently passing through their very midst."[76] Further, wisdom literature and concepts were spread by mendicant teachers and travellers.[77] Civilizations such as Judah were getting familiar with the outlook and culture of neighbouring countries, especially as these dominated the Levant, including the fertile crescent, over generations.

The Egyptian belief in the afterlife is complex. A human's body died and was mummified. The spirit rested in the underworld but could rise and observe the world.[78] The belief in the afterlife was also manifest in Mesopotamia.[79]

---

[76] B.M. Hoverland, *The Influence of the Egyptian and the Babylonian Wisdom Literature Upon the Hebrew Wisdom Literature* (thesis, later reprinted; London, 2018), at p. 10. And see the authoritative discussion by Greenstein, article, op cit., at pp. 287–320.

[77] Note that St. Paul was a tentmaker by profession. It seems clear that the making of tents, used by travellers and by caravans, was common in the 1st century CE. Note also that Jacob is described as one preferring living in tents to hunting: Gen. 25:27. The reference to "tents" suggests that travel was well-known in the Levant.

[78] In particular the Wisdom of Amenemope (8th century BCE), which has also impacted the Book of Proverbs. For a neat summary, see www.per-ankh.co.uk and Vicchio, op. cit., at p. 74. For an extensive treatment, see J.P. Allen, *Middle Egyptian: An Introduction to the Language and Culture of Hieroglyphs* (3rd ed., 2014), esp. at pp. 118 et seq., and by the same author: *The Ancient Egyptian Pyramid Texts* (Atlanta, 2005), esp. at pp. 8 et seq.

[79] The afterlife is described in the Epic of Gilgamesh. For a neat summary, see the Wikipedia article on She'ol. For a fine analysis and translation of Mesopotamian texts, see S. Dalley, *Myths from Mesopotamia* (1989).

Job: A Reassessment*,

These creeds differ from Judah's. With its exception, the religions of the ancient world were polytheistic. It was, thus, possible to designate a deity (or God) in charge of the underworld. Osiris and Hades come to mind. The belief in a single almighty God necessitated a different approach.

Notably, belief in an underworld (or She'ol) manifested itself in the Old Testament even prior to the composition of *Job*. By way of illustration, Samuel was "raised" by the Witch of Ein-Dor (Endor) [Samuel A, 28:6–20]. Angrily, he tells Sha'ul: "Why hast thou disquieted me [הרגזתני], to bring me up?" [Id.:15] By implication, the "underworld" is a place of peace.

In the 8th century BCE, the prophet Amos tells us that if sinners "dig into She'ol, from there shall my hand take them" [Amos 9:2]. Obviously God — and no other — is master of the place; and he can raise souls from there.[80] At the same time, the Psalms ask: "In She'ol who shall give thee thanks?"[81]

Job's concept of She'ol is in tandem with the prevailing outlook. When bemoaning his sufferings, Job tells us that, unlike in this world, "there [in She'ol] the wicked cease from troubling: and there the weary are at rest. There the prisoners are at ease together; they hear not the voice of the slaver driver. The small and the great are there; and the slave is free from his master" [3:17–18].

When a person descends to She'ol, he does not usually rise [7:9]. This point is underscored in the second round of debates. Job tells us: "There is hope for a tree, if it be cut down, that it will sprout again, and that its tender branch will not cease. Though its root grows old in

---

[80] Psalms 30:4; and see Sam. A, 2:6 (Hannah's prayer).
[81] Psalms 6:6; and see Isai. 38:18.

the earth, and its stock die in the ground: yet through the scent of water it will bud and bring forth boughs like a plant" [14:7–9]. He then asks, rhetorically: "If a man die, shall he live again?"[82]

At the same time, Job does not doubt God's supremacy and his ability to bring the dead back to life. He says to God: "Oh that thou wouldst hide me in She'ol, that thou wouldst keep me secret, until thy wrath is past, that thou wouldst appoint me a set time, and remember me" [14:13]. And, when He does, He can raise Job from She'ol.[83]

Job's three friends do not express a divergent view. Zofar tells Job: "Deeper than She'ol, what canst thou do?" [11:8] He does not suggest that Job's view of She'ol, as expressed in Chapter 3, is inaccurate or misguided.

Of particular interest is Chapter 28. As argued, this chapter was, in all probability, not part of the original text of *Job*. It was, however, included in the tome due to an error made either by the redactor or by a copier. It does reflect the view taken in antiquity of She'ol. In the eulogy of wisdom [28:12–28], we are told: "The depth says, it is not in me."[84] Accordingly, She'ol is not the domain of wisdom.

A similar view is expressed by the Ecclesiast, who tells us: "Whatever thou hand finds to do, do it with thy strength, for there is no work, nor knowledge, nor wisdom, in She'ol" [9:10]. She'ol is a place of darkness. Whilst an analysis seeking to date Ecclesiast is outside the scope of this

---

[82] *Job* 14:14. Cf. the LXX. *Job* does not indicate familiarity with Ezekiel Chapter 37 (the vision of the reviving dead bones). For a succinct discussion of the belief in afterlife in later Second Temple period in Israel, see C.A. Newsom, *Daniel — A Commentary* (Kentucky, 2014), at pp. 366–368.

[83] And see Hoshea,13:14.

[84] *Job* 28:14. Note that the text refers to "Thom" [תהום] and not to She'ol [שאול]. The words, though, are interchangeable. The author of *Job* would have used "She'ol".

paper, it is safe to assume that the MT version of this book is not earlier than *Job*'s.

The conclusion is that She'ol is a place of darkness where the souls of the dead are deposited. Whilst God has the power to raise them, *Job* does not manifest a belief in reward or punishment after death. In other words, She'ol is not hell; and there is no mention of Eden.

IX. Elihu's Assertions

In the version that has come down to us, Job's closing monologue is followed by Elihu's speeches (Chapters 32–37). Many scholars maintain that these are late additions. Vicchio,[85] who is of this view, supports it on nine grounds. These can be condensed as follows.

First, Elihu is mentioned neither in the prologue nor in the epilogue. This framework advises that Job's three friends came to call on him and discussed his misfortunes *inter presentem*. An outsider like Elihu could reply to the written work but was not a party to the initial debate. Indeed, in the epilogue God refers only to Job's three friends. Elihu is, thus, conspicuous by his absence from the mainstream of the book.

Second, none of the parties to the debate refer to Elihu directly or indirectly. Further, Job does not retort Elihu's arguments although some of them cover ground not discussed elsewhere in the book. Taken together, these points establish that Elihu is an outsider or a newcomer who deals with a written text he has read.

Third, Elihu's intervention in the first six verses of Chapter 32 is the only prose except the compiler's captions and the setting. If the

---

[85] Op. cit., at pp. 211 et seq., citing available authorities.

anonymous author of *Job* had intended to include Elihu as an integral contributor to the debate, these six verses (with the required alterations) would have been set out in the prologue. Alternatively, a reference to Elihu's words could have been set out in the epilogue.

Fourth, Elihu quotes Job's words verbatim.[86] In contrast, the three comrades refer to his views but do not cite him.

Fifth, Elihu refers to Job by name.[87] The three comrades refrains from doing this, although they address him in second person (e.g., "thou"). This, too, indicates that the relevant chapters [32–37] were not written by the author of other parts of the book.

Finally, *Job* is renowned for the use of hapaxes. Vicchio demonstrates that these appear more frequently in Elihu's speeches (and in Chapter 28) than in any other part of the book. Furthermore, the vocabulary and imagery of Chapters 32 to 37 differ from the language of the rest of the book.[88]

These points are adequate to support the view that the speeches of Elihu are late additions to the original version of *Job*. It is also noteworthy that, although the three comrades are gentiles, Elihu's name and lineage evidence his being Jewish. To start with, the name Elihu ("El is my God" [אליהוא]) is Hebrew. It is akin to Eliyahu [אליהו], the name of the acclaimed prophet, which conveys a similar meaning. Further, detailed pedigrees are set out mainly in late books of the MT (such as Chronicles). They describe the background of members of the tribe and distinguish them from outsiders.

---

[86] In 33:8–11, in which he refers to 13:23–24; and in 34:5–9 referring to 27:3; and in 35:3 referring to 7:20.

[87] 32:12; 33:1; 34:5; 36:16 and 37:13–14.

[88] And see S. Freehof, *The Book of Job: A Commentary* (New York, 1963), at p. 207, who points out that words of Aramaic origin are more common in Elihu's speeches than in the rest of *Job*.

Job: A Reassessment*,

Further, Elihu's speeches raise a theological point not covered by the three comrades. They, as well as Job, regard suffering as retributive. Elihu argues that God refrains from unjust acts[89] and that the sufferings of the innocent are the outcome of a predetermined divine plan. God alone decides when sufferings are to be inflicted or remedied.

Elihu also takes the view that Job sins by questioning God's ways. In his own words: "Would that [Job] may be tried to the end because he answers like wicked men. For he adds rebellion to his sin ... and multiplies his words against God" [34:36–37].

This point of view falls short of the assertion of a reward or redemption to be meted out after an individual's death. Neither Elihu nor any other party to the Jobian analysis manifests a belief in an "afterlife" [העולם הבא] in which transgressors are punished and people of faith are rewarded.[90]

Elihu's theological approach avoids the stand taken by Job's three comrades. He tells us that "against [Job] his anger burned, because [Job] justified himself rather than God. Also against his three friends did [Elihu's] anger burn, because they found no answer, and yet had condemned [Job]" [32:2].

Elihu challenges Job to dispute the theological point to be made by him. In his own words: "If thou canst, answer me; set thy words in order before me; stand up" [33:4]. He then explains that God himself does not deign to talk to people. He "speaks once, yea twice, yet man perceives it not. In a dream, in vision of the night, when deep sleep falls upon men ... then he opens the ears of men..." [33:14–16].[91]

---

[89] See, in particular, 34:10–12; and their translation by Greenstein, op. cit., at pp. 144–145.

[90] See, in particular, Job's denial of resurrection: 7:8–9; verse 8 is missing in the LXX version. *Contrast* Newsom, op. cit., at p. 168.

[91] Echoing Elifaz' first speech [4:12–15], discussed earlier.

Arrogantly he tells Job: "If thou hast anything to say answer me ... If not harken to me: hold thy peace, and I shall teach thee wisdom" [33:32–33].

Elihu's outlook is questionable. In other passages of the MT, God addresses individuals directly. His appearance to Moses, in which He gives explicit instruction to the prophet, is but one of them [Ex. 3:3–end]. God's eloquent initiation address to Jeremiah [Jer. 1:3–end] is another. Further, Elihu demands a reply from Job, although his speeches were written well after the conclusion of the debates and the compilation of the original version of *Job*. Does this make sense?

A detailed analysis of Elihu's speeches does not raise any further points.[92] Notably, the Qumran Scroll includes parts of Elihu's speech. Chapters 32 to 37 are also set out in the LXX, although certain verses thereof are missing. On this basis it is to be concluded that, although Elihu's speeches are late additions, they were composed at an early stage. As pointed out above, paleontologists have concluded that the Qumran Scroll was written in Herodian script. This means that Elihu's speeches were part of *Job* as circulated in the 1st century BCE. Further, scraps of the Hebrew text (including Elihu's speeches) were discovered amongst the Dead Sea Scroll.[93]

Elihu's viewpoint is in tandem with modern Christian and Jewish theology, which maintain that the ways of God are just and that everything is part of a divine plan. Earlier on, Jeremiah advises that God's principle is "to give everyone according to his ways, and according to the fruit of his doings" [Jer. 32:19]. In the circumstances, one might

---

[92] See the detailed discussion of Vicchio, op. cit., at pp. 227 et seq.; Greenstein, op. cit., at pp. 134 et seq. Greenstein's argument, to the effect that Chapter 28 is a sequel to Chapter 37, is unsupportable.

[93] Reproduced in Ulrich, op cit., at pp. 729–731.

enquire whether the bet of God and Satan (described in the prologue) was likewise retributive or preordained.

X. God's Replies

As has been shown earlier, originally the debates conclude with Job's monologue, in which he reasserts his innocence and once again requests an elucidation by God. This answer is set out in Chapters 38 to 41. These comprise two speeches, which God delivers from the whirlwind [סערה]. Greenstein points out that here God "assumes a hostile persona — that of the storm god".[94] He goes on to explain that, in Middle-Eastern mythology, the Storm God is a warrior. Undoubtedly, the retorts are both hostile and condescending.

In the first (comprising Chapters 38 and 39), God refers to his own magnitude. He tells Job that, as Job was not present when the earth was created, he is not in a position to criticise or raise queries respecting a divine plan of which he has no knowledge.[95] Job's replies thereto are muted. He says: "Lacking respect, how can I answer? My hand I place over my mouth. I have spoken once and I will not repeat; Twice — and I will (speak) no more" [40:4–5].[96] Here Job does not concede his having received an answer to his complaint. He avers that he has not doubted God's greatness, but that the theodicy issue has not been resolved.

God, thereupon, speaks once again [Chapters 40:6 to 41]. This second reply differs from the imagery of the previous one. Whilst His

---

[94] Op. cit., p. 165.

[95] Two verses of Chapter 40 poses a problem. God appears to ask again whether an accuser of divine justice deserves a reply. It is possible that these words are the commencement of an extra speech of God, which has not come down to us. They do not add anything to the discourse.

[96] Translation of Greenstein, op. cit., at p. 176.

first reply asserts His generic greatness, He now refers to two wonders, namely the "behemoth" and the "leviathan", and challenges Job to control them. God displays his anger at Job's words, asking him: "Wilt thou disavow my judgment? Wilt thou condemn me, that thou mayst be right? Has thou an arm like God?" [40:9]. However, as in his first speech, God does not explain why innocent people, like Job, suffer.

Job's reply thereto does, once again, falls short of conceding God's justice. In his own words: "As a hearing by ear I have heard you, and now my eye has seen you. That is why I am fed up. I take pity on "dust and ashes"!" [42:5–6]. Greenstein tells us: "Job understands the deity to be exactly as he had feared: a purveyor of power who cares little for people. Parodying the divine discourse through mimicry, Job expresses disdain toward the deity and pity toward humankind."[97] Job has done so earlier[98] and his reply to God's second speech does not depart from his original bitter and disillusioned stand.

It should by now be clear that *Job* does not resolve the theodicy issue. The inadequacy of the comrades' arguments is pointed out in Chapter 32:3, discussed earlier. Neither God's replies nor Elihu's speeches provide an adequate answer.

Nonetheless, Chapters 38 to 42:1–5 give rise to a number of intriguing issues. First, the vocabulary and the imagery of God's replies from the whirlwind differ from those of the poet who composed the setting and the debates. At the same time, the composer of the replies has read the earlier parts of the book. For instance, he refers to the

---

[97] Greenstein, op. cit., at pp. 184–185, which also sets out the passage from Job just quoted.
[98] In 9:22–23, cited above.

same heavenly constellations as Job.[99] Further, he replies to Job's complaints although he does not cite them verbatim.

Are these replies contemporaneous with the rest of the books or were they written later on? Passages of God's replies appear in the Qumran Scroll.[100] This establishes that they formed part of *Job* as circulated in the 1st century BCE. It is true that scraps of the Hebrew text on this point were not discovered amongst the Dead Sea Scrolls. The relevant chapters are, however, set out in the late Targum[101] and in the LXX.

Thus, the available sources do not provide a clear conclusion as to the date of God's replies. In view of the concluding sentence of Chapter 31, discussed earlier, it seems likely that the original version of *Job* ended with Job's seminal, final monologue. However, a book with such a conclusion would have been unacceptable to the Pharisee theology which developed after the destruction of Jerusalem in 71 CE. The book survived and was included in the MT due to the addition of God's replies from the whirlwind.

The second issue which arises as regards Chapters 38 to 42:1–6 is whether they were composed before or after Elihu's speeches (viz. Chapters 32–37). The point is of considerable difficulty. Both tracts postulate a divine order, which is beyond the scope of mankind's comprehension. Circumstantial evidence suggests that Elihu's speeches were added after the debate but prior to God's replies.

To start with, Elihu's discourse does not add much to *Job,* as comprising the setting, the debates and God's replies. It simply

---

[99] *Cf.* Chapter 9:9 with 38:31, both of which refer to Pleiades and Orion.
[100] DJD23, at pp. 149–168; Jongeling, op. cit., at pp. 57 et seq.; Sokoloff, op. cit., at pp. 86 et seq.
[101] See Mangan, op. cit., at pp. 83–90.

underscores or clarifies the notion that God's ways are just and beyond mankind's grasp. In addition, neither God's replies nor the epilogue refer directly or indirectly to Elihu's words. If the author of the replies had studied Elihu's analysis, his easiest way would have been to add a brief indication of God's agreement thereto.

Finally, Elihu's speeches and God's replies from the whirlwind do not cross refer. This, too, indicates that the respective authors were unfamiliar with the writings of each other.

The tentative conclusion, then, is that both Elihu and the composer of God's replies felt the need to retort to Job's bitter complaint and his negative assessment of divine justice. They worked independently, and it is only natural that the editor of the book included both God's replies after Elihu's discourse. He gave God the last word.

The tentative conclusion prescribed by this analysis is that an original version of *Job*, ending with Chapter 31 plus the epilogue, was "censored" by later compilers so as to save an apostate book, expressed in sublime poetry, from suppression or destruction.

XI. Greek Influences

It has been pointed out at the outset that *Job* was probably composed in the late 5th or early 4th century BCE. Is it possible that the anonymous author was influenced by Greek culture? The question is of considerable difficulty. The debating technique used in *Job* is not found in other books of the Old Testament. These comprise historical narration, prophecies of wrath, eschatological and apocalyptic messages and allegories. Terms and metaphors are not defined. It is assumed that the reader understands the meaning of words such as "God" and "justice"

For instance, in Ha'azinu [האזינו] we are told: "He is the rock, his work is perfect: for all his ways are justice: a God of truth and without iniquity, just and right is he" [Deut. 32:4].[102]

In contrast, the meaning of "justice" [צדק] is one of the issues debated by Socrates and his fellows in the *Republic*. Books I and II of the tome demonstrate a highly sophisticated and analytical examination of the term. But could this analysis have been known to the anonymous author of *Job*?

Socrates was born at around 470 and died in 399 BCE. Plato's dialogues respecting Socrates, including the *Republic*,[103] were composed between Socrates' death and Plato's first trip to Sicily in 387 BCE. It is believed that they became well-known throughout the Levant as indeed were other writings respecting Socrates, such as Xenophon's *Memorabilia* and Aristophanes' *Clouds*. However, and as stated earlier, these appear to have been composed after *Job*.

At first glance, this suggests that *Job* could not have been influenced by these works or by Greek philosophy. The dialectic, or debating approach, was however used in Greek politics even before it permeated into philosophy. It was the method used in debates at the Athens Assembly.

An attempt to unveil the origin of these Greek polemics is outside the scope of this investigation. Suffice it to emphasise that two friends of the young Socrates — Pericles and Alcibiades — were masters of

---

[102] הצור תמים פעלו כי כל-דרכיו משפט. אל אמונה ואין עול ,צדיק וישר הוא [MT Hebrew].

[103] For an authoritative examination seeking to date Plato's dialogues, see G. Vlastos, *Socrates: Ironist and Moral Philosopher* (Cambridge, 1991), Chapters 2 to 4. Greenstein, article., op.cit., suggests that a similar approach was used in early Canaanite and Mesopotamian texts.

rhetoric.[104] Notably, Pericles' consort, Aspasia,[105] was well acquainted with Socrates. It is likely that her skills influenced the young philosopher, were adopted by him during his later years and, in due course, became the basis of the debating or dialectic approach employed in Plato's dialogues. If this were the case, the technique of Athens' political leaders was likely to have been known to the author of *Job*.

That *Job* uses the debating, or dialectic, approach is clear. A proposition — namely theodicy — is posed and discussed at length. Undoubtedly, some books of the Old Testament have lengthy statements of an issue, such as the duty to observe law. *Isaiah* and *Jeremiah* are examples in point. Others concentrate on the praise of God. *Psalms* provides the best illustration. Other books still, for instance, *Judges* and *Samuel/Kings* are of the narrative gender. None of them uses the dialectic approach.

Further, the dialectic method is alien even to Biblical Books of Wisdom other than *Job*. *Proverbs* and *Ecclesiastes* set out sharp and usually concise epigrams, which prescribe an appropriate and wise norm of conduct. It is true that, in some instances, the advice or prescription encompasses a number of verses[106] but these do not question the issue.

It may be argued that the Talmud is renowned for the use of dialectics. This is, undoubtedly, true as regards the later part of the

---

[104] Aristotle's renowned *Rhetoric* was published late in the 4th century BCE, that is, well after the Peloponnesian Wars (431–404 BCE) and hence after the composition of *Job*. The discussion, though, deals with a technique well known in his time.

[105] For a brief and most interesting treatment, see W. Buckingham, "Aspasia, the Philosopher Who Taught Socrates Rhetoric" https://www.lookingforwisdom.com/Asapsia/ and M.M. Henry, *Prisoner of History: Aspasia of Miletus* (1955).

[106] Such as the lengthy warning against hedonism (in Prov. 31:2–5) and the doubts cast on wisdom (in Ecc. 9:13–16).

Talmud — the Gemara [גמרא] which was sealed in the 8th century CE. The earlier part of the Talmud — the Mishna [משנה] — does not use it. It is written in resonant Hebrew and was probably sealed by the end of the 2nd century CE. Basically it includes legal principles and short narratives. It supports the view that, in the period in which *Job* was written, dialectics (or the Socratic discourse) were not practised in Judaism. All this leads to the conclusion that, unless the author of *Job* invented the method on his own, he was influenced by a method common elsewhere, such as Greece at the relevant time.

The suggestion that *Job* manifests Greek influence is not novel. In 1918, Horace Kallen opines: "The Greek influence is ... beyond question." He then explains: "... we have in the Book of Job ... a Hebraized form of the Greek tragedy...."[107]

Kallen's opinion of the influence of Greek tragedy is to be doubted. The impact of the dialectic method is obvious.

XII. The Author's Personality

Who wrote *Job*? Some sages argue that the author was Moses.[108] However, the vocabulary and syntax of the Pentateuch (also attributed to Moses) differ from *Job*'s. Further, Moses describes God as the very source of faith and justice [Deut. 32:5]. Moses would not feel the need to discuss the theodicy issue.

Other sages[109] attribute *Job* to Jeremiah, who — as already pointed out — raised the theodicy issue [Jer. 12:1]. However, his query was

---

[107] H.M. Kallen, *The Book of Job as a Greek Tragedy* (New York, 1918), at p. 7. See also J. Kuriakose, "*The Book of Job*: A Greco-Hebrew Rhetorical Drama" in *English Language and Literature Studies* (2016), Vol. 6, No. 2, at pp. 72 et seq.

[108] Bava Batra, at p. 14b.

[109] Ibid., at p. 15a.

not favoured with a reply and was not discussed by him any further. There can, of course, be no doubt about Jeremiah's standing as a poet. All the same, Jeremiah's main objective was to deal with the issues of his era, namely the corruption of Judah and the military superiority of Babylon. In addition, the dialectic approach of *Job* was alien to Judah of Jeremiah's period (the 6th century BCE).

Greenstein[110] concludes that the text was composed by a Jew residing in Yehud and suggests that the author was more conversant with Aramaic than with Hebrew. However, a Jewish diaspora established itself in Damascus ever since the destruction of Samaria in 722 BCE.[111] Indeed, Diaspora Jews came to Jerusalem after hearing of the destruction of the First Temple by the Babylonians.[112] It is thus possible that the author was a Diaspora Jew, whose liturgical Hebrew was sparkling even if Aramaic was the language he spoke in his everyday dealings.

Admittedly, an identification of the author is speculative; but some clues about his personality are given in *Job*. To start with, the author is a scholar familiar with the dialectic approach to the examination of issues of ethics. He was, at the same time, a staunch believer in God's greatness and in His having created the universe.[113] He describes God as "… mighty in strength: who has hardened himself against him, and prospered?" [9:3–4].[114] Thus, he believed that God's wrath would impact transgressors. These words would not be uttered by a sceptic or a

---

[110] Op. cit., at p. xxvii.

[111] And note that the Book of Esther evidences the existence of a thriving Jewish Diaspora community during the 4th century BCE. And see Jer.: 40:11 and 41:4.

[112] Jer.: 41:5–8.

[113] See, in particular, 6:10, cited above.

[114] And see 31:23.

disbeliever. In reality, God's replies (Chapters 38–42:1–6) do not militate against Job's own creed.[115]

Another clue given to us is Job's familiarity with the pyramids,[116] his knowledge of the Egyptian wisdom writings and religion, and his approach to the concept of She'ol, discussed earlier on.

Was the author a priest? Probably, a member of this class would not utter Job's reproaches and negative statements respecting God's justice.[117] It seems more likely that the author was a member of a non-priestly patrician family. It is probable that he travelled throughout the Levant.[118] Herodotus, who lived in the 5th century BCE, was by no means the first voracious traveller. Ulysses of the Odyssey, who lived long before him, comes to mind. Sinuhe, the Egyptian, whose story was known as early as the 19th century BCE,[119] escaped from Egypt and travelled to what is Lebanon today. *Genesis* narrates the travels of Abraham, Jacob and Joseph. It is believed that, like these characters, the author was a traveller and that he had eyewitness knowledge of the Levant.

As already mentioned, Greenstein[120] maintains that the author was a resident of Judah from Jerusalem. "Yehud" of the Persian period,

---

[115] And note that Job does not believe in resurrection: 7:8–9.

[116] See 3:13 which, literally translated, refers to "ruins". Greenstein, op. cit., at p. 14 demonstrates that the Hebrew Haravot ought to be read as Haramot, derived from *mr* (pronounced "mer") which refers to the pyramids in Mid-Egyptian. And see P. Dickson, *Dictionary of Middle Egyptian* (California, 2006), at p. 164.

[117] But note that Jeremiah [12: 1–3] raised the theodicy issue.

[118] *Job* 6:18–19 confirmed his familiarity with caravans and travelling in general.

[119] For a neat exposition, see J.P. Allen, *Middle Egyptian Literature* (2015), at pp. 55 et seq.

[120] Op. cit., at pp. xxvii–xxviii. He concludes that the author was a highly educated man familiar with earlier biblical writings.

covering the 5th and 4th centuries BCE, was, however, underdeveloped.[121] In contrast, there were sophisticated Jewish settlements in Damascus[122] and — as demonstrated by the Book of Esther — in Shushan [Susa] and, of course, in Babylon.[123]

The author's familiarity with astronomy — mentioned earlier on — suggests that he might have been a scion of the Jews exiled to Babylon with King Yehoyakhin in 597 BCE.[124] Mesopotamia was renowned for its mastery of astrology. In contrast, astronomy and astrology were not practised in Judah or, later on, in Persian Yehud. [125]

Support for the view that the author was a Diaspora Jew is derived from three arguments. First, *Job* is one of the very few books of the Old Testament that does not refer, directly or indirectly, to Judah or Jerusalem. Job and his three comrades come from other countries of the Near East, and although Elihu's lineage is Jewish, he is not stated to have lived in "Yehud" or Judah.

Secondly, Job's patent bitterness and his fierce arguments respecting the theodicy issue are more likely to have been the fruit of an exile's bitterness than the utterances of one who returned to or lived in Yehud. A member of this second group would have been far more likely to sing the praise of the Almighty, who induced Cyrus the Great to sanction the return from the Babylonian exile.

---

[121] See Finkelstein, op. cit., at pp. 4 et seq.

[122] Note that Ben Hadad granted King Ahab the privilege of "making streets for thyself in Damascus": Kings I: 1:34. The Diaspora there would have grown following the fall of Samaria in 722 BCE.

[123] The sophistication of this Diaspora is demonstrated by Ezekiel's prophecies.

[124] Kings II: 24:8–15.

[125] Amos 5:8 also refers to heavenly constellations. But note that Amos prophesied mainly in the Northern Kingdom, which was not landlocked.

Thirdly, the author is highly sophisticated and well-read. He would appear to have been familiar with the wisdom literature of the Levant[126] as well as with weather conditions uncommon in Judah (or Palestine) but prevailing in regions such as Assyria.

Greenstein's view[127] that the book was originally meant for circulation amongst a limited circle of readers is supportable. This is especially so if the original version did not comprise Elihu's speeches and God's replies from the whirlwind. It is forcefully arguable that two separate members of this circle added these chapters. With their addition, *Job* did not militate against the creed of the day. When a council of sages, convened in Javneh in 90 CE, considered which books might have to be excluded from the MT, *Job* was not questioned.[128]

XIII. Conclusion

Job is a unique pearl of Jewish heritage. Its original version did not include Chapters 28, 32 to 37 (Elihu's speeches) and 38 to 42:1–6 (God's replies from the whirlwind). The final message of this original work is clear: the theodicy issue remains unsolved. Even a lengthy dialectic debate does not provide a satisfactory solution to it. Another wisdom book concedes its having arisen. The author of Ecclesiastes says: "… there are just men, to whom it happens according to the deeds of the wicked; again, there are wicked men, to whom it happens

---

[126] See Greenstein, article, op. cit.

[127] Op. cit., at p. xxviii.

[128] The canonisation of the MT is outside the scope of this paper. See, generally, McDonald and Sanders (Eds.), *The Canon Debate* (Michigan, 2019) and especially P.R. Davies, *The Jewish Scriptural Canon in Cultural Perspective* (2014), at pp. 36 et. seq. For the Javneh Council see J.P. Lewis, "Jamina Revisited" at pp. 146 et. seq.

according to the deeds of the righteous: I [say] that this is also vanity" [Ecc. 8:14–15].

Job's original version was written by a learned and well-travelled Diaspora Jew who, in all probability, was not of priestly origin. Initially, it was circulated to a limited circle of liberal intellectuals. To save this work from oblivion (that is, destruction or suppression) members of this group wrote Chapters 32 to 37 (Elihu's speeches) and 38 to 42:1–6 (God's replies from the whirlwind). Chapter 28 was included by error when the MT version was compiled for wider circulation.

In its final version, *Job* was included in the MT. Admirers of the Old Testament are fortunate to have it. The epilogue [42:7–end] assures them that honest questioning is preferable to abject hypocrisy.

To sum up, the author of the original version was a wunderkind. His poetic caliber remains unparalleled. He employed dialectic analysis long before it was adopted in the Gemara. It is believed that he became familiar with dialectics due to Greek influence. The splendour of his poetry manifests his genius. Judaism was enriched by the preservation of the book.

Kafka's Feet of Clay

I. Introduction

Franz Kafka died in obscurity about 100 years ago. After three decades, the worn-out cliché, "he was one of the greatest authors of the 20th century", was applied to him. I am dubious. For some, Kafka is good reading. His is the world of the bizarre, the phantasmagorical and the absurd: a reader can embrace it, admire it and enjoy Kafka's black humour. All in all, though, Kafka was an eccentric and unworldly writer.[1] Some readers are repelled by him.

My decision to express my views about him assumes that Kafka did not seek to confine his address to literary critics. If this had been his object, I would consider myself out of my depth: I am an ordinary,

---

[1] Of biographies the following are recommended: M. Brod, *Franz Kafka — A Biography* (1995; cited as K-MBB); R. Robertson, *Kafka — Judaism, Politics, and Literature* (1985; cited as K-RB); R. Stach, *Die Kafka Biographie in drei Bänden* (2023) (these include: i.: *Die Frühen Jahre*: K-RSFJ; ii. *Die Jahre der Entscheidungen* :K-RSJE; iii. *Die Jahre der Erkentnis*: K-RSL); R. Stach, *Is that Kafka? 99 Finds* (2012; in English, 2016; cited as K-99). Kafka's daily engagements are noted in R. Stach's excellent *Kafka von Tag zu Tag* (2024; cited as K-TT).

albeit widely read, middle-class person. This entitles me to form a view about books I study and their authors. The decision to go ahead is further motivated by my ability to read German (which means that I can read Kafka's originals) and by my being — like him — a Diaspora Jew.

My assessment is based on reviewing Kafka's oeuvre[2] and his achievements. As I intend to cover publications of Kafka's writings as well as leading discussions of his work, it appears best to refer to pieces cited by means of abbreviations. A list thereof is set out in an Appendix.

A brief explanation highlights the issues involved in this assessment. They stem from the fact that very few of Kafka's writings were published during his lifetime. Fortunately, he kept "octavo notebooks". He carried them with him but, from time to time, started a new notebook and, subsequently, reverted to an older, unfinished one. In these notebooks Kafka included diary entries[3] as well as aphorisms and drafts of literary works. These notebooks came either into the hands of Max Brod, his literary executor, or were acquired directly by publishers. The diaries and all other posthumous publications are generally arranged chronologically.[4]

This oeuvre is Kafka's contribution to the understanding of his age and of mankind. Prior to turning to an analysis thereof, it is appropriate

---

[2] All references are based on F. Kafka, *Gesammelte Werke* (Anaconda, Cologne, 2013; to be cited as K-GW); citations in English are from *Kafka's Collected Stories*, translated by W. Muir and E. Muir and edited by G. Josipovici (London & New York, 1971; cited as K-EST). Some lost writings were published in R. Stach, *Franz Kafka, The Lost Writings* (New York, 2020; cited as K-LW).
[3] F. Kafka, *Diaries 1910–1923* (edited by M. Brod, Schocken, New York, 1975; cited as K-DE); Franz Kafka, *Tagebücher 1910–1923* (details not given in copy; cited as K-DG).
[4] The exception is the new diary translation by Ross Benjamin (Schocken Books, New York, 2024; cited as K-KEB) which follows the order of the notebooks.

to provide some biographical details, a consideration of Kafka's Jewish heritage and a description of his period, which comprises the first decades of the 20th century.

II. Biographical

Franz Kafka was born in 1883 to secular Jewish parents. His city of birth, Prague,[5] was the capital of the Province of Bohemia, a domain of the Austro-Hungarian (Habsburg) Empire. Prague was a major city, next only to Vienna and Budapest. Kafka's father, Hermann, migrated to this city from his birthplace in rural Bohemia,[6] where the dominant language was Czech. He built up a successful business, which enabled him to give Franz a good education.

By moving to Prague, Hermann and his family became part of a twofold minority group. Czech was the language spoken by the population. Government employees and the gentry spoke German, which was the official language of the Habsburg Empire. Mass migration from rural Bohemia to the capital led to the Czech-speaking residents becoming the majority. Jews in Prague belonged to the German-speaking group but were not accepted as equals by the other German residents of Prague. The difficulty of moving into this type of class and being accepted by it is described in Arthur Schnitzler's *Der Weg in die Freie*[7]

---

[5] For photographs of Kafka's Prague, see J. Gruša (E. Mosbacher, Trs.), *Franz Kafka of Prague* (Schocken, New York, 1983).

[6] The negative aspect of this urbanisation trend amongst Jews is noted by Kafka, K-DEB, p. 193.

[7] A. Schnitzler, *Gesammelte Werke von Arthur Schnitzler* (Berlin, 1922, Vol. 3; reprinted in English: *The Way to Freedom*. Kafka saw a performance of a play based on this book on 19 November, 1911: K-DG, at p. 123. (Prior to Adolf Hitler's rise, anti-Semitism in Austria was generally non-violent; S. Zweig, *Die Welt von Gestern* (Frankfurt, 1944), pp. 83–85.)

and in Lion Feuchtwanger's *Judsüß*.[8] Kafka was, thus, born into a Jewish cultural ghetto circle. Although the Kafka family was not physically affected by antisemitic outbursts that took place in Bohemia during the late 19th and early 20th centuries, Kafka was keenly aware of his status.[9]

German was the language of instruction in the schools Kafka attended and at the university from which he graduated.[10] At home, the spoken tongue was a German dialect (spoken mainly in rural Bohemia), known as Mauscheldeutsch, which included words rooted in Yiddish.

An asset of Kafka's education was his acquiring knowledge of Greek and Latin. In addition, he studied French as a second language. He also acquired a command of Italian and a reading knowledge of English. His knowledge of the German slang spoken at home enabled him to comprehend Yiddish.[11]

Kafka's comments on his childhood are negative. An entry in his diary, of 26 December 1911, reads: "It is unpleasant to listen to Father talk with incessant insinuations about the good fortune of people today and especially of his children, [and] about the sufferings he had to entertain in his youth" (K-DB, p. 154). Kafka adds that his not having

---

[8] Jud Süß Oppenheimer was a Jewish merchant, who rose high in the court of Duke Carl Alexander in Württemberg in the 18th century. The story of his rise and fall is told in Feuchtwanger's book (originally published in 1916, current: Aufbau, Berlin, 1991).
[9] For antisemitic outburst when Kafka was 14 years old, see K-RSFJ, pp. 174–176; and note that on 7 July 1912, he was disturbed by the antisemitic remarks of playing children: K-TT, p. 162.
[10] The Friedrich Wilhelm University of Prague (German Division). Excellent photographs of Kafka as a pupil and as student can be found in K. Hagenbach, *Kafka's Prage* (Berlin, 2002), pp. 25 and 26, respectively. Kafka studied Czech as an optional subject in primary school: K-TT, p. 32.
[11] Kafka doubted his linguistic capacity: K-DEB, p. 266.

had to go through such sufferings "by no means leads to the conclusion that I have been happier than [father]" [id].

Max Brod confirms Kafka's complex relationship with his father. He tells us that "very early in life [Kafka] felt [that] his father's character was something foreign to his own ... [E]ven as he was growing older,[12] he still wished above all for his father's approval ..." (K-MBB, p. 30). Kafka appears to have loved his mother,[13] although she was active in Hermann's firm and spent most of her time away from home. Kafka was brought up by Czech-speaking governesses. It is due to them that Kafka became conversant in this language.[14] Further, from time to time he attended cultural events conducted in Czech.[15]

Kafka did not feel thankful for the fine education he was granted. He asserts that his education "had done [him] great harm in some ways".[16] He avers: "Parents who expect gratitude from their children ... are like usurers who gladly risk their capital if only they receive interest."[17] Despite this adverse stand, Kafka never freed himself from his parents' influence and failed to attain independence. In a diary entry

---

[12] But in a letter to Max Brod, of April 1921 (K-TT, p. 490), Kafka expressed doubts about his own maturity.

[13] But see his diary entries of 24 October 1911 (K-DE, p. 88), 5 December 1913 (K-EDB, pp. 318, 319) and 30 January 1922 (K-DE, p. 410) which raise doubts; and see K-TT, p. 236 referring to a diary entry of 15 August 1913, suggesting misunderstandings with her.

[14] A diary entry of 28 November 1911 reads: "I speak fluent Czech" [K-DE, p. 127].

[15] Such as Dr. Soukup's lecture: diary entry of 2 June 1913, K-DE, p. 203 and earlier a political meeting in March 1910: K-TT, p. 100. For a detailed analysis of Kafka's involvement with Czech culture, see A. Jamison, *Kafka's Other Prague* (Illinois, 2018). Kafka realised the importance of a small nation's memory: K-DE, p. 149 (meaning Czechoslovakia; see K-TT, p. 146).

[16] Diary entry of 19 May, 1910: K-D4, p. 15.

[17] Diary entry of 12 November 1914: K-DB p. 317; K-DG, p. 337.

dated 16 October 1916, he observes: "Father from the one side, mother from the other, have inevitably almost broken my spirit ... They have cheated me ..." (K-DE, p. 372). Three years later, in his famous *Letter to Father*,[18] written when Kafka was 36 years old, he seeks to blame his father for his own misfortune. The tone of this lengthy letter is reminiscent of Oscar Wilde's complaining tenor in *De Profundis*.

Records about Kafka's life during his early years of study are scanty. He made some early attempts at writing.[19] Whilst he had no interest in music,[20] he studied painting. Although he never attained fame in this field,[21] some of his art works have been preserved and published.[22] Throughout his life as a writer, he continued to draw[23] and, from time to time, supplemented letters or diary entries with sketches.[24] In a letter to his fiancé Felice Bauer, dated 10–12 February, 1913, which included some sketches, he explains: "I was once a great draftsman ... but then I started to take academic drawing lessons with a bad woman painter and ruined my talent" [K-LF, p. 389].

Kafka appears to have had an active life during his years of study. He took part in meetings of his circle, read out stories or extracts of works written by him and, in general, went to exhibitions and cultural

---

[18] K-GW, p. 459 et seq. It was composed in November 1919, K-LFR, p. 466 (n. 19).

[19] One of the pieces he started writing was *Description of a Struggle*, discussed subsequently.

[20] See his comment respecting a Brahms evening he attended on 11 December 1911: K-DEB, p. 150.

[21] One of Kafka's acquaintances was the artist Alfred Kubin; see entries of 26 September 1911, K-DE, p. 55 and of 12 June 1914, ibid., p. 289.

[22] A. Richter, *Franz Kafka — Die Zeichnungen* (Munich, 2nd ed., 2022).

[23] E.g., a caricature of his close friend, Max Brod, ibid., p. 250.

[24] See, e.g., the scribbles added to his letter to Felice Bauer of 11/12 February, 1913, ibid., p. 239.

lectures delivered in Prague.[25] He also attended some meetings of Czech circles and might have met Jaroslav Hašek, author of *The Brave [Good] Soldier Švejk [Schweik]* [K-RB, p. 140].

In 1906, Kafka obtained a Doctorate of Law. He served his year of apprenticeship at a law firm but his employment was with insurance companies. Due to the long hours of work (which did not leave him enough time for writing),[26] he resigned from his first post at an Italian-based company, and accepted employment at the Accidents Insurance Company run by the government (AUVA). His task was to examine and deal with applications of accident victims.[27]

Kafka remained in the employ of this company for the rest of his working life. He was one of the only two Jewish employees. Whilst he did not like his occupation, he distinguished himself and was promoted. He undertook several business trips on AUVA's behalf.

Kafka was concerned over the prevailing inadequate safety measures and took the side of the oppressed workforce. In his reports to the management, he advocated the introduction of methods aiming to improve the standard of care in industrial establishments.[28] Due to failing health, he was granted several periods of medical leave and eventually was pensioned early.

---

[25] Later on, in 1911, he attended Czech theatres: K-TT, p. 144.

[26] Kafka realised that he was unable to make a living from writing, see K-DE, p. 49.

[27] For a vivid description of his work, see K-RSFJ, p. 359. Together with Max Brod, Kafka saw a Yiddish theatre performance in Café Savoy on 4 May 1910: K-TT, p. 103. And on 27 October 1911, he saw there the performance of a play entitled *Kol Nidre*.

[28] He discussed the liability issue in a newspaper article, published on 4 November, 1911: K-TT, pp. 131, 138. See also his short story *New Lamps* [K-EST, pp. 390-1], which suggests that he often acted as spokesman when requests for innovation were made by the employees.

Kafka had an active life during his years of service. Max Brod mentions an early aviation demonstration attended by Kafka and himself. It was described by Kafka in an article entitled "The Aeroplanes at Brescia", published in a local periodical on 28 September, 1908 [K-MBB, p. 62, 104].[29] During vacations Kafka travelled — usually in the company of Max Brod — to Austria, Germany, the north of Italy and to Paris. His veneration of Johann Wolfgang von Goethe led to his staying for a few weeks in Weimar [K-DE, pp. 466–488; F-DG, pp. 499–522].[30] His Travelling Diaries [K-DE, pp. 425 et seq.; K-DG, pp. 454 et seq.] are perceptive and lively. He also spent time in natural health facilities, became a vegetarian and developed distrust in medicine and physicians [diary entry of 2 November, 1914: K-DEB, p. 333].

Of particular interest is his involvement with Yiddish theatre. Kafka befriended one of the actors, Yitzchak Löwy, and, despite his father's caustic remarks, supported the cause.[31] He studied Yiddish for a few months[32] but eventually discontinued at the beginning of 1912. Notably, on 18 February 1911, he gave a talk on this language to a meeting of Jews in Prague. Later, in a diary entry of 20 October 1911 [K-DE, p. 81], he refers to a session in which Löwy read out Yiddish stories of Shalom Aleichem and I.L. Peretz and a poem by Hayim Nahman Bialik,

---

[29] For an English translation, see Franz Kafka (M. Hofman, Trs.), *Metamorphosis and other Stories* (2007), pp. 287 et seq.; cited as K-MTS.

[30] Where he fell in love with the daughter of the warden of the Goethe House: K-TT, p. 161.

[31] During the period, he saw Löwy almost daily: K-DG, p. 155. Kafka's interest in Yiddish theatre might have been due to his infatuation with an actresses (Mrs. Tschissik): entry of 2 November 1911, K-DE, p. 106 [noted: K-TT, pp. 136, 138]; and see Isaac Bashevis Singer, *A Friend of Kafka* (New York, 2022); and diary entry of 19 December 1911, K-DEB, p. 154.

[32] Diary entry of 2 November 1911, K-DE, p. 103. And see V. Liska, *When Kafka Says We* (Indiana, 2009), pp. 26 et seq.

translated from Hebrew to Yiddish. All the same, Kafka treated Yiddish (and East European Jewry) as alien. He was unimpressed with the quality of Yiddish plays,[33] remained critical of the performances of some actors and, shortly after Löwy's departure from Prague, retreated into his own world [K-DG, pp. 177–178].

In 1911, Kafka was persuaded by his family to take part in an asbestos manufactory, named Prager Asbestoswerke & Co.[34] A diary entry of 7 November 1911 (K-DE, p, 110) indicates that he regarded the enterprise as intrusive and showed little interest in it.[35] He felt no remorse when it failed and was closed down in 1917.

In his spare time, Kafka wrote incessantly, often until very late at night.[36] He regarded writing to be his main task in life. His output included lengthy drafts of chapters of his novels and short stories, diaries (spread over 12 notebooks), extra notebook entries,[37] aphorisms[38] and letters to sweethearts and friends.[39] About 500 of them

---

[33] And see his detailed discussion of the Jewish theatre: K-NB, pp. 80 et. seq. In a diary entry of 17 December 1915 [K-TT, p. 315], he observed that these, and visits to the synagogue, did not affect his writing.

[34] See, Arthur Rose, "Recovering Franz Kafka's Asbestos Factory", *New Literary History* (2022), Vol. 53, No. 1, pp. 59–84.

[35] Entries of 14 and 28 December 1911 [K-ED, p. 137, 155; K-DEB, p. 368]; his family urged him to show interest: K-TT, p. 173.

[36] Having a negative effect on his health: diary entry of 21 November 1911: K-ED, p. 125.

[37] Max Brod (Ed.), *Kafka: The Blue Octavo Notebooks* (Cambridge, 1991; cited as K-NB). These notebooks were kept separate from others.

[38] H. Colyer (Ed. & Trs.), *Franz Kafka: Zürau Aphorism* (Middletwon, 2024; cited as K-ZAP).

[39] These are voluminous. They cover (i) E. Heller and J. Born (Eds.), *Letters to Felice* (New York, 2016; cited as K-LF); (ii) P. Boehm (Trs.), *Franz Kafka: Letters to Milena* (New York, 2015; cited as K-LM); and (iii) R. & C Winston (Trs.), *Franz Kafka: Letters to Friends, Family and Editors* (New York, 2016; cited as K-LFR).

were addressed to his first fiancée, Felice Bauer. A diary kept by him from about 1910 is extant. An earlier diary that he kept[40] was destroyed by him together with many writings.

Kafka had a harmonious relationship with his sisters but, as is clear from the passages cited, did not get on with his father, a self-made man who, according to Kafka, was a hard and domineering person. It is certain that Hermann was a self-assured and successful businessman who could be impatient with and hard on employees. He would have liked Kafka, his only surviving son, to take over the enterprise. There is little evidence supporting Kafka's negative assessment of his father's personality.

Kafka's biographers relate that he was a tall, good-looking and presentable man. The image gleaned from his writings — that of an introverted and lonesome man — differs from what is related by his acquaintances. They considered him a pleasant individual and a good mixer. Kafka was an active participant in small gatherings[41] but was overcome by shyness and reticence when in public gatherings. An entry in his notebooks indicates that he did not seek the attention associated with winning.[42] He felt compassion for those overtaken thereby.

Kafka's inner circle comprised well-known German-speaking Jewish intellectuals, such as the philosopher Hugo Bergmann,[43] the historian

---

[40] Entry of 15 August 1912 [K-DB, p. 206]. And see diary entry of 17 December 1910 [K-DEB, p. 67].

[41] He was a good listener, avoiding unnecessary contention: diary entry of 22 October, 1913 [K-DE, p. 235].

[42] The same is noted in his writings. See, in particular, his short story *Zum Nachdenken für Herrenreiter*: K-GW, at p. 25; K-EST, pp. 18–19.

[43] Later a professor at the Hebrew University of Jerusalem.

Oskar Pollak, the author Franz Werfel,[44] the musician Oskar Baum, the journalist Friedrich Welch and Kafka's close friend and biographer Max Brod. Quite regularly, Kafka read out some of his writings to these friends and commented on their efforts.[45]

Kafka liked the company of women.[46] A diary entry of 2 June 1916, reads: "What a muddle I've been in with girls, in spite of all my headaches, insomnia, grey hair, despair. Let me count them: there have been at least six since the summer" [K-DE, p. 362]. One of his early stories[47] suggests that he might even have contemplated accosting attractive girls bypassing him, except that, in many such cases, was overcome by shyness and diffidence. His Travel Diaries (published with his Diaries) confirm that he had an eye[48] for women although he was keenly aware of their imperfections and his description of them — in

---

[44] His opus magnum is *The Song of Bernadette*. His best known novel, *The Forty Days on the Musa Dagh,* deals with the massacre of the Armenians by the Young Turks. Kafka disliked and envied him: diary entry of 18 December 1911 [K-DE, p. 141].

[45] In 1903, Kafka was introduced to this circle by Oskar Pollak; they often met in Café Louvre: K-TT, p. 53.

[46] Letters to a Viennese girl (written from 1907 to 1909; K-LF 27–52) whom Kafka had met when she came over to meet her family in Triesch, indicate that they were never engaged; and see his diary entry of 12 January 2014, indicating that he noticed keenly good-looking waitresses in cafés: K-DE, p. 252; and see his diary entries of 10 April, 1922, K-DE, p. 413 and of July 1916, K-DEB, p. 421 (talking about early experiences); see also K-TT, p. 64, indicating that Kafka had an affair as early as 1905.

[47] *Die Abweisung*, probably written in 1908 [K-GW, p. 25]. And see his observations about women's education and emancipation: K-DEB, p. 143 (entry undated but probably from December 1911).

[48] See diary entry of 2 October 1911 [K-DEB, p. 27]. His first experience (with a salesgirl) was probably in July 1903: K-TT, p. 55; as from July 1907, he had a lengthy affair with Hedwig Weiler: K-TT, p. 73, 74.

his letters and writings — is usually unflattering.[49] He frequented brothels,[50] had numerous affairs but, at the same time, had reservations about lasting relationships and settling down.[51]

Whilst he bemoans a bachelor's loneliness and isolation, he tells us, in one of his first published works: "That's how it will be, except that in reality both today and later on, he [the bachelor] remains independent in his own body and head...."[52] This passage, as well as Kafka's conduct over the years, confirms that he had difficulties in committing himself to wedlock, in which a wife would become part of his inner life and aspirations.[53]

Kafka was engaged four times. In 1912 he met Felice Bauer, a relative of Max Brod [diary entry of 20 August 1912, K-DE, p. 207]. Despite finding her plain, he dated her.[54] A day was set for the formal engagement

---

[49] See S. Friedländer, *Franz Kafka* (Munich, 2012), pp. 109 et seq. [The English version is: *Franz Kafka: The Poet of Shame and Guilt* (2012)]; the author also discusses the issue of bisexuality. In a diary entry of 14 August, 1913, Kafka writes: "Coitus as punishment of the happiness of being together" [K-DEB, p. 301].

[50] See, e.g., his diary entries of 8 October 1911 [K-DE, p. 72]; and of 11 April 1922, [K-DEB, p. 489].

[51] And see his letter to Milena, of 8/9 August 1920 [K-LM, p. 151], in which he described his first sexual experience (with a salesgirl) and suggested that sex and lust are "disgusting".

[52] My own translation of *Der Kaufmann. Cf.* K-GW, p. 20 and the standard rendering: K-EST, 12–13. A similar message emerges from *Blumfeld, an Elderly Bachelor* [K-EST, p/ 342; see also diary entries of 14 November 1911, K-DE, p. 117, and of 27 December 1911, K-DE, p. 155]. In an entry of 9 October 1913, he wrote that if he ever reached the age of 40, he would marry an "old maid": K-TT, p. 134.

[53] In a chat with Milena, on 8 or 9 August, 1920, he suggested that sex and passion were "unclean" [K-TT, p. 467].

[54] For doubts respecting his love for Felice, see diary entry of 24 January, 1915 [K-DE, p. 328].

ceremony, which was to take place in Berlin.[55] In a diary entry of 8 March 1914, he observes: "I couldn't marry then; everything in me revolted against it, much as I always loved F.[56] It was chiefly concern over my literary work that prevented me, for I thought marriage would jeopardise it" [K-DE, p. 262; K-DEB, pp. 264–265]. Eventually, after acrimonious outbursts [diary entry of 23 July 1914: K-DE, p. 239; K-DG, pp. 309–310], she decided not to go ahead.[57]

Even thereafter, Kafka continued to write to her. They were re-engaged[58] but, in 1917, when Kafka was diagnosed as having succumbed to tuberculosis, their ways parted.[59] Kafka's letters suggest that, basically, he wanted to settle down and build up a family.[60] Felice was keen, although it is gleaned from Kafka's numerous letters to her that she was not deeply in love with him. Eventually, she married an

---

[55] Felice's father expressed his agreement to the match on 27 August 1913: K-TT, p. 238.

[56] Kafka's love of Felice has been questioned: S. Friedländer, op. cit., ante n. 49, pp. 109 et seq. Kafka's doubts are already reflected in a diary entries of 13 August 1913 [K-DEB, pp. 300–301], of 15 October 1914 [K-DE, p. 314], and of 24 January 1915 [K-DE, 329]; and see letter to Max Brod of 12–16 July 1916 [K-LFR, p. 117].

[57] An entry of 13 August 1913 [K-DE, p. 227] indicates that Kafka suffered badly when the engagement was in jeopardy. But note that, when one of Felice's girlfriends tried to help patch up, Kafka saw her home and might have had an encounter with her: K-DE, p. 239; K-DG, p. 309. As to his reaction when the engagement was terminated, see diary entry of 23 July, 1914 [K-DEB, p. 346 and K-DE, p. 293–294]. Still, in a letter of 18 January 1916 [K-TT, p. 322], he told her that he intended to move to Berlin after the end of the First World War.

[58] In July 1916; see his letter to Max Brod of 12–14 July 1916: K-LF, 116–117. His parents even found a suitable flat: diary entry of 6 May 1914 [K-DE, p. 267]. But Kafka continued to have misgivings: diary entry of 6 July 1916 [K-DEB, p. 419].

[59] Kafka took her departure hard: K-NB, p. 34.

[60] On 5 September, 1917, he asked Max Brod not to mention the diagnosis to the parents: K-TT, p. 375.

investment banker. When she faced financial reverses after having moved to the United States, she sold Kafka's letters to a publishing house.

In 1919 Kafka ignored his parents' disapproval, based on the lower status of the intended bride's family, and proposed to marry Julie Wohryzek, the daughter of a Jewish shoemaker. Julie was a vivacious and attractive woman. She had been engaged previously but her fiancé was killed in the First World War. She had met Kafka in Zürau and the two saw each other regularly. Kafka cancelled the engagement after the date for a wedding had already been fixed.[61] Thereafter, she continued to live with him for a while in Prague; but the relationship came to its end when, in 1920, he met Milena Jesenskā.

Milena was the wife of one of Kafka's acquaintances. Initially, she proposed to translate one of his stories to Czech; before long, their relationship developed into an affair. Kafka's closeness to her becomes clear from the voluminous letters[62] he wrote her and from his having given her — as parting gift when she decided to discontinue the relationship — his notebooks.[63] She explained the breach by advising that she had not got over her love for her estranged husband.[64]

Kafka's last association was with Dora Diamant, the daughter of a Polish Rabbi. The two met in 1923 in Hebrew classes Kafka attended

---

[61] See Kafka's letter to Julie's sister of 24 November 1919 [K-LF, pp. 215–220 (highly apologetic)]; as regards his only letter to Julie, see K-99, p. 69.

[62] The tone of their friendship is manifest by Kafka's form of address. In the early letters he addressed her formally (as "*Sie*"). Later on, he switched to informality (addressing her as "*Du*") and later still reverted to formality. Milena kept Kafka's letters.

[63] Diary entry of 15 October 1921 [K-DE, p. 392]. See also diary entry of 1 December 1921 [K-DE, p/ 397, indicating that Milena visited him during his period of illness]. And see her obituary: K-99, p. 279.

[64] She told him of her decision on 4 July 1920 [K-TT, p. 456].

at the time. Max Brod writes: "Franz came back from his summer holidays [having met Dora] full of high courage. His decision [was] to cut all ties [with his employers], get to Berlin, and live with Dora" [K-MBB, p. 197]. It would appear that these were the happiest days of Kafka's life. They stayed together for a while in Berlin but, due to the deterioration in his health, he had to move to a sanatorium.[65] Dora looked after him during the final days of his illness and wrote an obituary. Marriage was ruled out by Kafka's health and also because Dora's father opposed the match.[66]

Kafka remained in the service of AUVA until 1922. However, he took an extended period of leave in 1917, following two haemorrhages,[67] and spent most of it in Zürau, where one of his sisters — Ottla — managed a farm.[68] He liked the place and felt at home [K-LF, p. 137]. Whilst there, he composed aphorisms. He also set out his object in life: "I am not actually striving to be a good human being ... but rather quite the opposite, [my aim is] to survey the whole human and animal community, to recognise their fundamental predilections, desires, moral ideals, to trace them back to simple rules and to adapt myself to them ... so that I might carry out the vulgarities residing in me openly, before the eyes of all" [K-DEB, p. 446]. Readers of Kafka's works have to judge whether or not he achieved this object.

---

[65] Dora kept a diary in which she related the story of Kafka comforting a little girl who had lost her doll. The anecdote has not been verified; see K-99, pp. 193–194.

[66] It has been suggested that Kafka may have been a repressed homosexual: J. Hawes, *Excavating Kafka* (London, 2010); S. Friedländer, op. cit. n. 49 ante, Chap. 4. The point is dubious.

[67] In August, 1907; see his diary entry of 15 September, 1907 [K-DEB, p. 441 and n. 1025].

[68] He moved to the farm on 15 September, 1917: K-TT, p. 377.

Felice Bauer and Max Brod visited him during his months in Zürau. Kafka's health kept deteriorating even after his days in Zürau. In a diary entry of 16 January 1922 he tells us that he "suffered something very like a [nervous] breakdown" [K-DE, p. 398].

At the end of the First World War, the Habsburg Empire collapsed and Bohemia became part of Czechoslovakia. Thereupon, Czech replaced German as the official language. From then on, it was used by all government departments and bodies. As Kafka was proficient in the tongue, his services became of major importance. Still, his health kept declining and in 1922 he finally opted for full retirement. All the same, he made a last effort to recuperate. In the company of a physician, he spent a few weeks in Spindlermüle, in the Czech mountains. During his stay there he commenced the writing of his last unfinished novel: *Das Schloss* [*The Castle*].

Kafka was badly affected by the inflation of that period. Its severity is vividly described by Erich Maria Remarque in *The Black Obelisk* and *Der Weg Zurück* [*The Way Back*]. Kafka's pension, which was not index-tied, failed to provide adequate means for livelihood. He augmented his income with some royalties but, even so, needed the support of friends and parents.

In 1924 Kafka died of tuberculosis, which spread into his larynx and made the taking of food extremely difficult. He was but 41 years old and had not attained any recognition or fame. His most popular publication was *The Metamorphosis*. His last letter was written to his father on 2 June 1924 [K-TT, p. 577]. He died on the very next day [id.]

Kafka's name was saved from obscurity by the efforts of Max Brod,[69] whom Kafka constituted his executor. Although Kafka did not leave a

---

[69] Max Brod's writings, especially *Reubeni,* display a deep interest in and a commitment to Judaism.

formal testament, Brod found a note in which Kafka instructed him to burn his unpublished writings. Kafka had made the same request in an earlier encounter whereupon Brod told him that, if this were his wish, he ought to appoint someone else as executor. In tandem with this sentiment, Brod published Kafka's three novels within three years of his friend's demise. He also retained Kafka's other papers and even took them with him when he escaped to Palestine in 1939. Kafka's fame and renown is due to Brod's devotion. Two Nobel Laureates — Thomas Mann and Hermann Hesse — assisted by lauding Kafka's writings. The breakthrough came with the publication in 1931 of *The Great Wall of China* by Gustav Kiepenheuer Verlag in Berlin. It was reprinted in 1948, that is, after the end of the Second World War.

As already noted, Kafka's writings ought to be divided into those published during his lifetime and those that saw light posthumously. During his life Kafka did not publish any novel, although the draft of *Der Proceß* was practically complete.

Years earlier, Max Brod had encouraged his friend to publish a collection of short stories entitled *Meditation*. This appeared in 1913. In the same year, Kafka published two works. The first is *The Judgment* ["*Das Urteil*"], which he had written during the previous year in a single session that took place shortly after he had met Felice Bauer [diary entry of 23 September, 1912, K-DE, p. 212; and see K-DE, pp. 214–215, explaining the tome]; the second was *The Stoker*,[70] re-published posthumously as the first chapter of his *Amerika*.

The three years following 1912 were a highlight in Kafka's literary life. The novella, *The Metamorphosis* [*Die Verwandlung*] was written

---

[70] Kafka was pleased with it and read it out to his parents: diary entry of 24 May, 1913 [K-ED, p. 221].

during this period and saw light in 1915/[71] *In the Penal Colony* (discussed subsequently) was published in 1919 but was written on 5 October 1914; and Kafka read it to friends years before it saw light [K-TT, pp. 292, 295].

In December 1919, Kafka published another collection of short stories, entitled *The Country Doctor*. It included *Vor dem Gesetz* (*"Before the Law"*), later incorporated in Chapter 9 of *The Trial* (*Der Prozeß*). By then, Kafka was a sick man. His last publication, *A Hunger Artist,* including *Josefine, die Sängerin oder Das Volk der Mäuse*, appeared in 1924. Kafka had corrected the proofs but the tome appeared shortly after his death. An advance on the royalties was needed to settle the bills of the sanatorium in which he stayed at that time: Kierling on the outskirts of Vienna.

Kafka's three novels, *Amerika, The Trial* [*Der Proceß*] and *The Castle* [*Das Schloss*], as well as his *Letter to Father*, collections of his letters, diaries, short stories and aphorisms were published over and over again during the next three decades. Wilma and Edwin Muir's translations into English are outstanding and made Kafka's work available to monolingual readers in North America and the United Kingdom. In due course Kafka became a well-established and highly regarded writer. His works have been translated into many languages.[72]

Kafka was not a steady performer. Frequently, he started work on an opus, turned to another, returned to the first after a long break and

---

[71] An entry of 19 January 1914 [K-DE, p. 253] suggests that Kafka had misgivings about the ending.

[72] My initial reading of his works took place during my youth in Tel Aviv, where translations of his works into Hebrew were abundant. My appreciation of the corpus increased when I obtained his originals.

left the work in the form of an incomplete draft. *Beschreibung eines Kampfes* [K-GW, pp. 215 et. seq., translated as "*Description of a Struggle*": K-EST, pp. 253 et. seq.] is a case in point. Kafka started work on it in 1904 and came back to it from time to time until 1909. He then abandoned it and gave the rough draft to Max Brod. Another example is the novel *Amerika*. Kafka commenced work on it in 1911[73] but turned to other works after completing Chapter 8 in 1914.

As already mentioned, Kafka regarded writing to be his real vocation. He was a perfectionist. Works that appeared during his lifetime are meticulously fine-tuned and copy-edited. Although the text may be subject to varying interpretations, it is clear and can be read in one breath. This is not so in the case of some of the works published posthumously.[74] An assessment of his writings is undertaken subsequently. Before turning to it, it is necessary to examine his approach to Judaism.

III. Kafka's Outlook on Judaism

Antisemitism was prevalent all over 19th century Europe. Prague was no exception. An eruption of nationalism of Czech residents in 1894 which, ostensibly, was an uprising against the German population (and Habsburg supremacy) turned into a pogrom.[75] On a subsequent occasion, one of Kafka's friends, Oskar Baum, was hit by a stone and blinded. A few years later, when Hermann's Czech employees resigned en masse,

---

[73] Kafka published its first chapter as a short story, entitled *Der Heizer* ["*The Stoker*"] in 1913.

[74] A diary entry of 11 March 1912 affirms that Kafka "burned many old disgusting papers" [K-DEB, p. 209; K-TT, p. 154].

[75] Kafka was aware of the pogrom in Galicia of 1906: K-DEB, p. 409.

Franz talked them into resuming their posts.[76] Kafka was keenly aware of being a member of a minority. Whether his status affected his writing is disputed. The question is discussed in detail by Ritchie Robertson [K-BR, Cap. 1] and Reiner Stach [K-RSFJ, pp. 166 et seq.].[77]

Kafka's Jewish home was secular. In his *Letter to Father* [composed in November 1919: K-TT, p. 437; K-GW, pp. 459 et seq.], he complains that he was not given a traditional Jewish upbringing. He points out that his father went to the synagogue just about four times a year, but even on these occasions remained aloof. He adds that the traditional Passover Feast — the *Seder* — was perfunctory and, in effect, devoid of meaning; and that his Bar Mitzva – which encompassed the reading out in the synagogue of a *Parasha* (applicable passage of the Old Testament) — involved the learning of the text by heart. He feared this public performance, but it did not bring him close to the source [K-GW, pp. 484–486].

In an entry of 11 October 1911, Kafka tells us that he felt bewildered when attending synagogue on Yom Kippur (the Day of Atonement) and explains that there was a "[s]uppressed murmur of the stock exchange" [K-DE, p. 59]. He adds that he "was stirred more deeply by Judaism" in an Eastern European synagogue [id].[78]

---

[76] As regards the trip he took in order to talk to two of them, see: K-TT, p. 135; K-DE, p. 78.

[77] See also K. Wagenbach, *Kafkas Prag — Ein Reiselesebuch* (Berlin, 2022{?}), esp. p. 9.

[78] Kafka accompanied Max Brod to the synagogue on New Year Day in 1909: K-RT, p. 95. His orientation did not change. However, he noted that in "the Pinkas Synagogue [in the old Jewish quarter of Prague] I was seized incomparably more powerfully by Judaism" [diary entry of 1 October, 1911: K-DEB, p. 24]. And see "In unser Synaggoge," Franz Kafka, *Die Erzählungen und andere ausgewähle Prosa* (Frankfurt a.m., 2024), pp. 370–373. But note that occasionally, he also attended church services: K-TT, p. 164. In a letter to Felice, of 11 October 1916 [K-LF, p. 520] he mentioned that he found the Jewish New Year festival meaningless.

The contrast between secular Jews in Prague and East European Jewry is echoed in Kafka's description of two ceremonies. On 24 December 1911, his nephew was circumcised in a secular ceremony at the parents' home. Kafka tells us that "those present ... spent the time in dreams or boredom with a complete lack of understanding of the [*moule's* assistant] prayer". On the very next day he describes the "Kabbalistic" nature of circumcision in Russia [K-DE, pp. 147, 151]. The latter, he explains, leaves a deep impression; the former is ritualistic. Kafka was also impressed with the ritual bath — the *Mikveh* — of East European Jews [diary entry of 27 October 1911, K-ED, p. 91; and see K-DEB, p. 103 (regarding purifying by water)].

Kafka showed interest in Judaism as of 1911 and, as from July 1912, kept reading the Bible from time to time [K-TT, p. 163]. Apart from attending the Yiddish theatre and his long-term friendship with the actor Löwy, he read about Hasidic culture and its history.[79] He also became familiar with the studying in Yeshivas [K-DEB, pp. 183–184][80] and started to learn Hebrew.[81] Of particular interest is his analysis of the Enlightenment (the "*Haskalah*"). He tells us that the "*Maskilim*" wish to promote Hebrew but that, to "spread its ideas the Haskalah must use Yiddish ..., much as its hates the latter..." [K-DE, p. 174].

All in all, though, Kafka's interest vanished. On 6 January 1912 [K-ED, p. 167] he states: "My receptivity to the Jewishness in these [Yiddish] plays deserts me because they are too monotonous and

---

[79] See his detailed discussion of Hasidim in his entry of 6 October 1915 [K-ED, pp. 348–349; K-DEB, p. 405]. Kafka also read Grätz's history of the Jews: diary entry of 1 October 1911 [K-DEB, p. 109].

[80] And note that he attended lectures on the *Mishna*: K-DEB, p. 409.

[81] As from 12 July 1912, he read the Bible regularly: K-TT, p. 163; K-DEB, p. 398. On 16 November 1915 he referred to the Book of Judges. He started learning Hebrew again in May 1917: K-TT, p. 365.

degenerate into wailing that prides itself on isolated, violent outbursts. When I saw the first plays it was possible for me to think that I had come upon a Judaism on which the beginning of my own rested, a Judaism that was developing in my direction and so would enlighten and carry me farther along in my clumsy Judaism; instead it moves farther away from me the more I hear of it."

Two years later, on 8 January 1914, he summarises his conclusion about Judaism as a whole: "What have I in common with Jews? I have hardly anything in common with myself and should stand very quietly in a corner, content that I can breathe" [K-DE, p. 252].[82] The emerging picture is clear: a highly introverted man,[83] who does not find salvation in his people's culture and religion. It is thus not surprising that he declined to become an editorial member of Martin Buber's periodical (*Der Jude*).[84]

This conclusion is not shattered by Kafka's aphorisms. In one of his notebooks he states: "Man cannot live without a permanent trust in something indestructible in himself, though both the indestructible element and the trust may remain permanently hidden from him. One of the ways in which this hiddenness can express itself is through faith in a personal god" [K-NB, p. 29]. In the very same notebook, he avers: "The messiah will come only when he is no longer necessary, he will

---

[82] And note that even in earlier years, he was not attracted to Judaism. As early as 1900, he quarreled about the subject with Hugo Bergmann, expressing atheistic views: K-TT, p. 43. For a different view see, Liska, op. cit. n. 32 ante, pp. 15 et seq. But see K-DEB, p. 172, indicating that Kafka had doubts about religion as a whole. And see his comment in a diary entry of 13 March 1922, saying that a Purim celebration did not give him a Jewish feeling: K-TT, p. 518.

[83] And see his diary entries for 22 October 1913 [K-DE, 235]; and 16 September 1916 [K-DE, p. 343].

[84] Letter to Martin Buber of 29 November 1915 [K-LFR, p. 115; K-TT, p. 319].

come only one day after his arrival, he will not come on the last day, but on the last day of all" [ibid., p. 28].[85] The picture that emerges is that of a religiously inclined person who is not committed to a given faith. In essence, Kafka was a highly spiritual man but religiously undecided.[86] An entry in his diary, of 2 November, 1914 [K-DEB, p. 333], indicates that he doubted miracles.

This was, actually, the position of secular Central European Diaspora Jews, who had little in common with the traditionally inclined Jewry of Eastern Europe. Kafka's veneration of gentile authors such as Goethe and Fyodor Dostoevsky suggests that he put emphasis on orientation rather than on religion.

Kafka appreciated how the Enlightenment [*Haskalah*] led to Zionism [K-DEB, p. 188] but his approach to the movement was distant. As early as 1902 he made negative comments about it to his friend, Hugo Bergmann, who was an ardent Zionist and, actually, migrated to Palestine [K-TT, p. 48; K-DEB, p. 229].[87] From time to time, Kafka attended functions dealing with Zionism.[88] But he was not attracted to it. In a letter to a friend of 11 June 1914, he expresses his aversion to it [K-TT, p. 279]. When Bergmann promoted Zionism in his Bar-Kochba circle, Kafka did not join. In a letter to Felice of 12 September 1916 he

---

[85] The influence of Dostoevsky's Grand Inquisitor passage in *The Brothers Karamazov* is clear. And see Kafka's discussion of the devil: K-DEB, p.223. For another reference to religion, see diary entry of 9 August 1917 [K-DEB, p. 433]; on 14 July 1912, he attended a church service: K-TT, p. 164.

[86] And note that he said: "Christ suffered for mankind, but mankind suffered for Christ": February 1917 [K-NB, p. 49].

[87] He expressed disagreement with Bergman's Zionist orientations as early as 1900: K-TT, p. 43 and 1902; ibid. p. 48. But note that when Kafka met Felice, he discussed a plan to visit Palestine: K-TT, p. 166.

[88] E.g., on 23 February 1912 [K-TT, p. 152; D-DEB, p. 198].

writes: "I am not a Zionist" [K-LE, p. 501]. Kafka remained largely unaware of the initiatives taken by Theodor Herzl.[89] His orientation is neatly summarised by Ritchie Robertson: "[Kafka] always remained on the sideline of the movement and shunned practical involvement with it, however great his theoretical sympathy became" [K-RB, p. 143].[90]

Kafka studied Hebrew when Pua Ben Tovim came to Prague for a period of about two years for advanced studies. Kafka acquired considerable proficiency in the language[91] and thought of migrating to Palestine. In 1923, he arranged to accompany Bergmann's wife on her way back home to Jerusalem; but, at the last moment, he pulled out.[92] As Kafka was, at that time, a very sick man, his decision is understandable.

Kafka and other Jews in Prague were fortunate to obtain accomplished tuition in Hebrew. Whilst Hebrew became a literary (secular) language in the 19th century, its revival as a spoken means of communication involved a slow process.

The first school employing Hebrew as a teaching language was opened in Rishon LeZion in 1896; but Hebrew was not yet widely spoken. During the periods of the First and Second Ascents [*Aliyot*, viz. streams of migrants], many Jewish migrants continued to use their mother tongues. It was only after General Allenby conquered Palestine in 1917 that the country experienced massive migration — the Third Ascent — from Eastern Europe. The revival of Hebrew as a modern spoken language was promoted by Eliezer Ben-Yehuda's reforms, mainly after 1922.

---

[89] K-RSFJ, pp. 288 et seq.

[90] But note that from time to time he attended synagogue services. See, e.g., K-TT, p. 133 and also church services: K-TT, p. 164. For his negative reaction to Zionism, see his letter to Grete Bloch of 11 June 1914 [K-TT, p. 279].

[91] For a facsimile of Kafka's letter to Pua in Hebrew, see K-99, pp. 130–131.

[92] K-RSJL, pp. 533 et seq.

By then, Britain obtained its mandate over Palestine and, in due course, Hebrew became one of the recognised languages of the country.

Pua Ben Tovim came from one of the Hebrew-speaking homes of Palestine. During her lifetime Hebrew became the common language of the Jewish *Yishuv* (settlement) in Palestine. Modern Hebrew literature developed mainly after the foundation of Israel in 1948.[93]

To sum up, it would be unrealistic to regard Kafka a committed Zionist or an ardent Jew.

IV. Highlights of Kafka's Era

The first two decades of the 20th century saw major developments.[94] In 1900, Max Planck formulated the quantum theory and five years later, Albert Einstein came up with the theory of special relativity. Sigmund Freud's *The Interpretation of Dreams* appeared at the turn of the century. In 1901, Guglielmo Marconi set up the first radio communication between the United States and Europe. Commercially, his radio became available in the course of that decade.

Whilst Alexander Bell patented the telephone in 1876, the network was established only by the beginning of the 20th century. So did the cinema. The first "talking" film — a film incorporating synchronised soundtracks and dialogue — appeared in 1927. The silent film was, however, commonplace before then. Charlie Chaplin was scouted for the film industry in the United States in 1919. By then, he had become

---

[93] It grieves me to mention that although poetry of Bialik and Tchernichovsky were taught, our generation had to read works by Lea Porath, Nathan Alterman and Jonathan Ratosh privately.

[94] The main attainments are set out by Josipovici, in a fine chronology included in the English edition of Kafka's Collected Stories [K-EST, pp. xlii et seq.].

well-known. Early Sherlock Holmes films were in circulation from the start of the 20th century.

An important development of the period was the replacement of older propelling means by electricity. Whilst the "war of the currents" was won by Nikola Tesla and Westinghouse in 1893, the spread of the system was gradual. Similarly, in 1879, Thomas Edison patented the light bulb, but its spread to everyday use was slow. Electrical light was available in most urban settlements (including Prague) by the turn of the century, but it had not yet been available in rural communities.

The surge of motorcars — invented towards the end of the 19th century but popularised only at the beginning of the 20th — was yet another significant advance. The Ford Motor Company was founded in 1903 and its famous Model T car came onto the market in 1908. The trams in Prague were electrically propelled from 1891. By the turn of the century, they were fully operative. Other innovations included the gramophone and the rise of aviation. The Wright brothers' first flight took place in 1903.

There were also political developments. The English Labour Party was founded in 1900. In Europe, Germany maintained its military and political superiority, notwithstanding Otto von Bismarck's death in 1898. The first Russian Revolution, including "Red Sunday" in St. Petersburg, took place in 1905. So did the sad "Battleship Potemkin saga", involving a sailors' mutiny. In contrast to the weakening of Czarist Russia, the Habsburg Empire remained in force. Actually, in 1908, it annexed Bosnia and Herzegovina. All the same, sentiments for social reform were on the increase.

Bohemia — still part of the Austro-Hungarian Empire — underwent changes. In 1897, the Badeni Language Decrees sought to give Czech the status of an "internal official language". Opposition from the German minority prevented implementation. Eventually, a watered-down version thereof was adopted. The Young Czech Movement was reorganised by Karel Kramāf. Czech nationalism was on the rise.

Literature, too, was developing rapidly. For instance, H.G. Wells published *The Time Machine* in 1895. Oscar Wilde and Henrik Ibsen died shortly after the turn of the century. Romain Rolland, an ardent pacifist, started publishing in 1902. Joseph Conrad's *Lord Jim* appeared in 1900 and James Joyce's *Dubliners* saw light in 1914. Chekhov, Gorky, Thomas Mann, Pirandello, Rilke, George Barnard Shaw and Zola had established themselves.

Some leading plays were performed in Prague. Kafka often attended them.[95] His favourite authors, Fyodor Dostoevsky and Wolfgang von Goethe, belonged to previous centuries; but they had become household names and were celebrated.

These early decades of the 20th century were also significant for the growth of Zionism. Two affairs turned Jews to it. The first was the shameful Dreyfus affair, which involved the conviction of a Jewish senior French military officer on drummed up espionage charges. The absurdity thereof was pointed out in Émile Zola's famous *J'Accuse...!* in 1999. Although the conviction was later on quashed and Dreyfus was reinstated, the ensuing message was clear: Jews were aliens. Many felt the need to find a home of their own. Two assimilated German speaking Jews — Theodor Herzl and Max Nordau — became leaders of the movement.

The second affair was the Kishinev slaughter of 1903. This pogrom and the policy of Czarist Russia, as well as the rise of antisemitism in

---

[95] On 12 December 1911, for instance, he attended a play by Gerhart Hauptmann: K-TT, p. 143.

Central Europe, convinced many Jews of the need to find a new solution. The first Zionist Congress took place in Basel in 1897, and the movement gained strength at the beginning of the 20th century. Notably, Tel Aviv — an important centre of Jews in Palestine — was founded in 1909.

The evolutionary processes of the turn of the 20th century and the fermenting sociological drives were halted by the outbreak of the First World War (WWI). The event triggering it was the assassination of Archduke Franz Ferdinand, the successor to the Habsburg throne, on 28 June 1914 in Sarajevo by a Serbian fanatic.[96] Austria declared war on Serbia one month later.[97] The fateful WWI, which engulfed many countries in both the Eastern and the Western world, came to an end after the United States stepped in on the side of the Allies in 1917. The fighting, largely carried out in the trenches, ended with the Armistice of 11 November 1918. The Treaty of Versailles, signed on 28 June 1919, imposed heavy sanctions on Germany.

One of the consequences of WWI was the collapse of empires. The Ottoman Empire lost a number of Balkan countries and, under the takeover by the Young Turks, became a republic. In parts of the Middle East, including Palestine (which used to be part of the Ottoman Empire), the British rose to power. The Balfour Declaration made in 1917, prior to General Allenby's conquest, laid the foundation for a Jewish home in the country. The Austro-Hungarian (Habsburg) Empire collapsed and was replaced by a number of independent countries. Austria was transformed into a small landlocked state, with its government in Vienna. The Czarist regime in Russia was superseded by the Bolsheviks.

---

[96] Kafka did not refer to the event in his diary. See K-TT, p. 281.
[97] Events not noted in Kafka's diary: K-TT, p. 286.

Bohemia, which was no longer a province of the once mighty empire, became part of the new state of Czechoslovakia. Prague continued to be the seat of the government. German, though, ceased to be the official language. Czech replaced it.

WWI had far-reaching economic consequences. Hyperinflation commenced shortly after the surviving soldiers returned home from the battlefronts. Many found resettlement difficult. The period is vividly described by Erich Maria Remarque. The war had led to the destruction of agriculture. Food became scarce and expensive. Black markets thrived all over Europe.

How far did these developments and tribulations affect Kafka? In this regard, it is important to draw a distinction between the man and his writings.

On the personal level, Kafka was affected by this period. As from his days as a teenager, he was keenly aware of leading cultural and sociological developments. He attended lectures (including one by Albert Einstein on 24 May 1911 [K-TT, p. 125]), read widely and, in general, had sympathy for the fermenting spirit of the period. By way of illustration, he took part in launching the asbestos factory already mentioned. In February 1913, he obtained information about parlography — a precursor to tape recorders and dictating machines — and acquired prospectuses concerning them [K-TT, p. 202].

Kafka was familiar with the views expressed by Edison about the acquisition of American know-how in Bohemia in consequence of the return home by Czech migrants [K-DEB, p. 124]. But he took the view that their influence involved a slow process. On 25 December 1911 [K-DE p. 148], he tells us that "many benefits of literature, the stirring of minds, the doctrine of national consciousness, [are] often unrealised in public life".

Maybe a Swan Song: A Second Trip Down Memory Lane

All in all, Kafka's approach to the innovations of the period is ambivalent. On 10 December 1913, he tells us that "[d]iscoveries have imposed themselves on people" [K-DEB, p. 319]. All the same, he used them. For instance, on 17 February 1910, he watched together with Max Brod *The White Slave,* one of the early full-length films [K-TT, p. 118]. Similarly, he made full use of telephones installed by his employers. But he knew that the spread of the new instrument was slow. For instance, in the first chapter of *The Castle,* K is surprised to discover that a telephone had already been installed in an inn of a village. Similarly, his character in *The Country Doctor* uses a cart pulled by horses and not an automobile.

Was Kafka's life flow interrupted, or affected, by the outbreak of WWI? The Austrian ultimatum to Serbia was delivered on 23 July 1914. Most observers saw the writing on the wall. Kafka, in contrast, was so absorbed in his involvement with Felice that he did not refer in his diary to the then impending doom. But he was affected by the enlistment in the army of his two brothers-in-law.

On 31 July 1914, he noted the general mobilisation and added: "I am little affected by all the misery and am firmer in my resolve [to remain alone] than ever. I shall have to spend my afternoons in the [asbestos] factory; I won't live at [my parents'] home, for [sister] Eli and the two children are moving in with us. But I will write in spite of everything, absolutely; it is my struggle for self-preservation" [K-DE, p. 300].

In August 1914, Kafka left his parents' home and moved to a place of his own [K-TT, p. 303]. As his employers considered his services vital, he was not enlisted. In his spare time, he attended patriotic propaganda functions. On 6 August 1914, he wrote: "These parades are one of the most disgusting accompaniments of the war" [K-ED, p. 302].

Kafka's Feet of Clay

Yet, he bemoaned the reverses of the Habsburg army [K-TT, p. 291; K-DEB, p. 286].

In 1915 some of Kafka's colleagues, both at the insurance company and at the factory, joined the army. Kafka's workload was thereby affected [K-DEB, p. 284]. He was aware of the stream of Jewish refugees escaping from Galicia and helped to accommodate them. At about the same time he had to decide whether or not to purchase war bonds. In this context, he sensed the effect of the war. He tells us: "I felt myself directly involved in the war ... But gradually my excitement underwent a transformation, my thought turning to writings" [diary entry of 5 November 1915, K-DE, p. 351].[98]

A four months' break in Kafka's diary suggests that he was fully occupied with his own problems and with writing. The ongoing war did not disrupt his daily activities. Then, on 11 May 1916, he felt the need to join the army [K-DE, p. 361; K-TT, p. 326]. However, his application to enlist was declined due to his deteriorating health. Later on, around July 1917, his sputum turned red. On 11 August, he had his first haemorrhage.

The most significant political development of the time was Tomáš Masaryk's Announcement on 27 November 1918 that Bohemia had become part of the newly founded Czech Republic, which constituted part of Yugoslavia. Antisemitic outbreaks took place a few days later [K-TT, p. 422]. Kafka was not affected. A subsequent antisemitic outburst in Munich [ibid., p. 448] is discussed by him in two letters of May 1920, written whilst recuperating in Meran. In the first, he made sarcastic comments about an editorial in a local newspaper, referring

---

[98] Note that Kafka had bemoaned Austria's defeat in battles: diary entry of 13 September 1914 [K-DE, p. 314].

to *The Protocols of the Elders of Zion*, and described the passages involved as "at once stupid and frightening" [K-LFR, p. 236].

In his second letter (to Max Brod), he wrote: "the Jews are not spoiling Germany's future, but it is possible to conceive of them as having spoiled Germany's present. From early on they have forced upon Germany things that she might have arrived at slowly and in her own way, but which she was opposed to because they stemmed from strangers. What a terribly barren preoccupation anti-Semitism is..." [id].

Obviously Kafka was aware of the wave of antisemitism.[99] His resistance, though, remained passive. He did not attend the Jewish National Congress held in Prague at the beginning of the next year [K-TT, p. 425].

Kafka continued in the employ of AUVA. On 19 December 1919, he was constituted a "Secretary": a promotion entailing a rise in his salary [K-TT, p. 439]. On 1 March 1920, he was issued a Czech passport, naming him "František Kafka". His orientation, though, was not thereby affected . Whilst he took out a subscription of a periodical devoted to the promotion of the Czech language and culture, he continued to write solely in German.

During this entire period Kafka did not make diary entries. Instead, he polished his Zürau Aphorisms and entered sayings in extra octavo notebooks. It will be recalled that this is also the period in which Kafka intensified his studies of Hebrew and befriended Dora Diamant. Notwithstanding his deteriorating health, it was a happy period in his

---

[99] A reminder for Kafka was the antisemitic manifestations that took place in March 1918, before the end of WWI: K-TT, p. 408; and in November 1920 [ibid., p. 478]. Kafka had doubts about intellectuals preaching antisemitism without hatred: diary entry of 16 June, 1922 [K-DE, p. 421–422].

life. The octavo notebooks confirm that he was meandering about life after death. At the same time, he did not commit himself to any given religion. This may have been his strength; or, perhaps, his weakness.

Did technological and political developments affect his writings? His style — and a model one at that — remained unchanged. The mastery discernible in his late works can already be seen in *The Aeroplanes at Brescia*. The theme, too, has remained basically the same. Kafka deals with the individual's plight at the hand of an entity or a group stronger than he. He also bemoans, years before George Orwell, the bureaucratic "red tape" encountered by members of the public.

His orientation remained unaltered in yet a further respect. His writings continued to address one and the same group. It may be objected that Kafka wrote only for himself. This plea — encountered in the case of many writers and other artists — must, however, be taken with a pinch of salt. Undoubtedly, some individuals write solely because they wish to get "things" off their chest. But once an author looks for a publisher, he (or she) manifests the wish to share the product with "others".

In some cases, these "others" are easy to define. By way of illustration, take the author of the Book of Deuteronomy. His words are directed at the Israelites. His objective is to induce them to obey divine law. Similarly, when Greek playwrights composed their masterpieces, they sought the approval of the audience entitled to determine the winner. Modern writers too select their audience. William Shakespeare sought to appeal to the patrons of the theatre. Charles Dickens addressed the reading population (basically the literate middle-class) of London.

Who then was the group addressed by Kafka? The answer is transparent: he read out some of his works, or parts thereof, to members of his inner circle, to friends and to family members. In addition, his letters to publishers, such as Kurt Wolff, indicated that he wanted to see his works in print. He hoped that they would appeal to their German-speaking, alphabetic readers. The fact that his writings have been savoured by a much wider group of readers — attained worldwide appeal — is a bonus. All the same, it is important to bear in mind that Kafka continued throughout his life to primarily address people who were able to read the original written by him in German.

V. Assessment of Kafka' Oeuvre: The Novels

As already mentioned, very few works of Kafka were published during his lifetime. Purists seek to confine their reading to these. In their opinion, Max Brod's posthumous publications involved a betrayal. The point is debatable but, as already noted, Max Brod felt entitled to publicise his late friend's works. Furthermore, it will be recalled that Kafka gave his extant notebooks — comprising *inter alia* his diaries — to Milena as a parting gift. He knew full well that she was engaged in promoting literary works. Their very friendship commenced when she offered to translate *The Stoker* into Czech. He ought to have realised that he gave her the ownership and full possession of the items gifted. He did not swear her to secrecy.

Even if these arguments were rejected by the purists, they ought to consider *Der Proceß* as part of Kafka's completed works. All that Max Brod had to do in respect of this outstanding work was copy-editing or, in other words, due diligence.

For those who feel free to read all of Kafka's writings, the oeuvre need be divided into three components: (i) the novels, (ii) shorter works, comprising novellas, short stories and tales, and (iii) parables and epigrams. All of them bear Kafka's kenmark: they are phantasmagoric and surreal. They are also imbued with the author's black — perhaps even macabre — humour.

Two of Kafka's novels remained incomplete. The first is *Amerika*, as the work was entitled when Max Brod facilitated its publication in 1927. Kafka called it *Der Verschollene* (*The Disappearing Man*). He started work on its second (extant) version on 26 September 1912 — amidst his first literary outbreak — and finished the first six chapters by that year's end [K-RSEJ, p. 192–193; K-TT, pp. 171, 178]. Later, he lost his enthusiasm for the novel.[100] On 9 March 1913, he told Felice in one of his letters that only the first part of the novel was good [K-LF, p. 218]. On 28 May 1913, Max Brod obtained the manuscript of the chapters completed by then [K-TT, p. 223]. Still, as gleaned from Kafka's diary, he continued to write fragments during 1914 [K-TT, pp. 273, 291] and on 6 July 1916, [K-DE, p. 364]. The last available chapter, dealing with the Oklahoma theatre, was written on 5 October 1914.

During this period, Kafka might have been satisfied with the work [T-KK, p. 311]. Subsequently, doubts crept in. In a diary entry of 8 August 1917, he observed that "[t]he Stoker {viz. Chap. 1 of *Amerika*} is a clear imitation of Dickens, the projected novel even more so" [K-DE, p. 388; K-DG, p. 411].[101] A few months later, after he had initially declined to give completed manuscripts of the work to Max Brod, he eventually delivered them [K-TT, pp. 400, 406].

---

[100] He stopped working on it on 24 January 1913: K-TT, p. 199.

[101] At one time Kafka considered the possibility of publishing it in a book entitled *The Sons*: letter to Kurt Wolf of 11 April 1913 [K-LFR, p. 96].

Amerika has been described as Kafka's most readable novel. It is, at the same time, difficult to discern its message. Further, whilst Dickens' novels are reader-friendly, *Amerika* is not.

The plot is simple. Karl Rossman, a 16-year-old Czech boy, is sent by his parents to America after having been seduced by the family's cook, who made herself pregnant by him. The parents' objective is to avoid the ensuing scandal and to obviate an action for alimony. Whilst proceeding to disembark in New York, Karl encounters the Stoker, who had been dismissed on drummed-up charges. Karl decides to plead the Stoker's case before the captain. In the latter's room he meets his uncle, who had migrated from Prague a few years earlier and had risen to the rank of a senator. The uncle recognises Karl and adopts him. Karl leaves the ship with his uncle, whilst the Stoker yields to his own inappropriate sentence. Later, the uncle banishes Karl when, notwithstanding the uncle's objection, Karl accepts an invitation extended by one of the uncle's friends.

Karl then befriends Robinson and Delamarche — European migrants who became tramps in New York — and, after falling out with them, accepts the post of a liftboy in a local hotel. He is dismissed after Robinson turns up drunk, and Karl puts him up in a dormitory. Thereafter Karl becomes the servant of Delamarche, who has become the kept man of a fading woman called Brunelda.[102] Karl attempts to escape Brunelda's flat but is prevented by force from departing and has to spend the night on a balcony. A student, who is studying throughout the night in the balcony of a building next door, advises Karl to stick to his post because jobs are hard to get [Kafka worked on this episode in August 1914: K-TT, p. 290].

---

[102] Kafka's sketch of 19 April 1916 may be of Brunelda and Delamarche [K-DE, p. 354].

In the last chapter of the novel [composed in October, 1914: K-TT, p. 292], Karl finds employment with the Oklahoma Theatre, which advertises its being able to find a job for everybody. This last chapter is unconnected with the earlier part of the novel. A reader may wonder how Karl managed to escape the snares of Delamarche and Brunelda and start a new life.

Dickens often portrayed vivid characters, like Sam Weller, the Artful Dodger and Miss Havisham's lawyer, Jaggers. The reader feels close to the heroes and celebrates their breakthroughs, for instance, David Copperfield's success or Oliver's salvation. Further, Dickens was a master narrator. Each of his books has a clear message; and he describes only venues known to him.

Yet another strength of Dickens is his ability to adjust to dialects. The Artful Dodger, Sam Weller and all lawyers portrayed by Dickens express themselves in a vocabulary suitable to them. This is not so in Kafka's writings. His characters — including the chambermaid Peppi in *Das Schloß* — express themselves in *Hochdeutsch* (viz., BBC German). In consequence, their addresses appear tedious.

Kafka had never set foot outside Europe. His descriptions of American places, such as New York, is based on seeing photographs and his characters are, predominantly, European migrants of the early 20th century. It is possible that his aim was to dispel the myth about America being the land of universal success. Karl's uncle, for instance, is fiscally successful but, at the same time, fails to develop as an individual. Robinson and Delamarche invoke the reader's disdain rather than endorsement.

Finally, it is difficult to comprehend Brunelda. Her vulgarity comes across but, in all other regards, she remains *sui generis*. She and the hotel's cook, who initially wished to protect Karl, do not come to life.

To sum up, Kafka's attempt to write a Dickensian novel was misguided. Dickens celebrated humanity. His art was to discern a positive streak even in negative characters. He believed in the eventual victory of the human spirit. Kafka emphasised weakness, dents in human nature and hopelessness. A novel, in which the hero manages to surmount obstacles put in his way, is alien to Kafka's agenda.[103] In a novel by Charles Dickens, Karl might have started a new life after joining the Oklahoma Theatre. A diary entry, quoted beneath, suggests that Kafka had a sad ending in mind even for this novel.

People may, nevertheless, read the novel in order to comprehend the position of migrants in America of the early 20th century. However, a more authentic picture thereof is provided by Upton Sinclair in *The Jungle* and in Elia Kazan's *America America* film. The immigration story of East European Jews is masterly narrated by Shalom Aleichem. Kafka is not a reliable authority in point.

Kafka's best achievement was the composition of *The Trial (Der Proceß)*. He started writing it on 15 August 1914 — after WWI had commenced [K-DE, p. 303] — and finished the first and the last chapter in the same year. Chapter 9 — the high point of the book — was composed in September 1914. The ending was clear in his mind. On 10 September 1915, he writes: "Rossman [of *Amerika*] and K. [viz. J.K. of *The Trial*] the innocent and the guilty, both executed without distinction in the end, the guilty one with a gentler hand, more pushed aside than struck down" [K-DE, pp. 343–344].

Max Brod had to cobble together the different parts of the novel. It is possible that *A Dream* [K-GW pp. 170–173; K-MTS,

---

[103] And note that a sad ending was contemplated by Kafka; diary entry of 10 September 1915, cited post.

pp. 222–224] — published in 1919[104] — was meant to be juxtaposed as a penultimate chapter. It would have been an excellent intermezzo between Jospeh K.'s talk with the chaplain, who indicated that the hero's case was indefensible, and the latter's execution.[105] Notably Kafka did, occasionally, publish parts of full-length works as short stories. *The Stoker* is a case in point. In respect of *The Trial*, Max Brod did not feel entitled to carry out the amalgamation of the extant manuscript and the short story.

The Trial's plot is straightforward. After waking up, Joseph K. (J.K.), who occupies a senior position in a bank, is told by two strangers that he is under arrest. They are wardens of the "authority" but have not been told the nature of the charge brought against him. The wardens' supervisor arrives in due course and, again, is unable to advise J.K. about the charge. J.K. protests his innocence and the unreal nature of the proceedings. To his surprise, he is told by the supervisor that he may proceed to his bank and that two of his subordinates have been summoned so as to accompany him.

After work, J.K. returns to his flat and attempts to find out further details about the case from his landlady, who had let the warders in. She is unable to give him any details but opines that the matter is not "serious".

---

[104] As one of the short stories in the book, entitled *The Country Doctor*. First published in an almanac issued by *Selbstwehr* (a Jewish periodical in Prague) on 15 December 1916, and in January 1917 in a periodical in Berlin.

[105] In a new edition of the book, i.e., S. Lück's translation of 2012, two extracts composed by Kafka are inserted between Chapter 9 and the final one. The first is entitled "Journey to His Mother" and the second "The House". Both refer to characters appearing in the original publication, but neither refers to the meeting with the chaplain. Max Brod's composition of the manuscript is preferable.

J.K. receives a message advising him to appear before the court on a Sunday. The case is set on this day so as not to interfere with J.K.'s work schedule. J.K. goes to the stipulated address. To his surprise, the court is situated in a dilapidated building. As the relevant room had not been properly described, he has difficulty finding it. When he finally arrives, the examining magistrate scolds him for being late but listens to his protestations of innocence. J.K. departs without having gleaned any further details respecting the charge.

A few days later, J.K.'s uncle calls on him at the bank. The uncle, who had heard about the case, persuades J.K. to employ an advocate. J.K. agrees and is taken to the advocate's premises.[106] The latter is bedridden. Still, he agrees to take on the case and implies that he will seek to sort it out through his contacts. The advocate's nurse seduces J.K., who leaves the premises without a clear understanding of what the advocate proposes to do.

Later still, one of the bank's clients advises J.K. to seek the help of an Italian, who turns out to be the court's painter. He, too, agrees to assist J.K., but makes it clear that a full acquittal is out of the question. J.K. may be granted a "temporary acquittal", which means that the case may be reopened at any time, or a postponement, which means that the case will drag on indefinitely. The painter, like the advocate, can assist by pulling strings. J.K., who considers all the relevant facts, concludes that the advocate is unable to tackle the case and dismisses him.

Next, J.K. is asked by his superior at the bank to take an important customer on a tour of the local cathedral. The customer does not turn up. Instead, J.K. has a conversation with a chaplain. The latter refers to an episode that had been narrated by Kafka in *Before the Law*, a short

---

[106] Chapter written on 1 September 1914: K-TT, p. 290.

story published in 1919 in *The Country Doctor* [referred to earlier].[107] The story tells of a gate, before which stands a doorkeeper. A peasant comes up and asks to be admitted. The doorkeeper says that he cannot "admit him just now" [K-MTS, p. 197]. The peasant waits in front of the door for years. When he is about to pass away, he sees that the doorkeeper intends to close the door. In reply to the dying peasant's question, the latter explains: "No one else could gain admission here, because entrance was intended for you alone."

In response to J.K.'s complaint that the doorkeeper had misled the peasant by not telling him this fact earlier on, the chaplain replies that the peasant had not asked the decisive question. J.K. finally accepts the hopelessness of his case.[108] An even clearer condemnation of the system is voiced in *The Problem of Our Laws* [K-EST, pp. 404–406; K-GW, pp. 371–372]. In it, Kafka states: "Our laws are not generally known; they are kept secret by the small group of nobles who rule us." In the last chapter of *The Trial*, J.K. is executed by the wardens. He shows no resistance. His last words are: "Like a dog."

The Trial has been given different constructions. Max Brod takes the view that Kafka searches for God. There is no doubt that Max Brod's views are of major importance. However, he was a deeply religious man and ardent Zionist. It is possible that he read his own views into his late friend's oeuvre.

A more widely held view is that *The Trial* voices Kafka's bitter complaint about the individual's struggle with the "establishment", such as the state or those in charge of it. J.K. is deemed guilty not in consequence of any offence or transgression on his part but simply

---

[107] First published in *Selbstwehr* (a Zionist periodical in Prague) on 7 September 1915.
[108] Chapter written on 15 September 1914: K-TT, p. 290.

because the state deems him so to be. His protestations of innocence are irrelevant; the very arrest establishes his guilt. This concept of guilt is also manifest in Kafka's *In the Penal Colony*, where the ageing officer takes the view that he is empowered to be both judge and executioner. The same notion is explored much later by George Orwell in *1984*.

In *The Trial* Kafka protests against the "red tape" or bureaucratic obstacles put in a citizen's way when he seeks "justice" or an answer to a query. The term "Kafkaesque", which has been accepted in modern English, is based on this understanding of the author's works.

It is believed that when Kafka wrote *The Trial*, he had in mind the complex and often ineffective system of the Habsburg Empire. Although this collapsed after WWI, it was in force at the time Kafka wrote this novel.

A remaining puzzle concerns publication. *The Trial*'s manuscript was practically complete well before Kafka succumbed to his last illness. Why, then, did he not seek to publish it during his lifetime? Max Brod did not tackle the question. Neither did later biographers.

Whilst there may not be a conclusive explanation, two possibilities need be considered. First, Kafka worked only when he was engulfed by the creative spirit. This induced him to pursue new texts. He may not have experienced an urge driving him back to this novel. Secondly, Kafka was a perfectionist. It is possible that he preferred to attend to the publication, and the editing, of shorter works. It is fortunate that the manuscript was preserved and that *The Trial* saw light.

Kafka's third novel — *The Castle* [*Das Schloß*] — remained unfinished. He started it on 27 January 1922, during a period of medical leave which he spent in Spiendelmühle (in Bohemia). About two months later, he read out part of it to Max Brod [K-TT, pp. 512, 518]. He continued to work on it but, on 6 May, expressed serious doubts about it [K-TT, p. 522]. Later in the month he turned to one of his short stories but also continued work on his novel, completing Chapter 16 [K-TT, p. 524]. However, on 11 September 1922, he told Max Brod: "I will evidently have to drop the Castle story forever, cannot pick up again" [K-LFR, p. 357; K-TT, p. 532]. In the event, he broke off in mid-sentence! His muse, though, had not left him. He completed the writing and the publication of other works.

Initially, Kafka wrote *The Castle* in first-person, but subsequently struck out the "I" and substituted "K." The plot is Kafkaesque. Late one evening a stranger — K. — arrives at the B Inn and introduces himself as the land surveyor.[109] There are at that time no vacant rooms, but the landlord allows him to sleep in the hall. K. is woken up by an official, who advises him that the village is governed by the Castle and that staying anywhere in the village is subject to permission thereof being granted. Initially, a telephone conversation with an authority of the Castle suggests that K. is an impostor. A subsequent call affirms that a land surveyor had been summoned.

The next morning, K. proceeds to the Castle but is worn out by the heaps of snow in his way. Eventually, he finds temporary refuge in a house but, after a short sleep, departs and is told that strangers are usually not wanted. On his way back to the B Inn, he encounters two assistants provided by the Castle. On arrival, a messenger delivers to K. a message from Klam — a senior officer of the Castle — in which K. is assured of Klam's goodwill, but is advised that K.'s immediate superior is the village's mayor.

---

[109] For a variant of this beginning, under which K.'s arrival is anticipated, see K-GW, pp. 965–966. The current text was preferred by Max Brod. As to fragments not included in the current text, see ibid., pp. 967 et seq.

Thinking that the messenger intends to return to the Castle, K. accompanies him. K. is surprised to discover that the messenger has walked back to his own home. Olga (the messenger's sister) takes K. to the H Inn — the second inn of the village — which is reserved for the temporary visits of the Castle's occupants. In this inn, the barmaid Frieda (who is that time Klam's mistress) allows K. to observe Klam through a peephole. Shortly thereafter she becomes K.'s mistress and, the next morning, returns with him to the B Inn. It then turns out that she is very friendly with the B Inn's landlady, who had — in the past — also been Klam's mistress.

K. reports to the mayor, who advises him that his appointment had been approved in consequence of a misunderstanding between different departments of the Castle. On the mayor's behest, K. is offered the post of a school janitor, which Frieda persuades him to accept.

Thereafter, the messenger delivers K. a letter from Klam, praising K.'s successful land surveying work as well as the assistants' contribution. Puzzled, K. continues with his attempts to encounter Klam but to no avail.

K. tries hard to carry out his duties at the school, notwithstanding the disdainful and unfriendly conduct of the principal and a female teacher. He resolves to stick it out until he manages to clarify the position.

Initially, Frieda is of great help but, due to insinuations voiced by the B Inn's landlady about K.'s motives, Frieda becomes disillusioned. She abandons K. after he goes to the messenger's house to see whether the latter carries any further messages.

In that house, Olga tells K. all about the family's misfortune. They have been shunned by all friends and acquaintances after Amelia,

Olga's sister, spurned the advances of a member of the Castle and had torn his letter of summons, delivered by a messenger, to pieces.

When K. finally departs after Olga finishes her lengthy discourse, K. encounters one of his assistants, who advises that he himself had by then won Frieda over. K., who is summoned to the H Inn by one of the officials of the Castle, goes over but, by error, enters into a room occupied by another official. The latter embarks on a lengthy and rambling monologue in which he talks about the grandiose nature of the officials. Thereafter, K. is summoned by the official who had subpoenaed him and who delivers the simple message to the effect that Frieda ought to be told to go back to the bar.

K. remains on the premises. This is forbidden, and he is forced back to the H Inn's bar, where he falls fast asleep. When he wakes up, Peppi — Frieda's temporary relief — embarks on a petty-minded and vindictive discourse about Frieda, whom she envies. Peppi, who has to return to her post as chambermaid, invites K. to secretly join her and her two friends in their tiny accommodation. At this stage, the H Inn's landlady enters the bar and, after some exchanges, tells K. she might invite him to come over to see her next new dress. At this very point Kafka stopped writing.

The Castle has been given many diverse interpretations. Max Brod sees in it a further religious[110] tome but, as already pointed out, his view is unsupportable. Another fancy construction is that Kafka predicted the Holocaust.

---

[110] Edwin Muir, one of the first translators of Kafka's oeuvre, has compared *The Castle* to John Bunyan's *The Pilgrim's Progress*: Franz Kafka, *The Castle* (London, 1947), pp. 6 et seq.

Yet another explanation is that Kafka voiced the sad fate of Jews in Central Europe. K. is an outsider who seeks to remain in residence in the village. Max Brod advised that Kafka had indicated that the proposed end was that K. received a communication in which the Castle advised that, although a formal permit of residence remained unavailable, his stay in the village would be tolerated. This, however, is exactly what the mayor had told K. in their interview. The mayor confirmed that nobody would dare to evict K.

Perhaps the best way is to emphasise what the novel seeks to tell, and to accept that the ending has remained a puzzle — a puzzle not sorted out by Kafka. His objective was to narrate the capriciousness and absurd conduct of "the elite". Support for this view can be found in *The Knock on the Manor Gate*, published posthumously [K-GW, pp. 350–351; K-EST, pp. 387–389]. In that story, the narrator and his sister were "passing the gate of a great house on [their] way home". The sister knocked on the gate or might have just made a knocking gesture. The villagers thereupon warned the narrator that they, or either of them, could be charged by the manor. The narrator convinces his sister to proceed to their home and change her dress. He himself is arrested and imprisoned without trial. Contextually, it is clear that the narrator and his sister are not ordinary members of the village. Nobody questions or protests against the arrest. Just as in *The Castle*, the village and the "manor" are separate entities. The narrator is dealt with so harshly because nobody would seek to aid a stranger.

Admittedly, this construction is debatable. A clear, incontestable point is that in this tome, just as in *Das Schloß*, Kafka mocked the establishment. The mayor's lengthy tirade, which seeks to justify the muddle caused by miscommunications between various departments of the Castle, is a sharp satire. So is the soliloquy of the official, whose room K. enters by error in the H Inn, in which this worthy sings the praise of the Castle's high officials. Of particular comic impact is his assertion that these officials are so exhausted by loafing about during the day that they have to deal with supplicants late at night.

Another absurdity is the veneration in which the villagers hold the Castle's inmates. Questioning their way is regarded as forbidden. Further, the women of the village regard it a privilege to be possessed by such officials and are proud to become mistresses and brag about it. Amelia's rejection of an official's summons is condemned in the village and her entire family is disgraced.

The irrationality of the villagers' veneration of the Castle's prowess is even more clearly demonstrated in *The Refusal*, published posthumously [K-GW, pp. 367–370].[111] The tax collector, who is the small village's undisputed principal (originally commissioned by the capital and its elite), is approached by the villagers with a request that taxes be waived for a one-year period because one district had been destroyed by fire. The delegation is so awed by the tax collector's presence that, initially, its spokesman finds it difficult to voice the petition. When it is rejected, the decision is not questioned by anybody except members of the younger generations. They, though, are a minority and, at that stage, of no significance.

Here, as in *Das Schloß*, the upper class is venerated by the population. It is feasible that Kafka was lampooning the bureaucratic machinery and the class structure of the Habsburg Empire. It is of course true that by the time Kafka started to write his last novel, this

---

[111] This story is not included in G-EST. It is published in F. Kafka (Glatzer, Ed.) *The Complete Short Stories* (New York, 1971), pp. 263 et seq. (trs. by T. & J. Stern). And see *The Lamps* [K-EST, pp. 390–391], showing how petitions for the improvement of working conditions were handled by AUVA.

empire had collapsed. He might, however, have satirised the society that was in power prior to the end of WWI.

Support for this view is to be found in the description of the Castle. Far from being described as a mighty palace, Kafka tells us: "It was neither an old stronghold nor a new mansion, but a rambling pile consisting of innumerable small buildings closely packed together and of one or two stories; if K. had not known that it was a castle he might have taken it for a little town."[112] It is possible that this was precisely its nature: a township up the hill occupied by the elite and out of bounds for the villagers.

Regrettably, Kafka does not refer to any women living in the Castle. It is possible that the H Inn's landlady was, originally, an occupant of this township. Still, we have no information about any other females originating from there. In particular, we are not told how they might have felt about their husbands' involvements with women of the village. For instance, did Klam have a wife and how did he explain to her his peccadillos at the H Inn?

It is possible that this lacuna is explainable by the statues of women in Europe during the early decades of the 20th century. Their emergence as enjoying rights and full equality eventuated later in that century. However, female authors — such as Virginia Woolf — left their marks during Kafka's lifetime. His approach is, arguably, old-fashioned.

VI. Assessment: Kafka's Shorter Works

Kafka's shorter literary compositions — novellas and short stories — comprise works published during his lifetime and many that saw light

---

[112] Cited from F. Kafka (trs. by the Muirs), *The Complete Novels* (2019; cited as K-CN), p. 449.

posthumously. The former have been the subject of acclaim. The style is uniform and cohesive. The stream of consciousness technique — immortalised by authors like Virginia Woolf and James Joyce — was not utilised by Kafka or, indeed, by any member of his circle.

Very little is known about Kafka's early writings. Some such publications, scattered amongst German language periodicals, are set out in some of his collected works [e.g., K-GW, pp. 215 et seq.] Most of the unpublished pieces, written before 1912 ,were destroyed by him.[113] Two, however, have survived.

One, "*Shamefaced Lanky and Impure in Heart*", was attached to a letter of 20 December 1902 to Oskar Pollak [K-LFR, pp. 6–7]. The second is *Description of a Struggle* [K-GW, pp. 233 et seq.; K-EST, pp. 253 et seq.]. Kafka worked on the latter intermittently from about 1904. He abandoned work in 1909 and gave the manuscript to Max Brod. An American author described these works as repellent. "Hard to understand" would be a more appropriate conclusion.

Kafka's first book was the collection entitled *Meditation* [K-EST, pp. 3 et seq.; *Betrachtung*: K-GW, pp. 13 et seq.]. It included 18 very short pieces, some of which had been published in a periodical entitled Hyperion. Max Brod encouraged Kafka to republish them as a book. They were accepted in 1912 by Rowohlt Verlag and saw light in 1913.[114]

The stories are, it is believed, poems set out in prose style. Each of them describes an internal struggle of the writer who pours out his emotive reaction. This is particularly evident in *The Wish to be a Red*

---

[113] See Kafka's letter of 6 December to Oskar Pollack, 1903 [K-LFR, p. 8], indicating that he aimed to send his friend a bundle with all his early writings for their destruction. And see K-TT, p. 113.

[114] Dedicated to Felice Bauer: K-TT, p. 188.

Indian [K-EST, p. 20], in which the writer expresses his desire to escape his current, dreary, existence and materialise in another realm.

Two further stories need to be dealt with. *The Tradesman* [*"Der Kaufman"* K-GW, pp. 201–202; K-EST, pp. 13–15] describes the unsatisfactory existence and inner turmoil of the narrator, who has gained wealth but has, nevertheless, remained lonely and unsatisfied. In *Unhappiness* [*"Unglücklichsein"* K-GW, 27–31; K-EST, pp. 20–24], the narrator has a chat with a female child ghost that appears late in the evening in his lonely room. The exchange of words leaves an impact on the narrator. He goes out but a neighbour, whom he meets on the stairs, convinces him that if one does not believe in ghosts, there is no need not to fear them. Thereupon, the narrator decides to return to his room and goes to bed. The encounters helped him to overcome his misery.

A reader may conclude from these pieces that the author enjoys his misery and loneliness. It is a state to which he is used to and which actually agrees with him. This view derives some support from *The Judgment (Das Urteil)*, composed in a single session proximate to his first engagement with Felice Bauer. About the composition, he tells us: "I wrote [the story] in one sitting on the night of 22–23 [September 1912] from ten o'clock at night to six o'clock in the morning. I was hardly able to pull my legs out from under the desk, they had got so stiff from writing. The fearful strain and joy ... as if I were advancing over water" [K-DE, p. 212]. He adds: "Only *this way* can writing be done, only with such coherence, with such a complete opening of the body and the soul" [ibid, p. 213].

In this story [K-GW, pp. 32 et seq.; K-EST, pp. 27 et seq.; K-MTS, pp. 35 et seq.], a young merchant, G, who has effectively been running the family's business since his mother's demise, writes a letter to a friend, who has settled in a foreign country, informing the friend of G's recent engagement. Having doubts about informing his friend about the development in G's life, G decides to discuss the letter with his father prior to dispatching it. The father, who has aged perceptively and has been in a foul mood ever since his wife's demise, accuses G of sidestepping him in the business and cheating him. He then discloses that he himself has an active correspondence with the friend, who reads the father's letters and discards G's. The father then avers that G is a disappointment and orders him to drown himself. G, who feels rejected by both his father and his friend and whose world collapses on him, jumps to his death off a bridge.

At the instigation of Max Brod, *The Judgment* was published in Kurt Wolff's *Arcadia* Yearbook in 1913. Kafka emphasised its autobiographical elements in a diary entry of 11 February 1913 [K-DE, pp. 214–215]. The construction of the story is debated. On plain reading, it tells the reader that not everybody who is regarded as a friend is really one. It also reflects Kafka's troubled relationship with his father and relates that once a person loses his illusions, his entire world collapses on him.

Kafka's writer's outburst or inspiration resulted also in the composition of his most famous novella: *The Metamorphosis* [K-EST, pp. 73 et seq.; K-MTS, pp. 85 et seq.; *Die Verwandlung*: K-GW, pp. 70 et seq.]. The idea of writing it came to Kafka on 17 November 1912 [K-TT, p. 182], during the period in which he was still working on *Amerika*. He read out parts of the novella to friends and family, whilst continuing to work on it during the next few weeks.[115] Although he submitted it for publication in March 1913 [K-TT, p. 207], it was not

---

[115] He completed it on 6 December 1912 [K-TT, p. 186], and read out the final part to Max Brod on 1 March 1913.

Maybe a Swan Song: A Second Trip Down Memory Lane

published until October 1915.[116] In a diary entry of 19 January 1914, Kafka expressed an antipathy to the story and doubts about the ending [K-DE, p. 254; K-TT, p. 254]. Later generations disagreed.

The first line of the work is famous: "As Gregor Samsa [G.S] awoke one morning from uneasy dreams, he found himself transformed in his bed into a gigantic insect" [K-EST, p. 75]. The German original refers to "*ungeheueren Ungeziefer*" [K-GW, p. 70], which literally means "huge repulsive bug".[117] Being a commercial traveller, G.S. feared being late to work and missing his train. His firm's chief clerk came over to remonstrate and, with an effort, G.S. managed to open his locked bedroom door. Shocked by the apparition, the chief clerk fled.

G.S.'s transformation led to an upheaval in his family. Ever since the bankruptcy of his father's firm, G.S. became the family's breadwinner. The transformation turned him into a dependent. The family started to shun him and confined him to his own room. The father had to take the job of a night porter and the pampered sister became a secretary.

Initially, the family members tried to look after G.S. His sister, in particular, was sympathetic. As time lapsed, they became antagonistic. The sister cleaned his room perfunctorily. The father bombarded G.S. with apples when the latter emerged from his prison-room. Eventually, the sister removed all the furniture and turned his cell into a rumpus room. To improve the family's finances, they let out some rooms. The tenants gave notice to quit when they saw G.S. Shortly thereafter the family held a council, in which the sister — who had grown from a child into a good-looking young woman — took the view that they

---

[116] First in a periodical and then in a book published by Kurt Wolff; see Franz Kafka (N.N. Glatzer, Ed.), *The Complete Stories* (New York, 1971), p. 469.

[117] The phrase has been translated in different modes. Hoffman rendered it as "monstrous cockroach" [K-MTS, p. 87 (which conveys the meaning)].

should get rid of "it". G.S., who listened, starved himself to death. The family thereupon decided to move to a cheaper flat. All its members were relieved.

Kafka does not relate the cause of G.S.'s transformation. Contextually, it may be gleaned that the uninspiring and monotonous job turned G.S. into a sort of beetle. On a plain reading,[118] *The Metamorphosis* deals with family dynamics.[119] Once the caregiver becomes a caretaker, he has outlived his usefulness. Family members,who are supposed to be friends and well-wishers, turn against him. It is the very message of *The Judgment*: beware of fair weather friends. All in all, man is alone. The only being which he can trust is he himself.

A point that tends to be overlooked is the novella's humour — albeit black humour. G.S.'s struggle to open the locked door is amusing. As his numerous petite legs are unsuitable for the task, he has to use his mouth. Friends and family to whom Kafka read out the story appreciated the point. So should current readers. They ought to comprehend that humour, like grammar and syntax, may undergo changes with time.

Another novella written by Kafka during this period is *In the Penal Colony*. He wrote it on 5 October 1914 [K-TT, p. 292],[120] although some fragments were added in 1917 [ibid, p. 372]. Publication was delayed.[121] In July and August 1916, the Kurt Wolff publishing house and Kafka himself were dubious about the inclusion of the story in a new book [K-TT, pp. 335–337, 348]. Finally in October 1918, Kafka agreed to

---

[118] Like much of Kafka's writing, the novella has given rise to many varying constructions. Max Brod, for instance, regarded it as a religious text.

[119] And see one of his late sayings, which deals with family dynamics: K-ZAB, p. 169.

[120] The day on which he also wrote the Oklahoma Theatre chapter in *Amerika*.

[121] On 4 September 1917, he asked Kurt Wolff to defer publication due to unease about the end: K-LFR, p. 136.

its publication [K-TT, p. 418]. It saw light a year later in book form [K-TT, p. 416].

The plot is restricted to four persons: (i) the semi-official explorer, who is paying a visit to the penal colony; (ii) the ageing officer; (iii) the soldier; and (iv) the prisoner. Two further characters are referred to: the Old Commandant and his Successor. The officer acquaints the explorer with a torture machine, conceived and used by the Old Commandant.Inmates of the penal colony were frequently summarily condemned by the Old Commandant and tormented to death: the burrow of the device executed the condemned man by the repetitive inscription on his bare body of the offence of which he had been convicted, e.g., "thou shalt not steal".[122] Usually such a scene took approximately 12 hours and was attended by a cheering crowd. The Successor disapproved of this procedure and the machine had fallen into disrepair.

The officer seeks to convince the explorer of the legitimacy of such proceedings and wants to demonstrate the working of the machine by executing the prisoner, whom he has condemned because the latter had shown disrespect to his superior. The soldier's only role is to act as guard of the shackled prisoner. Neither of them appreciates what is going on. When the explorer disapproves of such proceedings, the officer straps himself to the machine, which stabs him to death.

The explorer is then taken to a cafeteria in the colony and is told that the Old Commandant had been buried beneath its ground. The officer's numerous die-hard attempts to dig him out and bury him elsewhere had been unsuccessful. Thereafter the explorer leaves the colony but bars the soldier and the prisoner from accompanying him.

---

[122] The procedure is reminiscent of medieval punishment methods, such as burning the letter V (for Villain) onto a convict's body.

This novella, too, has been given varying constructions, including the strange argument that it is a religious text. On a plain reading, the story deals with progress. Whilst members of the old generation continue to respect the tenets applicable during days gone by, their successors reject outdated dogma and oppressive policies. The explorer, a man of the new age, is not prepared to accept either the unrestrained powers assumed by the Old Commandant or his method of brutal execution. When the officer, a remnant of days past, gleans that his doctrines and outlook are rejected, he opts for death.

The ending of the novella has been ignored by critics. It is significant that the explorer prevents the soldier and the prisoner from leaving the penal colony. No reason is given for his act. Is it possible that Kafka wanted to tell his readers that society at large ought to be protected from the influx of unwanted individuals?

Like most of Kafka's other works, *In the Penal Colony* has a comic element. The officer's ramblings, the prisoner's bearings and the festive nature of the Old Commandant's ceremonies manifest black humour.

Kafka's next tome was his second short stories collection: *The Country Doctor [Der Landarzt]*. Like his previously mentioned novella, this collection was published by Kurt Wolff, appearing in May 1920 (bearing 1919 as publication date).[123] Kafka dedicated it to his father. It comprised 14 pieces. Most of them were written in 1917 after Kafka's sad diagnosis. It is noteworthy that, when Kafka composed them, he ignored the turmoil resulting from WWI.

The first story in this collection is "The New Advocate". Kafka composed it on 10 February 1917.[124] The new advocate, named Bucephalus, was (in times of old) Alexander the Great's charger. This

---

[123] K-TT, p. 446. For details, see K-RSJI, pp. 189 et seq.
[124] K-TT, p. 360; it was originally published in a periodical in Berlin, ibid., p. 377.

hero was willingly admitted to practice because "modern society being what it is, Bucephalus is in a different position, and therefore, considering his importance in the history of the world, he deserves at least friendly reception" [K-EST, p. 163]. Kafka points out that in his own days, "there are still plenty of men who know how to murder people" [id]. The technological advances of modern times have not changed mankind's negative core. This short and pungent tale is Kafka's only literary protest about the carnage of WWI.

The second story, which bears the same title as the collection, was composed by Kafka in December 1916 [K-TT, p. 356]. It was initially published in an almanac published by Kurt Wolff in Leipzig in 1918 [ibid, p. 399]. Later that year, the publishing house decided to include it in the short stories collection and sent Kafka the proofs [ibid., p. 403].[125]

In "The Country Doctor", the narrator, the district's medical general practitioner, is summoned by a sick man's family residing in a village other than his. He is facing difficulty because his own horse died on the previous day. His maid's (Rosa's) attempt to borrow a horse is unsuccessful and so he feels desperate. Then, unexpectedly, a groom with two horses turns up in the doctor's pigsty. The groom harnesses the horses to the buggy. The doctor fears to leave him alone with Rosa, but the horses take off despite the doctor's protests and deliver him forthright at the patient's house.

To start with, the doctor believes the patient is shamming. He then discovers a nasty wound at the patient's side and notes that worms have penetrated it. The parents of the sick man and some villagers in

---

[125] For an Alfred Kubin illustration respecting it, see Gregor-Dellin (Ed.), *Das Wachsfigurenkabinett* (Munich, 1974), esp. p. 9.

attendance strip the doctor and place him in the bed beside the patient. The latter, though, expresses his death wish. Unable to help or to fulfil the role of a priest, who would have been able to give the final anointment, the doctor gets out of the bed and flees. This time the horses proceed in slow motion. The doctor realises that he will freeze to death before getting back home and that, in any event, he is bound to lose his practice. The sacrifice of Rosa was fruitless.

On a plain reading, the story makes three points. First, as the people have lost their faith, they expect a physician to have magic remedial powers. His mere touch ought to help a patient to recover. Secondly, mankind needs prejudices. Once it loses faith, it needs another type of belief. Thirdly, Kafka tells the reader that man cannot defeat fate. When overcome by circumstances, he is unable to resist. It is difficult to discern any humour — black or satirical — in this story. It is bleak. Nevertheless, Kafka experts loud it. Their reason for doing so is unclear.

Three other stories of the collection require mention. In February 1917, Kafka wrote "Jackals and Arabs" [K-TT, p. 360; K-EST, pp. 175 et seq.]. In the following October, it was published in *Der Jude*, a periodical run by Martin Buber. Three months later, it was published in a daily newspaper in Vienna [K-TT, p. 392] and in Berlin in December [ibid, p. 419].

This story, too, is ephemeral. The narrator travels to a Middle Eastern country. During the night, a senior Jackal approaches him and asks him to lead "them" out of the bondage or slavery imposed by the Arabs. He assures the narrator that Jackals do not fear the Arabs. Yet, when the Arabs appear in the morning, the Jackals disperse. The scene is left to the Arabs.

It is easy to discern the satirical, perhaps even comic, aspect of the tale. The Jackals proclaim their strength and independence yet are unable to live up to their leader's brave assertions. On a plain reading, Kafka expresses his doubts about the oppressed class's ability to stand up to their masters. This, too, is a story imbued with pessimism. Kafka doubts the propaganda of the self-appointed freedom preachers. The disappointing developments of totalitarian regimes during the 20th century indicate that he had a point.

The third story of the collection meriting discussion is "A Report to an Academy" [K-GW, pp. 172 et seq.; K-EST, pp. 195 et seq.]. Kafka wrote it on 6 April 1917 [K-TT, p. 363] and first published it in *Der Jude* [ibid, p. 387].[126] The narrator, a chimpanzee dubbed *Rotpeter* (viz. Red Peter), lost his freedom when caught in the jungle. Being keen to get out of the captivity cage, he transformed himself into a human being by learning how to drink, to smoke and to spit. He even managed to utter some sounds akin to words. He thereupon became a celebrity. People flocked to watch his performance in the circus. He advises the Academy that he has come to terms with his lot and enjoys his new existence. But the freedom he had experienced in the jungle is far in the past. He has forgotten virtually everything about it.

This story is Kafka's sharp satire about the nature of the common man. He also tells us that people often prefer a comfortable but regimented existence to freedom. Freedom and the wild go in tandem.

The last story is "Ein Altes Blatt" [K-GW, p. 152; translated as "An Old Manuscript" [K-EST, pp. 171–172]. It was first published in a

---

[126] Publication in Martin Buber's periodical led to attempts to construe the work as seeking to discuss Diaspora Secular Judaism. This analysis is not supported here. Notably, Franz Werfel lauded the story: K-TT, p. 395.

periodical in Berlin [K-TT, p. 377]. After its publication in the new collection, it was republished in a Zionist periodical (*Selbstwehr* of Prague) in September 1921 [K-TT, p. 501].

This is one of Kafka's bleakest stories. An alien military has overtaken a country. The nomads do not converse with the local populace, emitting only sounds akin to the chirping of magpies, exploit the citizens, and even the emperor is unable to drive them out. In effect, the locals have to bear them and adjust to them.

On a plain reading, Kafka bemoans the fate of advanced populations, beaten by, or even overtaken, by barbarians. History furnishes examples of such developments. The destruction of the Western Roman Empire by swarms of German tribes is a case in point. Fortunately, such conquerors often develop a culture of their own. That of Germany is but one instance.

The remaining stories in the collection, too, demonstrate Kafka's negative assessment of mankind. As already discussed, "Before the Law" became the gamut of Chapter 9 of *The Trial*. "A Dream" was, it is believed, meant to constitute the penultimate chapter of this book. "An Imperial Message" [K-GW, p. 163; K-EST, p. 183], in which the emperor's messenger is unable to deliver it because he is bogged down by the labyrinthine structure of the seat of government, viz. red tape, reiterates Kafka's distrust of bureaucracy.

A story that was originally meant for inclusion in the collection, "The Bucket Rider" [K-GW, p. 228; K-EST, 205], was composed in January 1917 [K-TT, p. 359] and published in a daily in Prague on 25 December 1921 [ibid., p. 509]. It is Kafka's darkest message about human nature. A destitute resident of Prague proceeds to the house of a merchant, from whom he purchased coal in the past. He begs for some coal on credit so as to survive the freezing spell. The merchant's wife convinces her husband that nobody is calling on them. They ignore their fellowman's desperate appeal for assistance.

Kafka was lucky that, when he himself was down and out, his friends stood by him and did not shrink away. His dark verdict of man's nature may therefore be regarded as an unwarranted dismissal of humanity. In Kafka's pessimistic portrayal, the good Samaritan is absent.

Kafka's third and last collection of short stories, *A Hunger Artist*, appeared in 1924. The publishers, Verlag Die Schmiede of Berlin, entered into contract for its publication in March [K-TT, p. 566]. Kafka needed the royalties to facilitate payment of outstanding accounts. He corrected the proofs in May. The volume saw light in August, after Kafka's demise.

The volume includes four stories, dealing principally with the vainglory issue. "First Sorrow — *Erstes Leid*" was written in March 1922 [K-TT, p. 517], first published in January 1923 in a local periodical and a year later in Berlin [ibid., p. 580]. It deals with a trapeze artist, who stays up "high in the vaulted domes of the great theatres" [K-EST, p. 211; K-GW, p.181] and, when the circus moves from town to town, insists on travelling up the luggage rack in a compartment of the train occupied only by the manager and himself. On one such occasion he asks, sobbingly, that he be given two trapezes. The manager is pleased to comply but worries about the artist's fate once he loses the ability to perform.

The second story, "A Little Woman", written in December 1923 [K-TT, p. 560], was initially published in a local daily on 20 April 1924 [ibid., p. 572]. It is the odd story out in this collection. Apprehension of vainglory is not its subject. The narrator, who has noted his being

Kafka's Feet of Clay

immensely disliked by "the little women", finally resolves to ignore her moods altogether. In this instance, Kafka shows how ordinary people, just like artists who had fallen out of favour, ought to be disregarded when their behaviour is unreasonable.

The third story bears the name of the collection: "Der Hungerkünstler" [K-GW, pp. 190–199; K-MTS, pp. 252–264]. It was written on 23 May 1922 [K-TT, p. 523] and initially appeared in dailies in Berlin and in Prague [ibid, p. 534].

The narrator tells the reader that during his heyday, people flocked to observe the hunger artist and enjoyed taking meals whilst he fasted. He found his falling out of fashion and being side-stepped unbearable. Death was the only appropriate end.

"Josephine the Singer, or the Mouse People" [K-GW, pp. 199–214; K-MTS, pp. 264–283] is both the last story in the collection and Kafka's final literary piece. He wrote it on 17 March 1924 and had it published initially in a local daily on 20 April.

The plot is straightforward. During her zenith, Josephine's whistling was regarded as high art, although many other "mice" were able to pipe like her. Still, she became a public figure, was excused from doing any common work and enjoyed her popularity. When she lost her gift, as well as the public admiration she had become used to, she simply faded away.

Is there an autobiographical element in this story or, perhaps, in the collection as a whole? The point is debatable. It will be recalled that, on the one hand, Kafka disparaged the competitive elements in pursuits such as racing. On the other hand, if a person did not seek fame or recognition, why would he lament its expiration or, in other words, why would he sympathise with the victims of their own vainglory?

VII. Posthumously Published Stories

Kafka's remaining short texts were published posthumously. In respect of them, it is essential to bear in mind that Kafka ought to remain "an author to be read, not someone for experts".[127] This sentiment advocates extreme caution in respect of a discussion of Kafka's stories published posthumously. Some are outstanding. Others raise the reader's eyebrows. In all such cases it is, of course, crucial to bear in mind that these texts did not undergo the meticulous revision and copy-editing notable in works that saw light during Kafka's short life.

Kafka started "Description of a Struggle" [K-GW, pp. 231 et seq.; K-EST, pp. 253 et seq.] in 1904 [K-TT, p. 61]. A first version was completed in 1907 but did not come down to us. In June 1909, extracts — later included in the current version — appeared in a periodical published in Prague at that time. They were entitled "Conversation with a Supplicant" [K-GW, pp. 217 et seq.] and "Conversation with a Drunkard" [ibid., pp. 223 et seq.]. Later on, in the autumn, Kafka started to work on the novella that has come down to us [id.].[128] He continued to work on it but then abandoned it and, as already mentioned, gave the draft to Max Brod.

Another story which met with the same fate is "Wedding Preparation in the Country" [K-GW, pp. 233 et seq.; K-EST, pp. 298 et seq.]. Kafka embarked on it in August 1905 [K-TT, p. 64] and turned back to it in the summer of 1909 [ibid., p. 90]. Max Brod lauded it in a public lecture delivered on 28 January 1910. Thereafter, the piece is not mentioned during Kafka's days.

---

[127] M. Hofmann in his introduction: K-MTS, p. vii.

[128] For the current publication, see Franz Kafka (based on Pasley, Ed.) *Beschreibung eines Kampfes* (Schocken, N.Y. & Frankfurt a.m., 1994). The introductory entry by Pasley explains departures from Max Brod's edited text.

The two stories are significant for an assessment of Kafka's progress as an author. In the former, he talks about an individual's struggle to free himself from the company of an intruder who forced himself on the narrator. The latter is the story of a groom, who makes the preparation for his trip to the wedding ceremony. Both are arguably the domain of the professional critic. An ordinary reader may remain perplexed to the very end of these pieces. The same applies in respect of many stories published posthumously.[129] Some, though, have remained relevant and instructive.

"The Village Schoolmaster — The Giant Mole" [K-EST, pp. 327 at seq.] deals with the spotting of a giant mole by the village's schoolmaster. His discussion of his find is ridiculed by the scientific community. So is the pamphlet of the narrator — a local businessman who embarks on his own investigation of the matter and comes down in support of the schoolmaster's assertion. The schoolmaster feels threatened by this support because he suspects that the narrator attempts to "steal" his discovery. The message is clear: an individual's genuine discovery is often discredited by the ones in power. Supporters of a theory rejected in such a manner risk falling out with those they seek to back.

In "The Hunter Gracchus" [K-EST, pp. 366–370], Kafka deals with the issue known as the fate of the "Eternal Jew" or the "Flying Dutchman". The twist in Kafka's story is that Gracchus was not sentenced to the fate of perpetual wandering by a superior entity. He was unable to reach the shore of the netherland because his boatman fell asleep whilst they were crossing "the Stych". This error by a being over which Gracchus had no control resulted in this hero's infinite odyssey.

---

[129] Amongst them are: "The Student" [K-EST, pp. 323–324]; "The Angel" [ibid., pp. 324–326]; "Blumfeld, an Elderly Bachelor" [ibid., pp. 342–365].

An amusing piece is "The Proclamation" [K-EST, pp. 371–372; *"An Alle meine Hausgenossen"* K-TT, p. 361], written in February 1917. A resident of a large house invites "all my co-tenants" to participate in the arrangement for the disposal of toy guns. As nobody pays attention to this proclamation, the resident issues a new one, expressed in the same ponderous style, advising that nobody had taken up his offer. This is one of Kafka's sharpest lampooning of the bureaucratic mode of expression employed by the Habsburg Empire, which was still in existence at the time of writing. Notably, the same verbose and clumsy style continues to be used by the Republic of Austria for such simple documents as probate orders.

A novella which Kafka wrote on 8 March 1917 [K-TT, p. 362] — *The Great Wall of China* [K-GW, pp. 338 et seq.; K-EST, pp. 374] — was published by Max Brod in a collection of the same name, which appeared in 1931.[130] The plot is simple. The narrator — an ageing building worker — tells the story of the construction of the Great Wall. Historically, the narration leaves much to be desired. Research has established that sections of the Great Wall were built before China's unification by Qin Shi Huang, whose capital was Xianyang (on the outskirts of modern Xi'an) and not (as implied by Kafka) Beijing (Peking). Kafka's objective though was not to discuss the Great Wall, but to decry the blind obedience in which the people used to hold the emperor, often without even knowing his identity. They might worship an emperor who had been long deceased and whose dynasty was no longer in power. The novella incorporates another story, "An Imperial

---

[130] In Berlin; a reprint appeared in 1948. The German title of the work — *Beim Bau der Chinesischen Mauer* — emphasizes the construction of the wall rather than the wall itself.

Message" (discussed earlier on), which (like the one under discussion) condemns the untoward repercussions exercised by an unwieldy government and its machinery. When the novella was written, the Habsburg Empire was intact. Kafka lampooned the intricate bureaucratic machinery and the people's blind obedience to it; he did not seek to convey any message about the Kingdom of the Heaven.

Some readers may wonder what had induced Kafka to keep repeating the same message. In reality, though, such an approach is quite common. By way of illustration, take D.H. Lawrence. His message about sexual emancipation comes up in most of his writings.

Literary texts deserve a plain reading. If a message is clear, there is no need to search for camouflaged meanings. Experts may object on the basis that such an approach is uncultured. In response, attention may be drawn to Hans Christian Andersen's *The Emperor's New Clothes*. Was the little boy who pointed out that the emperor was naked a philistine?

In my opinion it is unreasonable to read rarefied meanings into works by Kafka that were published posthumously. Such works were written down on the spur of a moment's inspiration. Kafka did not revise them or refine them for publication. This approach may, of course, deprive experts of their freedom of speculation; they may even claim that their muse is being fettered. But then, do they really believe that Kafka's objective was to aggrandise them?

Two posthumously published stories illustrate the point respecting spontaneity. "The Bridge" [K-GW, p. 332; K-EST, pp. 372–373, probably written in 1917] tells the reader how it fears collapsing when a person tries to cross it. The bridge expresses human feelings and fears for its own safety. Attempts have been made to construe it as an autobiographical

Maybe a Swan Song: A Second Trip Down Memory Lane

tale. But Kafka never gave such an indication. The remarkable aspect of the story is that Kafka attributes consciousness to an inanimate object.[131]

The second piece is "The Student" [K-EST, 323–324],[132] in which Kafka tells us that "[e]very evening for the past week my neighbour in the adjoining room has come to wrestle with me" [ibid, p. 23]. The story goes on in this vein and, on a plain reading, does not tell us any more than these lines. The question is: why did Max Brod see fit to publish such a curtailed sketch and why do other pundits seek to read an ulterior message into it?

Some of Kafka's stories published posthumously are excellent sketches and, when read on this basis, are both informative and revealing. By way of illustration, take "A Common Confusion" [K-EST, pp. 396–397; "Eine altägliche Verwirrung": K-GW, p. 396], which tells readers a great deal about human nature. "A" wants to conclude a transaction with "B". Confusion arises because each travels to the other's business quarter so that they miss each other. In the ensuing turmoil, the deal falls through, although both men initially had the intention of concluding it. The story advises that mankind is unable to control unpredictable events.

A similar message is conveyed by "The City Coat of Arms" [K-EST, pp. 400–401; "Das Stadtwappen": K-GW, pp. 361–362], which advises that the Tower of Babel could not be completed due to the confusion

---

[131] And see his aphorisms No. 16, [K-ZAB, p. 16]: "A cage went to find a bird"; and No. 59 [ibid, p. 62], in which he said: "In its own eyes a stair not worn deep is just barren wood".

[132] The piece is not included in K-GW; it was translated by Martin Greenberg and Hannah Arendt; they also translated "The Angel" [K-EST, pp. 324-6], which tells us how the narrator imagined that, in the wake of a tremor, an angel visited him.

arising from the fact that each generation destroyed the work of its predecessors by improving it on the basis of technological developments. The building work, though, went on because the bureaucratic state machinery did not wish to call an end to it. Both stories[133] are in tandem with Kafka's philosophy, which is that mutations cannot be controlled by planning. The story also satirises red tape, which used to be so common in the Habsburg Empire.

An even sharper satire is the very short sketch of "Poseidon" [K-EST, pp. 401–402; K-GW, p. 363], written in September 1920 [K-TT, p. 471]. We are told that, far from launching ocean storms, Poseidon was always sitting at his desk. He could have had as many assistants as he wanted, but "since he took his job very seriously, he insisted on going through all the accounts again himself" [K-EST, p. 401]. Whilst he did not enjoy his work, he carried it out because it had been assigned to him. In consequence he had never sailed on the oceans he commanded. He postponed such a trip to the "end of the world". Like the Habsburg administrators, Poseidon was bogged down by paperwork of questionable importance.

The conclusion about such frailty of mankind is underscored by Kafka's animal stories, which tell the reader that when fate and planning are in conflict, the former prevails. Thus, in *The Metamorphosis*, Gregor Samsa cannot undo the transformation effected by destiny. A similar message is conveyed by "The Burrow" [K-EST, pp. 467 et seq.; *"Der Bau"* [K-GW, pp. 427 et seq.], written in 1923 [K-TT, pp. 558, 560]. In this incomplete lengthy short story (or short novella), the narrator — an anthropomorphic rodent — relates how he constructed an underground labyrinth but, despite the care taken in the construction

---

[133] First published in 1931 in *Beim Bau Der Chinesischen Mauer.*

work, he continued to fear a hidden — unspecified — enemy, who would be able to defeat him when attacking. In this instance, too, Kafka advises that dangers triggered off by fate cannot be defeated by careful and elaborate planning.[134]

The same message, in a slightly modified form, can be derived from "The Vulture" [K-EST, pp. 410–411; K-GW, p. 378], written at the end of September 1920 [K-TT, p. 475]. The narrator, a human being, is tortured by a vulture, which keeps hacking his feet. A passer-by, described as a gentleman, offers to fetch his gun and kill the beast. As he departs, the vulture, which understood the man's words, "thrust its beak through [the narrator's] deep, into [him]" and kills him. Once again, man is unable to escape the vicissitudes of fate. The story also highlights the danger of relying on helpful promises made by strangers.

This second point is made in yet another brief sketch, entitled "A Little Fable" [K-EST, p. 414; K-GE, p. 381]. A mouse laments that the world is getting smaller and that proceeding along lengthy walls would lead it to a trap. It accepts the cat's advice to change course, whereupon the latter eats the mouse up. Obviously, the mouse had no escape route and its reliance on the cat's, a seemingly friendly stranger's, advice was misguided.

It is believed that the best way to understand Kafka' writings is based on plain reading. His dislike for fables is expressed in "On Parables" [K-EST, p. 466; "Von den Gleichnissen": K-GW, p. 426]. Expressing doubts about the sayings of "the wise", he tells us that "[a] these parables set out to say [is] merely that the incomprehensible

---

[134] *Investigations of a Dog* [K-GW, pp. 386 et seq.; K-EST, pp. 420 et seq.] is a rambling tale by a dog, who has attained human consciousness, about the misuse of animals by circus performers. Kafka wrote the piece in September of October 1922, after abandoning work on *The Castle* [K-TT, p. 533].

is incomprehensible" [K-EST, p. 466]. He adds: "If you only followed the parables, you yourselves would become parables" [id.]. This perceptive statement leads to the conclusion that many writings that Kafka jotted down on the spur of a moment should be taken at face value. Reading hidden messages into them is unrealistic and contrary to Kafka's spirit.

VIII. Kafka's Aphorisms

It will be recalled that in 1917, Kafka spent a few months in a farm run by his sister in Zürau. During this period, as well as in 1918, he composed sayings (or aphorisms) and some brief sketches. The latter are usually published together with his short stories. Some of the aphorisms were included in 1931 by Max Brod in *The Great Wall of China* collection but are currently available in a separate publication.[135]

A typical sketch of this period is "The Truth about Sanscho Panza" [K-EST, p. 397; K-GW, p. 357]. Written in 1917 [K-TT, p. 385], it comprises just 12 lines. It relates that Don Quixote was nothing but Sancho's demon, whom he set out on the maddest exploits. The message is clear: an ordinary man — like Sancho Panza or any other Tom, Dick or Harry, who goes in the morning to his work, returns in the afternoon and thrives in this well-defined existence — often has phantasies of grandeur, in which he ceases to be one of the crowd and becomes a knight errant.

Another amusing sketch, written at about the same time, is "A Common Confusion", discussed earlier. The confusion, which can arise in the course of the life of simple persons, ties in neatly with one of Kafka's aphorisms, which reads: "There are two great sins from which

---

[135] Note that the story by that name has been discussed.

all others follow — impatience and indolence. Due to impatience, they were thrown out of Paradise; due to indolence they don't go back. But perhaps there's just one cardinal sin — impatience. Due to impatience, they were thrown out of Paradise; they don't run back due to impatience" [K-ZAB, p. 3].[136]

This remarkable saying suggests that the seven sins, viz. pride, greed, lust, envy, gluttony, wrath and sloth, spelt out by Pope Gregory the Great and analysed by Thomas Aquinas, stem from impatience or indolence. Kafka further suggests that impatience and indolence go hand in glove. It remains an open question whether, in a revision that never took place, Kafka might have elaborated on the connection between impatience and indolence which, on their face, appear to be distinct faults.

The Zürau aphorisms resemble Kafka's meditations, published years earlier. Both are the reflections of a lonely man, who despairs of life although he finds it amusing and who has retained a sceptic outlook. In aphorism No. 13, he states: "The first sign of the dawn of wisdom is the wish to die. This life seems unbearable, another unreachable" [K-ZAB, p. 11].[137] In No. 25 he avers: "How can you rejoice in the world except by fleeing to it?" [ibid., p. 23]. Sheer contemplation and observation cannot bring you a sense of fulfilment. Your own endeavours to set yourself free are bound to fail. Accordingly, "[i]n the struggle between you and the world, back the world" [aphorism No. 52, ibid., p. 54]. In aphorism No. 57, he advises that communication cannot get

---

[136] Howard Colyer, ante n. 38, n. 1, points out that at some point after writing his aphorisms, Kafka re-read them and put a line through a number of them, including the one cited. It is possible that Kafka meant to revise these.

[137] But note his reflections about the feasibility of another world: diary entry of 30 January, 1922: K-TT, p. 513.

Kafka's Feet of Clay

you out of the morass. "Language can only hint at things beyond the world of senses, it can't even be used for a crude comparison, because language comes from the physical world and so is bound to possessions and all that goes with possession" [K-ZAB, p. 60].[138] This despair, or negation of hope, dictates loneliness. The point is underscored by No. 70: "Dealing with people tempts self-reflection" [ibid., p. 79]. Staying on one's own is preferable.

A similar sentiment is expressed in "Resolution" [K-EST, p. 11; K-GW, p. 18] — the fifth *Meditation*: "So perhaps the best resource is to meet everything passively ... and, if you feel that you are being carried away, not to let yourself be lured into taking a single unnecessary step ... in short, with your own hand to throttle down whatever ghostly life remains in you, that is, to enlarge the final peace of the graveyard and let nothing survive save that." A similar sentiment is expressed in aphorism 103, which tells us that "[y]ou can turn from suffering of the world, you're free and it would be natural for you, but perhaps this turning away is the only suffering you might avoid" [K-ZAB, p. 106].

In Kafka's opinion self-sacrifice is pointless. It may have an unexpected outcome. "Martyrs don't undervalue the body, they allow it to be raised to the cross — this unites them with their enemies" [aphorism 33, K-ZAB, p. 33]. It follows that it might be best to join your enemies before being crossed.

In general, Kafka advocates humility. He opines: "Humility gives everyone, even those lonely and in despair, the strongest bond with others" [aphorism 106i, K-ZAB, p. 110]. The same maxim emphasises that prayer is strongly connected with "the power to strive", and is only a means of communication. Some of Kafka's stories, like

---

[138] But note that a different view is expressed in his letter to Felice of 15 February 1913 [K-LF, p. 198; K-TT, p. 205].

"The Description of a Struggle" and "Unmasking a Confidence Trickster",[139] show that when these sentiments are taken to their extreme, they may deter an individual from getting rid of unwanted company.

In some of his aphorisms, Kafka dealt with evil. In No. 19 he says: "Don't believe what Evil says, you can't keep secrets from him" [K-ZAB, p. 17]. Further: "Evil doesn't ask for faith once it is sunk deep into you" [No. 28, ibid. p. 27]. In another saying, he tells us: "Your hidden motives when accepting Evil, are not yours but those of Evil" [No. 29i, ibid., p. 28].

A sad aspect of Kafka's belief is that evil — which is not defined — is the natural state of mankind. He concludes his 85th aphorism by advising that "this world is made of Evil" [K-ZAB, p. 87]. In his opinion, "[s]in is our condition regardless of guilt" [ibid., p. 85]. This saying, which is reflected in *The Trial*, makes it difficult to distinguish between good and evil. "In a certain sense the good is desolate" [No. 30, ibid., p. 30].

None of the aphorisms deals with religious belief as a concept. As pointed out earlier, Kafka realised that a human being needs to have trust in something indestructible. In the same vein, he confides: "What's more cheerful than believing in a household god!" [No. 68; ibid., p. 70]. His approach to sin is equally ambiguous. He observed: "We aren't only sinful because we ate from the Tree of Knowledge, but also because we did not eat from the Tree of Life" [No. 83, ibid., p. 83]. Accordingly, there is no need to lament the fall: "We weren't banished from Paradise because of this {meaning the eating fruit of the Tree of Knowledge}, but because we might have eaten of the Tree of Life"

---

[139] In *Meditation* [K-EST, p. 5].

[No. 82, ibid., at p. 84]. Finally, in aphorism No. 100, we are told: "The ways of the Devil can be known, but there can be no faith in them, the Devil stands before us and there's nothing more to believe in" [ibid., at p. 103]. The influence of *Faust* and of *Job* is self-evident.

All in all, the impression gained from Kafka's sayings is that his assessment of life did not undergo a transformation as he advanced in age. The person staring at us is a benevolent sceptic, who craves for loneliness and a quiet existence,[140] yet had a need for company or an audience. In one of his very last sayings, his position was neatly summarised by himself: "Low vitality, an upbringing full of misunderstanding, and being a confirmed bachelor result in scepticism, but this isn't necessary, and to protect the scepticism some sceptics marry — at least they marry an idea and become believers" [K-ZAB, p. 182].[141]

Kafka was too realistic, too imbued with self-knowledge, to become "a believer". Although he was intrigued by religious issues, he did not come down in support of any specific religious dogma. Further, he did not draw a clear distinction between heavenly and physical love. In his own words: "Sensual love distorts our view of heavenly love; by itself it couldn't, but unknowingly sensual love has a trace of the heavenly — so it can" [aphorism No. 79, K-ZAB, p. 81]. His embracing absurdity becomes clear from aphorism No. 16 [K-ZAB, p. 16]: "A cage went to find a bird".

---

[140] As regards Kafka's abhorrence of noise, see "The Silence of the Sirens" [K-EST, pp. 398–399] and "*Grosser Lärm*" [K-GW, p. 227], initially published in October 1912 in *Herderblätter*, a Jewish periodical in Prague.

[141] The significance of these telling words has been overlooked by many commentators. Our thanks are due to Howard Colyer for giving publicity to these late aphorisms.

IX. Kafka's Standing and Readability

Having analysed Kafka's writings, it remains essential to consider his standing. The statement that Kafka is one of the greatest novelists of the 20th century is unsupportable. Two of his novels, *Amerika* and *The Castle*, remained incomplete. Whilst *The Trial* was virtually complete, and is a fine book, it does not constitute Kafka a celebrated novelist. Further, Kafka was active during the second (and the beginning of the third) decade of this period. He did not live to see the Great Depression, WWII and the sociological and technological revolutions that took place thereafter. He dealt mainly with the social conditions prevailing before the end of WWI.

Kafka's strength is in his short stories and novellas. *The Metamorphosis* is an outstanding novella and secures Kafka's position as a significant writer. This and *The Trial* are masterpieces and constitute his finest contributions to literature. In both of them, as well as in most of his short pieces, he opens a window which enables readers to have a glimpse of his inner life. In this regard, his writings are unique. Their influence on later writers like George Orwell, Jean-Paul Sartre and Albert Camus are well known.

Earlier on it has been shown that Kafka was neither a convinced Jew nor a Zionist. Can Kafka, nevertheless, be regarded as having contributed to Judaism or Jewish literature? The point is debatable and depends on definitions. In one view, three factors have to be taken into account when seeking to answer the question: the writer's origin, the topic he discusses and the reading audience. In another view, the issue is to be determined solely on the basis of the topics dealt with in the oeuvre under assessment.

Some notable cases support the latter opinion. In many of his works, Arthur Schnitzler dealt with social issues which were of relevance in his days, such as sexual mores and "honour". In *Reigen* (often referred to as *La Ronde*), he dealt with the former. In *Liebelei*, he discussed both class distinctions and "honour" (which used to lead to duels and killings). Neither of these can be regarded as a contribution to Judaism or Jewish culture, although Schnitzler was — and remained — Jewish. At the same time, in *Professor Bernhardi* and *Der Weg ins Freie*, Schnitzler discussed issues faced by assimilated Jews. So did his posthumously published *My Youth in Vienna*.[142] This leads to the conclusion that in some of his literary works, Arthur Schnitzler influenced the understanding of assimilated Diaspora Jews.

Another significant case is Siegfried Sassoon, a poet of semi-Jewish origin.[143] His poetry constitutes a contribution to the pacifist literature of the post-WWI period and to English literature. It does not impact Judaism or to Jewish culture. The same can be said about Marcel Proust. Whilst the influence of his Jewish mother is paramount, Proust was brought up as a Roman Catholic.[144] Although he refers — in *Swann's Way* — to antisemitism in France, his contribution is to French and world literature. He did not influence Judaism or Jewish Literature.

Erich Maria Remarque's writings demonstrate that such influence would not necessarily depend on the writer's origin. Whilst Remarque's early novels, such as *All Quiet on the Western Front* and *Three Comrades*, are pacifist writings and bemoan the horrors of war, some of his later works, such as *Flotsam*, discuss the life of Jewish middle-class persons

---

[142] Published posthumously by his son, Heinrich Schnitzler. Translated into English by Catherine Hutter.

[143] Siegfried Sassoon's father married out. Sassoon converted to Roman Catholicism in 1957.

[144] Marcel Proust's father was Roman Catholic. Marcel was brought up in that faith but eventually became either an agnostic or an atheist.

displaced during the Holocaust. This constitutes a significant contribution to Jewish culture, although Remarque was not a Jew.

These illustrations support the view that, in determining impacts on Judaism, it is important to concentrate on the topic discussed in the work. The author's origin is a secondary consideration. In some cases, Jewish authors made contributions to the culture of their Diaspora environment. In others, gentile authors have left a mark on Jewish culture.

Is the writer's audience of importance? Most people read works recommended by authorities and by media outlets they respect. Here again, Remarque is of significance. He is widely read in Israel and by Jewish communities in the Diaspora. His being of gentile origin has not affected his popularity in such circles. Siegfried Sassoon and Marcel Proust, on the other hand, are not widely read. The reason is simple: they are too difficult.

What then is the conclusion respecting Kafka? Did his work impact Judaism or Jewish culture? A careful examination suggests that it did not. Kafka's writings deal with ordinary members of the middle-class regardless of their affiliation. There have been attempts to construe *The Metamorphosis* as dealing with a Jewish family. This suggestion is baseless. Gregor Samsa is a *sui-generis* person and the family dynamics covered in the novella have nothing to do with Judaism.

Some writers propose that some of Kafka's short stories are allegorical or, in other word, discuss assimilated Jews. "Jackals and Arabs", "A Report to an Academy" and "Josephine the Singer, or the Mouse Folk" have been cited in support. The answer to such chauvinistic arguments is simple. What would be the reaction of Jewish organisations if a gentile writer published a paper likening Jews to jackals, apes or mice?

Kafka's contribution is to the world's literature as a whole. His style and metaphors are distinct and readers can share his insights into human nature. Further, as German was his sole medium of literary expression, he is also to be seen as a contributor to German culture.

Should Kafka's oeuvre be treated as recommended reading? To answer this question, it is necessary to divide potential readers into four groups. The first comprises potential experts and students who would like to immerse themselves in a literary corpus so as to advance their career. For them Kafka is godsent. The ambiguity of Kafka's writings and the controversies respecting it mean that a suitable topic for a doctorate or a seminal and original essay can usually be detected.

This recommendation is, however, subject to a number of caveats. To start with, such an aspirant ought to study the available learned corpus. In particular, Reiner Stach's three-volume biography should be consulted. All in all, such a process can take up to two or perhaps even three months. This, however, is time well spent. It would be unwise to embark on a study only to discover in its midst that the field has been exhausted.

Another important caution concerns language. A person who wishes to study Kafka's oeuvre ought to be able to read the author's originals. To this end, he should have a command of German. Further, he ought to secure access to documents. Kafka's handwriting is clear and readable, and some of his works (such as letters) were produced on a typewriter. Reading them is easy. Regrettably, Kafka's manuscripts are scattered in libraries around the world. A Kafka student must be prepared to travel.

Another warning concerns analysis. Many scholars are inclined to embark on a psychoanalytical investigation of an author's personality. Would-be experts ought to remember that psychoanalysis has developed into a discipline. Unless a person has the relevant qualifications, he better avoid speculations based on it.[145] A hair-raising "discovery" is the suggestion that a wound in a patient's side is symbolic of a vagina. This starling assertion has led to a speculation as to whether Kafka was bisexual. Idle discussions of this type are, it is believed, to be avoided.

Finally, any person seeking to discuss Kafka's works must familiarise himself with the period in which the author was active. In other words, he (or she) has to study the early decades of the 20th century. If he (or she) fails to do so, he (or she) may miss sarcastic or topical points made by Kafka.

The second group, to which I belong, comprises persons who love books and read literary works in order to gain insights and satisfy intellectual curiosity. Some members of this group may decide to avoid reading Kafka because they are not interested in the relevant period. Further, they may dislike Kafka's sarcasm, black humour and pessimistic outlook.

My advice to them is to give *The Trial* and *The Metamorphosis* a try. If these tomes are not to their liking, their best course is to avoid reading Kafka's other works. If they decide to persevere, they ought to acquire a collection of his writings. The available works are set out in the Appendix.

Personally, I enjoyed "A Report to an Academy" [K-EST, pp. 195 et seq.]; "A Common Confusion" [ibid., pp. 396–397], "Poseidon" [ibid., pp. 401–402] and "The Truth about Sanscho Panza" [ibid., p. 397]. The choice, though, is individual. Other readers may prefer different pieces.

---

[145] Kafka's aphorism No. 93 avers: "Psychology never more!" [K-ZAB, p. 95]. This is a stern warning in point.

The third group encompasses those who read mainly for entertainment or in order to experience a thrill. Admittedly, the boundary between the last two groups is elusive. Some individuals may have a foot in each camp. For those who fall fairly and squarely into this third group, my advice is straightforward: avoid Kafka. A good 'who's done it' is likely to be more satisfying. I must confess that I have really enjoyed novels of Agatha Christie and Raymond Chandler, although I am aware that characters like Hercule Poirot and Philip Marlowe are larger than life.

Finally, there is a substantial group of people — male and female, middle-aged and old — who suffer from chronic insomnia. I strongly recommend that they read *The Castle* (including passages struck out by Kafka) or "Description of a Struggle" [K-EST, pp. 253 et seq.] whilst seeking to fall asleep. This proposed therapy is likely to be more effective (as well as cheaper and less addictive) than pills prescribed by the doctor.

Appendix to Kafka's Feet of Clay

Abbreviations

K-CN   Kafka's Complete Novels (Muir translation)
Franz Kafka (W. & E. Muir, Trs.) *The Complete Novels* (Penguin, UK, 2019)

K-DE   Kafka's Diaries (Max Brod Ed.)
Franz Kafka (Max Brood, Ed.) *Diaries, 1910–1923* (Schocken, New York, 1976)

K-DEB   Kafka's Diaries (Ross Benjamin Ed.)
Franz Kafka (Ross Benjamin, Trs.) *The Diaries* (Schocken, New York, 2022)

K-DG   Kafka's Tagebücher
Franz Kafka *Tagebücher 1910–1923* (German, Amazon, no date)

K-EST   Kafka's Collected Short Stories
Franz Kafka (W. & E. Muir, Trs.) *Collected Stories* (Knopf, UK, 1993)

K-GW	Kafka's Gesammelte Werke
	Franz Kafka *Gesammelte Werke* (Anaconda, Cologne, Germany, 2012)
K-LF	Letters to Felice
	Franz Kafka (E. Heller & J. Born, Ed.) *Letters to Felice* (Schocken, New York, 2016)
K-LFR	Letters to Friends
	Franz Kafka (R. & C. Winston, Trs.) *Letters to Friends, Family & Editors* (Schocken, New York, 2016)
K-LM	Letters to Milena
	Franz Kafka (P. Boehm, Trs.) *Letters to Milena* (Schocken, New York, 2015)
K-LW	Kafka's Lost Writings
	Franz Kafka (R. Stach, Ed; M. Hofmann, Trs.) *The Lost Writings* (New Direction, New York, 2020)
K-MBB	Max Brod's Kafka Biography
	Max Brod *Franz Kafka: A Biography* (Da Capo, US, 1995)
K-MTS	Metamorphosis and other Stories
	Franz Kafka (M. Hoffman, Trs.) *Metamorphosis and Other Stories* (Penguin, UK, 2008)
K-NB	Kafka's Blue Octavo Notebooks
	Franz Kafka (Max Brod, Ed.; E. Kaiser & E. Wilkins, Trs.) *The Blue Octavo Notebooks* (Exact Change, Cambridge, 1991)
K-RB	Ritchie Robertson's Kafka Biography
	R. Robertson *Kafka: Judaism, Politics & Literature* (Clarendon, OUP, 2001)
K-RSFJ	Reiner Stach's Kafka Biography, Vol. 1
	R. Stach *Kafka: die frühen Jahre* (Frankfurt a.m., 2016)

K-RSJE	Reiner Stach's Kafka Biography, Vol. 2
	R. Stach, *Kafka: die Jahre der Entscheidungen* (Frankfurt a.m., 2023)
K-RSJL	Reiner Stach's Kafka Biography, Vol. 3
	R. Stach: *die Jahre der Erkenntnis* (Frankfurt a.m., 2023)
K-TT	Reiner Stach's: Kafka von Tag zu Tag
	R. Stach: *Kafka von Tag zu Tag* (Fischer, Frankfurt a.m., 2024)
K-ZAB	Kafka's Aphorisms
	Franz Kafka (H. Colyer, Trs.): *Zürau Aphorisms* (Lulu, North Carolina, 2021)
K-99	Reiner Stach: Is that Kafka?
	R. Stach (K. Beals, Trs.): *Is that Kafka? 99 Finds* (New Directions, New York, 2012)

www.ingramcontent.com/pod-product-compliance
Lightning Source LLC
Chambersburg PA
CBHW070045250525
27076CB00004B/18